Burning at Europe's Borders

ISSUES OF GLOBALIZATION
Case Studies in Contemporary Anthropology
Series Editors: Carla Freeman and Li Zhang

Labor and Legality:
An Ethnography of a Mexican Immigrant Network,
Tenth Anniversary Edition
Ruth Gomberg-Muñoz

Marriage after Migration:
An Ethnography of Money, Romance, and Gender in Globalizing Mexico
Nora Haenn

Serious Youth in Sierra Leone:
An Ethnography of Performance and Global Connection
Catherine E. Bolten

Low Wage in High Tech:
An Ethnography of Service Workers in Global India
Kiran Mirchandani, Sanjukta Mukherjee, and Shruti Tambe

Care for Sale:
An Ethnography of Latin American Domestic and Sex Workers in London
Ana P. Gutiérrez Garza

Waste and Wealth:
An Ethnography of Labor, Value, and Morality in a
Vietnamese Recycling Economy
Minh T. N. Nguyen

Haunted:
An Ethnography of the Hollywood and Hong Kong Media Industries
Sylvia J. Martin

The Native World-System:
An Ethnography of Bolivian Aymara Traders in the Global Economy
Nico Tassi

Sacred Rice:
An Ethnography of Identity, Environment, and Development in
Rural West Africa
Joanna Davidson

City of Flowers:
An Ethnography of Social and Economic Change in
Costa Rica's Central Valley
Susan E. Mannon

Listen, Here Is a Story:
Ethnographic Life Narratives from Aka and Ngandu Women of the
Congo Basin
Bonnie L. Hewlett

Cuban Color in Tourism and La Lucha:
An Ethnography of Racial Meanings
L. Kaifa Roland

Gangsters Without Borders:
An Ethnography of a Salvadoran Street Gang
T. W. Ward

Burning at Europe's Borders

An Ethnography on the African Migrant Experience in Morocco

ISABELLA ALEXANDER-NATHANI

New York   Oxford
OXFORD UNIVERSITY PRESS

Oxford University Press is a department of the University of Oxford.
It furthers the University's objective of excellence in research, scholarship,
and education by publishing worldwide. Oxford is a registered trade mark of
Oxford University Press in the UK and certain other countries.

Published in the United States of America by Oxford University Press
198 Madison Avenue, New York, NY 10016, United States of America.

For titles covered by Section 112 of the US Higher Education
Opportunity Act, please visit www.oup.com/us/he for the latest
information about pricing and alternate formats.

Library of Congress Cataloging-in-Publication Data
Names: Alexander-Nathani, Isabella, author.
Title: Burning at Europe's borders : an ethnography on the African migrant
    experience in Morocco / Isabella Alexander-Nathani.
Description: First edition. | New York : Oxford University Press, [2021] |
    Series: Issues of globalization : case studies in contemporary anthropology |
    Includes bibliographical references and index.
Identifiers: LCCN 2019035386 (print) | LCCN 2019035387 (ebook) |
    ISBN 9780190074647 (paperback) | ISBN 9780190074654 (epub)
Subjects: LCSH: Immigrants—Morocco—Social conditions—21st century. |
    Refugees—Morocco—Social conditions—21st century. | Refugees—Africa,
    Sub-Saharan—Social conditions—21st century. | Africans—Migrations. |
    Blacks—Morocco—Social conditions—21st century. | Ethnology—Africa. |
    Morocco—Race relations. | Morocco—Emigration and immigration—Social
    aspects. | Africa, Sub-Saharan—Emigration and immigration—Social aspects.
Classification: LCC JV8978 .A45 2021 (print) | LCC JV8978 (ebook) | DDC
    305.896/064—dc23
LC record available at https://lccn.loc.gov/2019035386
LC ebook record available at https://lccn.loc.gov/2019035387

Printing number: 9 8 7 6 5 4 3 2 1
Printed by Sheridan Books, Inc., United States of America

DEDICATION

The space that exists between Africa and Europe has become a graveyard. It now claims more than six lives every day. But behind every number, there is a name, a face, and a story that goes untold.

This book is dedicated to all those who remain unnamed.

May they finally find the refuge they were seeking.

CONTENTS

....

List of Illustrations   xii
Acknowledgments   xiv
Prologue   xxi

CHAPTER 1   **The Question of Ethnography**   1
              Introduction   1
              New Forms of Riutal   4
              Mapping Morocco   8
              A Rooftop Home Away from Home   16
              A Place at the Table   21
              A Note on Chapter Structure   23

CHAPTER 2   **At the Crossroads: Africa on the Map
              of Human Migrations**   31
              Introductory Case Study: a Transnational Moroccan
                 Family Network   31
              The Homes Remittances Buy   34
              Who Has the Right?   37
              Refugee "Crises" in the Headlines   41
              From Early Models to Contemporary Studies
                 of Human Migration   43
              Slave, Soldier, "Seasonal" Laborer   49
              Measuring Migrations: How Far Or How Strange
                 Is the Destination?   51

Morocco's Critical Place at the Crossroads   54
An Island Surrounded by Land   63

CHAPTER 3   **Colony, Monarchy, Muslim Democracy: Morocco as the New "Destination" for African Migrants**   **69**
Introductory Case Study: Two Sides to Every Story   69
The War on Migrants, the War on Drugs   77
Aid from the Other Side   79
The Long Road Home   81
Trapped at the Gates of Europe   86
A Brief History of the World's Oldest Monarchy   88
The Arab Spring and the Moroccan Exception   94
The (Il)Legalization of Morocco's Newest Subjects   96

CHAPTER 4   **Vulnerability and the Gendering of Political Status**   **100**
Introductory Case Study: A Neighborhood No One Calls Home   100
Doing "Man's Work"   105
Strangers Sleeping Side by Side   107
Mother, Sister, Daughter, Wife: The Vulnerability of the Female Migrant   110
Neither Mother, Nor Sister, Nor Daughter, Nor Wife: The Role of the Female Researcher   113
Migrants as the "New" Muslim Men   117
Learning from Comparative Studies of Migration   122
When Is the Migrant a Refugee?   129

CHAPTER 5   **Burning Yesterday for Tomorrow: Images from the In Between**   **137**
Introductory Case Study: A Journey to the Space In Between   137
Memory Making: How One Man Builds a Narrative (and One Researcher Rebuilds it)   142
Traditional Life History Collection and a Call for Visual Data   144
Phino: A Visual Life History   149
Santigie: The Digitization of Visual Life History   155
Mapping Migrants' (Dis)Location   160

CHAPTER 6   *"Le Peril Noir"*: The Racialization of
             Political Status   165
             Introductory Case Study: The Senegalese Exchange   165
             University Village: A Space for Here and Now   171
             New Racisms on the Rise   173
             The Language of Difference   176
             Race as Nationality: Placing Black Moroccans   181
             How We "Other": From Racialization to Legalization   186
             Inside and Outside of the Lines   191

CHAPTER 7   **Where The Story Ends**   195
             The Legality of Undocumented Movement   197
             Policy and Practice on the other Side of the Border   199
             Border Externalization: A Modern Spanish Ruling
                 of The Moroccan Border   205
             The Weight of their Journeys   208
             At the Threshold: Migration as a Sacrificial
                 Rite De Passage   213
             A Return to the Beginning   214

Epilogue   223
Glossary   231
Bibliography   234
Index   244

LIST OF ILLUSTRATIONS

Figure 0.1   Bambino sits on a rock at the edge of his camp, looking down over the Spanish enclave of Melilla, the Mediterranean Sea, and mainland Spain in the distance. Morocco, 2015. *Photograph by the author.*

Figure 1.1   Map of primary migratory routes between Africa and Southern Europe. *Image is based on a 2012 version of MTM i-Map (imap-migration.org).*

Figure 1.2   Map of Africa with Morocco and primary research sites highlighted.

Figure 1.3   Author and a Guinean brotherhood share their one daily meal of rice in the hidden forest camp they call home. Morocco, 2016. *Photograph courtesy of* The Burning.

Figure 2.1   Map of colonial era Africa following the Berlin Conference of 1884.

Figure 3.1   *Je ne m'appelle pas Azzi"/"Ma smeeteesh Azzi"* antiracism campaign poster. *Campaign archives.*

Figure 4.1   A sampling of images of rock art created by the brotherhoods in the hidden forest camps surrounding the Spanish enclaves of Ceuta and Melilla. Morocco, dates vary. *Photograph by the author.*

Figure 5.1   A collection of "departure day" portraits of Phino and his two friends. DRC, 2000. *Photographs courtesy of Phino Ngiaba and copied with his permission.*

Figure 5.2   A collection of "sending ceremony" photographs from Phino's departure day. DRC, 2000. *Photographs courtesy of Phino Ngiaba and copied with his permission.*

Figure 5.3   A collection of photographs Phino sent home to his family in the DRC. Morocco, dates vary. *Photographs by Phino Ngiaba and copied with his permission.*

Figure 5.4   Santigie's UNHCR asylum application and attached photograph. *Note*: Sensitive information has been removed. *Image copied with Santigie Achuo's permission.*

Figure 5.5   Santigie's Facebook profile page. *Note*: Sensitive information has been removed. *Image copied with Santigie Achuo's permission.*

Figure 5.6   *Constellations* by Bouchra Khalili. *Image courtesy of the artist.*

Figure 6.1   "*Le Peril Noir*" magazine cover. *MarocHebdo archives.*

Figure 7.1   Tourists enjoy a break in front of the "*Barca Nostra*" exhibit by artist Christoph Büchel. Venice Biennale, Spring 2019. *Photograph courtesy of Martin Herbert.*

Figure E.1   A sampling of the 39 photographs collected for author's "Names not Numbers" campaign, which included the names, images, and stories of the 47 victims of the February 4th tragedy and can be viewed in full at www.twitter.com/isabella_writes. Places and dates vary. *Photographs courtesy of the victims' families.*

ACKNOWLEDGMENTS

First and foremost, to the men, women, and children whose stories bring this book to life and to the countless others whose stories remain untold, thank you for inviting me into your journeys. As I remember one young boy named Luca telling me, "The road is long and hard, so we learn to laugh with hope." You have taught me what it means to hold on to light in darkness. You have welcomed me with astounding courage, warmth, and generosity—into your homes, camps, and prison cells, into your families, brotherhoods, and smuggling rings—and I have learned more from you that you will ever know. You are the reason behind all of the work that I do. *Merci, Shoukran, Jaaraama, I'ni'ce, Botondi,* in every language that I know and from the depths of my heart—Thank you. Sharing your stories with the world is the great honor of my life.

To my mentor, Carla Freeman, who guided this project from my earliest phases of research, I owe a deep gratitude. Carla was not only the chair of my doctoral committee and the Dean of Faculty at Emory University throughout my time as a faculty member there, I am also fortunate enough to include her in my closest circle of friends. Carla, your mentorship has shaped me as a researcher, a writer, and a woman. Thank you for always believing in me and teaching me to believe in my own voice. This project is a testament to the fierce love that you pour into your roles as teacher, scholar, and friend.

To the other members of my doctoral committee, Oussama Cherribi, Peter Little, and Michael Peletz, who also guided this project from the beginning, I am grateful for the immeasurable value you added to the following pages. To Sam, who first taught me how to navigate the foreign country I now call home, to Peter, who grounded my research in the rich history of the continent he loves, and to Michael, whose friendship saw me through the countless trials that come with work in crisis zones, thank you for helping to shape me into the anthropologist I am today.

My time as a faculty member at Emory University, where this project came to its conclusion, was influenced by the generous support of my colleagues and students there. To Rob Barracano, Aaron Stutz, and Liv Nilsson Stutz, thank you for making the Departments of Anthropology and Film Studies feel like home. To every one of the students who I have been fortunate enough to teach over the past years, please know that you were the light when my work was full of darkness, and I am grateful for you. I often tell people that it is *you* who give me hope that, as Dr. Martin Luther King Jr. famously said, "The arc of the moral universe is long, but it bends toward justice." You are the change makers of tomorrow, and I know that you will do great things with all of the gifts you have been given.

To the cherished friends and fellow social scientists who I have been fortunate enough to study, write, and work alongside over the past decade, I owe a special gratitude. To Badre Abdeslam, Elizabeth Buckner, Melissa Creary, Jason Derby, Sarah Franzen, Hemangini Gupta, Hilary King, Wendell Marsh, Matthew Reilly, Jennifer Sarrett, Gabriela Sheets, Megan Tabag, Tawni Tidwell, and Mael Vizcarra, thank you for continuing to teach me, through your own inspiring work, what it means to be an engaged researcher in today's world. You make me proud to be a part of our community of new scholars.

I remain grateful to the faculty at New York University's Gallatin School of Individualized Study and the University of Chicago's Department of Anthropology, where I received outstanding training, and I thank my earliest mentors there, including Kesha Fikes, June Foley, Kelda Jamison, John MacAloon, Bella Mirabella, and Laurin Raiken. To the late Rekha Eanni, who first taught me what it means to fight for social justice, I cannot wait until your son is old enough to appreciate all of the incredible stories about you that I have to share.

Countless other scholars played vital roles in the development of this project through their support of my nontraditional research, and I thank this broader community for showing me the possibilities of work at the intersection of social science, activism, and the arts. Ruth Behar,

Nicholas de Genova, and Jason de Leon, although you may not know it, your work has deeply impacted not only this book but my desire to do ethnographic research in the first place. I thank each of you for teaching me how to keep both the heart and the humanity in the following chapters. To Ava DuVernay, Valarie Kaur, and José Palazón, whom I turn to as sources of continual inspiration, thank you for giving me something to strive for. Through your creative approaches to activism, you have shown the world that art can be powerful, love can be revolutionary, and human rights have no meaning until they are granted to all.

The various phases of research and writing that culminated in this book were generously supported by a range of grants and institutions, for which I am grateful. My field research was supported by funding from the National Science Foundation (NSF), the American Institute for Maghrib Studies (AIMS), the West African Research Association (WARA), the U.S. Department of Education's Fulbright-Hays Program, Emory University's Visual Scholarship Initiative, and the Saharan Crossroads Research Fellowship, awarded annually by AIMS and WARA. Emory University's ORDER (On Recent Discoveries by Emory Researchers) Fellowship and a second grant from NSF afforded me the time and space to complete my writing. I remain grateful to these institutions for their commitment to advancing new voices in the field of anthropology, their support of work at our world's most critical borders, and their willingness to take a chance on a project that challenged the boundaries of traditional research.

My field research was further made possible by the generous support of Morocco's *Université Mohammed V* and the hospitality of my colleagues there. I owe a special thanks to Mohammed Boudoudou, my Morocco-based adviser, and Mohammed Haytoumi, my fellow social scientist in the field, who each added new depths to my analysis and provided me with support when I needed it the most. To Hicham Echerfaoui, Adil Barihsina, and your families, thank you for giving me the immeasurable gift of finding home in a foreign place. *Barak Allahu feekum.* You represent all that is exceptional about your country, and because of you, *qalbi fi almaghrib.*

Despite all of the humbling support that I have received along the way, if it were not for the quiet fight of one man, these words would likely have remained trapped along with those whose stories I am sharing. To Reverend Jesse Louis Jackson, who negotiated my release from a prison sentence in Algeria and made the completion of this project possible, it is difficult to find the words. You freed me and made it possible for me to free these stories, and so from all of the men, women, and children whose words bring this book to life, I say thank you. You have taught me that change does not come without struggle and sacrifice, and you have challenged me to wear my scars with pride. Through your example, you have taught us all what it means to be a "freedom fighter." We will continue the good fight in your name.

The completion of this project would also not have been possible without Oxford University Press and the team of women who lead the Issues in Globalization Series. It is an honor to be published alongside such rich contemporary ethnographic works, and I am grateful to Carla Freeman and Li Zhang for seeing the potential in my book when it was still in draft form. I owe thanks to Sherith Pankratz for her dedication to this project throughout its long path to publication, to Olivia Clark for her support in our final months of work together, and to Betty Pessagno for her expertise in refining the pages before you. This project was greatly enriched by OUP's thorough review process and by the thoughtful comments of the following reviewers: Asale Angel-Ajani, City University of New York; Madeline Campbell, Worcester State University; Katie Nelson, Inver Hills Community College; Georgina Ramsay, University of Delaware; Anna Reed, Iowa State University; John Schaefer, Miami University. I thank each of them for their time, knowledge, and encouragement, which helped make this book what it is.

From the beginning, this book project has been deeply intertwined with my latest documentary film project, *The Burning* (www .smallworldfilms.org), and I cannot fail to thank those who have seen the importance of telling the untold story of Africa's migrant and refugee crisis in both written and visual formats. To the wide community of supporters who made this film possible through your donations of time, resources, and talent, thank you. I could not have done it without you. To my mentor and executive producer, Joe Berlinger, thank you for believing in *The Burning* from day one and standing by me through all of the challenges of bringing it to life. To my other executive producer, Regina Scully, thank you for seeing the potential of this film to bring global change and making its completion possible. To my co-producer Eric Esrailian, I am grateful that you share my belief in the power of film to reform policies, expand human rights, and improve the lives of the most vulnerable, and I thank you for working with me to see that this film does all three. *The Burning* has been supported by an exceptionally talented and committed team of student interns, and to every one of you, I am grateful. To Adama Kamara, who has been instrumental in designing a curriculum to bring this film and book into classrooms and introduce human rights to a new generation of change makers, thank you for making our world a better place one student at a time. To the incredible team of creatives whom I have been fortunate enough to work with over the years, Pedro Pinto, Ellen Goldwasser, and Matthew Shehata, thank you for giving pieces of your own hearts to this project. To say that you gave only your blood, sweat, tears, and broken bones would not be enough. To the late Andrew Berends, my lead cinematographer and cherished friend, thank you for giving your life in the pursuit of telling the untold stories. *The Burning* will be your final project, and I promise, we will make you proud.

Most importantly, to the individuals who courageously invited me and my small team along on your journeys toward safer shores, thank you. Engraved on my heart forever are your words: "*Demandez aux oiseaux si des frontières font partie de la terre.*" To the brotherhood— Thierno "Moneba" Barry, Ibrahim Jalloh, Thierno Mamadou Jalloh, Mamadou Saliou Diallo, and Alseny "Bambino" Diallo—*Jaraama wakkilarè madhen.* To the Kone family—the late Jah Kone, Kia Kone, Mariam Kone, and little Mahama Kone—*I'ni'ce I ka ce sirila.* And to those who continue to guide me on my own journey—Phino Ngiaba and Myriame Niangadou—*Merci d'être mes guides, ma tante et mon oncle chéris.* Even with oceans between us, we are together, and together we will win the good fight.

To those who make the other side of my world feel like home, thank you for supporting me in my own long journey to tell the untold stories. To my parents, whose adventurous spirits and generous hearts were my earliest map of the world, thank you for providing the foundation that pushed me to ask the questions I set out to ask. To my closest circle of friends, thank you for standing by me through all of the highs and lows, not just of writing, but of life. To Julian Cyr, Rafael Duran, Jordi Fallon, Veronica Finch, Julian Mitton, Jordan Reeves, and Cubby West Spain, thank you for loving me like only brothers and sisters can. To Willow, who sat by my side and listened to more iterations of this book than everyone else in my world combined, thank you for seeing it through. Your quiet support has been my heartbeat. And lastly, to my grandparents, Dottie and Billy Sam Baldwin, I wrote these words with you in my heart, and I know you would have been proud.

Lastly, to my husband and partner in all things, Amit Alexander-Nathani, who taught me that great love gives you both roots and wings, thank you for bringing me depths of joy I never knew were possible. I am grateful to you for always believing in me, believing in my work, and helping me believe, even on the darkest days, in the possibility of stories to change the world. Your support has made the completion of this book and film project possible. I love you more than words could ever say.

And to our child, thank you for teaching us, before you have even arrived, why we must never forget how to "laugh with hope." For you, more than anyone, we hold on to our hope for a better tomorrow.

PROLOGUE

....

"In Guinea, you grow up thinking about escape. When I was little, no one asked me what I wanted to become. They asked me where I wanted to go."

—"Bambino," M, 13, Guinean migrant

B ambino is 13 years old. He sleeps on a blanket in the forest, he eats what he can scavenge from trash piles in the town at the base of the mountain, and he is not alone. He is one of thousands of boys who live hidden at Europe's southernmost borders, awaiting their chance at what they call "the crossing."

Morocco, curving around the northwest corner of Africa, is less than 8 miles from the coast of southern Spain. But the European border is even closer. Morocco is still home to two small Spanish enclaves, making it the only African nation to share land borders with an internally borderless European Union (EU). The Spanish enclaves of Ceuta and Melilla make Morocco one of the most trafficked border regions in the world today and a primary crossing point for African migrants, refugees, and asylum seekers—hundreds of thousands of men, women, and children, like Bambino, who travel from across the continent dreaming of escape every year. Only a series of fences separate those fleeing conflict and poverty in their home countries from the promise of a better life on the other side of the Mediterranean Sea.

Bambino's makeshift camp is impossible to find without a guide, and he hopes to keep it that way. He and his "brotherhood" change location every few weeks, pushing their camp further and further into the woods, further and further from the town of Nador below. "The longer we have to walk past the last road, the longer the police have to run to catch us," he said, explaining how raids on their home drive their movement up the mountainside. "The police don't like to run this far." For those living in the mountains surrounding Ceuta and Melilla, life has become a tireless attempt to evade the Spanish-supported Moroccan police forces that are tasked with keeping Africans from reaching European soil. In this region of Morocco, police raids routinely leave a trail of bruised and bloodied bodies behind, and the bandaged men and boys scattered around the camps are evidence of how officers target the hands and feet first. "You can't climb without them," Bambino explained. The police know these forest camps are home to men, women, and children preparing for the crossing, and they know to target what the crossing requires—strength, agility, and the ability to climb.

When living in camps across the valley on Mount Gourougou back in 2010, I learned how the brotherhoods construct "tents"—searching for pieces of discarded plastic and attaching the plastic over bent tree limbs with "rope" they make by ripping apart old T-shirts. I saw how they pile into these tents every night to protect themselves from the harsh elements. Each tent, no larger than the square footage of a small closet, holds twelve or more bodies. I also learned how routinely their shelters are burned to the ground in weekly raids, as officers decimate whatever food, water, and other supplies they can find. "Everyone used to sleep in tents," Bambino explained, as we walked past rows of tattered blankets laid out across the rocky forest floor, "but tents make us easier to find, so we no longer build them." I have countless photographs of plastic melting over the few possessions that boys like Bambino have to their names—a blanket, a few spare articles of clothing, and if they had not already been burned, a photograph of their parents or the younger siblings they left behind. In the summer months, with temperatures in the 90s, the lack of shelter means increased exposure to animals and poisonous insects. In the winter months, as temperatures plummet below freezing with frequent rainfall and occasional snow, the lack of shelter brings the risk of hypothermia and other critical medical issues.

Nador is less than 10 miles from the border with Melilla, and the mountains surrounding this Moroccan town are dotted with hidden camps, visible only when you catch a glint of sunlight reflecting off a piece of repurposed plastic or see the flickering of small bonfires between the shadows of trees at night. Each brotherhood is formed along lines of nationality—the Senegalese living together in one camp, the Malians, Sudanese, Nigerians, and Congolese in others. They range in size from a few dozen to a few hundred. Although women and girls are occasionally present, the brotherhoods are comprised primarily of young men and boys, 10 to 25 years of age. The chief of the Guinean camp where Bambino lives is a soft-spoken young man by the name of Moneba. He explained how he decided to stop building tents after their last move up the mountainside. "Now, more than half of the people in my camp are children—boys only 12, 13, 14 years old like him," he said, looking affectionately toward Bambino. "I have to make a greater effort to keep them safe." At 25, Moneba is the oldest in his brotherhood, and he gained his status of chief through his age, his resourcefulness, and the knowledge he acquired in his impressive number of attempted crossings. "Every time you cross, you learn something new about yourself. You test your will to survive."

The rhythm of life in each camp centers on survival. Although the small communities are transient, with new members arriving every day and groups regularly breaking off for attempted crossings, the chiefs maintain consistent structure within the boundaries of their camps. Under Moneba, every brother is assigned a daily duty that keeps their camp running—"food duty," which involves scavenging through trash sites and occasionally begging for money with outstretched hands on busy street corners in Nador, or "water duty," which involves trekking several miles with plastic jugs to be filled at the creek on the other side of the mountain or, when the creek runs dry, at the spigot behind an unsuspecting stranger's house in town. Any job that brings one into contact with the public is dangerous. For Morocco's rapidly growing population of African migrants, refugees, and asylum seekers, beatings at the hands of locals loom as a constant threat, just like those at the hands of raiding police officers. "We live in the forest like animals," Bambino explained, "because Moroccans don't accept us living beside them. They don't want to see us in their towns. When they do, they throw rocks at us and shout 'Azzi!'" (Azzi is a racial slur used to denigrate blacks.) Although I have witnessed more than one instance in which foreigners were welcomed in Moroccan communities over the years, I have also witnessed countless instances that unfolded exactly as Bambino described.

As the sun began to set over his camp, Moneba busied himself preparing the one daily meal he and his brothers would share, combining the previous day's scavenging in a large cast-iron pot over an open fire he brings to life with the friction of rocks every night. "One summer before I left home, I cooked in a restaurant," he said with pride in his eyes, surveying the ingredients he had to work with. "I can make food out of almost anything." He combined a rotten onion and several bruised tomatoes with what remained in the sack of rice beside the fire-pit. A few half-eaten loaves of bread would be served on the side. Salt and sugar are among the most prized possessions in Morocco's hidden camps, but Moneba explained, "This week, we have none." Police make an effort to pour out spices, along with the bags of rice and jugs of water they find in their raids. In most camps, the job of cooking goes to the younger boys, or to the women, if any are present. It is not the job of a chief. Yet Moneba savors the opportunity to create sustenance for his brothers out of what little remains. When he is not cooking, his other primary responsibility is preparing his brothers for the final leg of their long journeys to a new home. This task no chief takes lightly.

The crossing is planned and trained for like a military mission, and the chief of each camp stands as the officer in charge. "It is a great responsibility," Moneba said. "I go into each crossing knowing I may lose some of my brothers, and in the hours before we leave, I always question—Did I do enough to prepare them? Did I build our ladders strong enough? What if the guards are out in force this time?" Boys like Bambino sleep in the forest for months, sometimes years on end, awaiting their chance to escape. As time passes, each camp grows in number, making it more and more difficult to evade the police who threaten to capture and deport them to the Moroccan-Algerian border over 100 miles away. But the brothers know that in order for them to stand any chance at success, they need numbers on their side. "If 500 of us start out, maybe fifty of us will cross the first fence, maybe five the second, and maybe one of us will make it all the way," Moneba explained. Despite the discouraging odds, he works to build morale in his brotherhood as they train, constructing ladders from tree limbs and makeshift rope, running test missions at nightfall, and subsisting on what little they have left. "The longer it takes for our group to grow, the weaker our bodies get," said one recent arrival to the Guinean camp. He knew it would take both training and strength to master the physically grueling feat of the crossing, and as Moneba told me many times, "it takes God on your side."

Although Spain has invested in multiple rings of razor-wire fences around the enclaves of Ceuta and Melilla, Morocco's hidden camps are alive with stories of success. On the small cracked screen of an old cell phone, Bambino and his friends pulled up photograph after photograph of "heroes" for me to see. They showed me brothers who had made it to the detention center for unaccompanied minors in Melilla, their feet bleeding and clothes torn. They showed me others who had finally made it through the asylum application review process after years spent in the detention center and who were rebuilding their lives in mainland Europe. One of the brothers is pictured in the uniform from his "good job," where he works as a prep cook in a bustling kitchen. Another is pictured beside a cement mixer on a dusty construction site. "They are living our dream," I heard one boy say over my shoulder. As the sun disappeared from the sky and the fire began crackling, I looked toward Bambino. Small, but strong, he is young and tired and hungry and hopeful. In training, I had seen him run quickly, his eyes always fixed on the path in front of him. He runs without fear. Moneba once told me, "Bambino has God on his side."

Bambino fled his home more than one year before I first met him in Morocco. By the age of 12, he had lost both of his parents and had no way of providing for the younger brother and sister who were left in his care. In the Mano River region, which includes Guinea, Liberia, Côte d'Ivoire, and Sierra Leone, two major civil wars and the ensuing political crises have led to more than 500,000 deaths and the destruction of once-functioning state institutions. In Guinea, the ongoing crises are both political and economic in nature, including active ethnic conflict, pervasive political corruption, and a majority of the population trapped in extreme poverty.

"My father was killed in the fighting when I was young, and for a while, my mother and I took care of our family," Bambino explained. His mother worked the small patch of land beside their home, and they sold what little excess they had in the marketplace—just enough to supplement their diet of *foufou* and plantains with some sugar and goat's milk. "On special occasions, like when someone in the village got married, we ate goat's meat, too," he remembered. Their home was constructed in the traditional way, with mud bricks and a metal roof, but Bambino described a village landscape that was far from traditional. It was overcrowded with homes, the homes were overcrowded with people, and struggling crops were squeezed into every open patch of dry earth. The crumbling infrastructure led to failing irrigation and sewage systems. Spoiled harvests and sick residents soon followed. "We had no money for the hospital, no money for doctors, no money for medicine, so we had to watch my mother die at home," he said one morning as we walked down a rocky path with our empty water jugs in hand. "I tried to busy my brother and sister with chores outside of the house, so they wouldn't see her suffering." Tears filled his eyes as he described his mother's final days. After she died, Bambino struggled to keep his siblings alive:

> I didn't make a choice to leave. I had no choice. I could stay in Guinea and watch my brother and sister starve, or I could leave and try to find a new home for us. I dreamed about finding a home where I would be able to go to work, they would be able to go to school for the first time, and we would all eat well at night. First, I traveled to the bigger cities, but I couldn't find any work there, not even in Conakry, so I traveled past my country's borders. I had never left my village before, and suddenly, I was alone in a strange country. I walked for days and hitched rides on passing trucks. I slept on the streets and begged for change. Sometimes, people would leave scraps of food at my feet, and I would find them when I woke up. I met many other boys like me on my journey. We had all left our homes in search of something better. It seemed like no countries wanted us, so we kept traveling north together. Now, we are here at our final border crossing. We have all traveled so far, we have lost so much, you can ask any one of us, and we will tell you the same thing: We will make it to Europe, or we will die trying. There is no other way home.

Thinking about the brother and sister he left behind, Bambino grew serious. "I worry about what will become of them." He left them with a distant cousin, promising, as many departing migrants do, that he would repay his cousin richly once he reached Europe. "I thought, I will get a good job, and I will send all of my money home to him. Then, my cousin will be happy." But Bambino is aware that his cousin's house already had too many hungry children to feed before he added two more. He worries that with every passing day, his siblings become a heavier burden for his extended family to carry.

Standing at a lanky 5 feet 6 inches tall, Bambino keeps his black hair closely cropped with Moneba's razor blade. His face is round and full, his skin a smooth, deep ebony, his eyes wide and amber in the light.

He looks at least two years younger than his 13 years and better suited for beginning middle school in the fall than crossing international borders on his own. Yet I know from all of my time spent listening to the stories of those who traveled before him that Bambino has been aged by his years on the migratory route. Extortion and abuse always accompany long journeys like the one he took—first paying smugglers to help him cross jihadist-controlled regions of Mali and then trekking across the vast Sahara Desert to the heavily militarized border between Morocco and Algeria, where gangs armed with dogs and machetes hide out waiting to attack. "When I have a good job in Europe," he said, "I will buy my brother and sister plane tickets, so they don't have to do the crossing like me. Someday, I will tell them my stories, and they won't believe all of them, but they will be so thankful for me."

When you have sacrificed everything to arrive where you are standing, when you have no home to return to or the people you left behind are depending on your success for their very survival, the stakes are high. At 13 and 25, both Bambino and Moneba speak about

FIGURE 0.1 Bambino sits on a rock at the edge of his camp, looking down over the Spanish enclave of Melilla, the Mediterranean Sea, and mainland Spain in the distance. Morocco, 2015.
Photograph by the author.

their lives like a game of chance. Their pasts have toughened them. Their present tries them. And they hide their fierce determination for a better future beneath faces that give way a little too easily to a smile. "We have suffered great things," Bambino, pictured in Figure 0.1 above, said. "But we know that someday the suffering will end." Sitting at the northern lookout point of their camp, he focuses his eyes on the waters of the Mediterranean just below. Mainland Spain is a shoreline in the distance, Melilla a lush green pasture almost reachable past the razor wire.

They wait until the darkest hours of night to storm the fences. It is a daunting ring of three 20-foot-high razor-wire barriers, and every inch of the border is under video surveillance by the Guardia Civil, Spain's oldest law enforcement agency. The Guardia Civil is a national military force carrying out police duties, tasked primarily with patrolling Spain's southern borders and controlling the flow of migrants, refugees, and asylum seekers from Africa. Bambino had trained for this moment. His brotherhood had hidden their newly constructed ladders in the brush at the base of the mountain. Their order had been selected. They had practiced again and again. "It is an honor to be in the first round of stormers," Moneba explained. "It means that you are one of the strongest, one of the fastest—but it is also a sacrifice." The older and more experienced brothers are expected to go first. They accept this position, knowing there will be no one in front of them guaranteeing their safety, even if they succeed in crossing all three fences. They will be the first to absorb the baton blows from the Guardia Civil. Touching foot to Spanish soil no longer grants individuals even their most basic human rights.

I have seen it many times before. The first round of stormers runs in unison toward the first fence. They throw their ladders over their heads, aiming the hooks they have made from bent nails and affixed to the tops of the ladders to catch on the crest of the fence. With their shoes removed for greater dexterity on the chain link, they clamber, all fingers and toes, up the fence until they can grasp the lowest rung of the ladders that are hanging above them. Once they have reached the top of the first fence, they wait, positioned to help the second round of stormers following behind them. Only after the third and final round of stormers has reached the top of the first fence, they toss their ladders down to the dusty trench between the first and second fences. Then they repeat the exercise, again hooking their ladders and clambering up and down the second and third fences. The first round of stormers are expected to pull up and ease down those who grow weak or tired behind them. After they have reached the top of the final fence, their hands and feet now open wounds and their clothing shredded by the razor wire, the real sacrifice begins. Leaving their ladders suspended on the back side of the third fence, those who have not yet been beaten off the fence by the Guardia Civil on their descent make a perilous jump to the ground. "If we are lucky," Moneba said, "there may only be one guard for every five of us. But if we aren't lucky, then there will be five guards for every one of us." This is when the batons start striking flesh.

Ceuta and Melilla represent the front lines of Europe's fight against what is commonly called "clandestine" or undocumented migration. Yet there is little discussion of the fact that many of the men, women, and children, like Bambino, who arrive at Europe's borders in North Africa have legal claims to asylum. Inside of Morocco's Spanish enclaves, the bodies of those fleeing conflict and poverty in their home countries are stripped of their human rights. They are routinely beaten and occasionally killed at the hands of Spanish authorities, with minimal media coverage given to the ensuing cases. Chiefs like Moneba are well aware of the risks. He explained that Bambino would be placed in the third round of stormers. "I think I am strong enough to run in the front," Bambino countered, "but the younger boys always get placed behind their brothers."

The camp fell quiet as Moneba spoke, giving last-minute instructions and reassuring his brotherhood with the knowledge he gained in his previous attempts. "I have crossed six times now," he said with humility in his voice. "So the boys listen to me." There was mounting excitement as dusk fell and the group prepared for their trek down the mountain, where they would stage themselves in the bush alongside their hidden ladders. I heard Moneba speak to them in fragmented whispers. "Don't let your body feel pain. Pain will slow you down. Hold the ladder steady for the ones behind you. Don't drop it until you are certain that everyone has reached the top." And most importantly, "If you reach the other side, RUN."

Moneba instructed his brothers to put one bloodied foot in front of the other and run as quickly and directly as they could toward the two cement structures that serve as detention centers—the places they have been taught to recognize as "Europe." In fact, anyone touching foot in Melilla is firmly planted within the borders of the EU—a group of nations that were foundational in creating our current international human rights laws. Yet within the confines of Spanish Morocco, legal conventions are being twisted in the name of "border enforcement," and even unaccompanied minors with legal claims to asylum are routinely pushed back across the border and into the hell they just risked their lives to escape. The rare ones among them who reach the safety of a detention center are granted a review of their cases. The process takes an average of 24 months and often longer for unaccompanied minors, but if their claims to asylum are approved and they are given official refugee status, then they will be resettled to mainland Europe. Migrants whose claims are denied should be properly repatriated to their home countries at the end of the review process.

"In all of my attempts," Moneba said, once we were alone, "my journey ended in the hands of the Guardia Civil. If you are lucky, they beat you, open the doors in the fences with their keys, and push you back to the other side. If you aren't lucky, they deport you to the desert and you must start again at zero." As chief, Moneba lives in constant fear of his brothers being illicitly "repatriated" to the desolate stretch of the Sahara that runs along the border between Morocco and Algeria, where he knows all too well the chances of survival are slim. But he had a good feeling about this crossing.

Bambino was wearing his one pair of tattered jeans and one of two T-shirts he had to his name. It was his favorite, the one with "Lacoste" printed in large letters across the back. "I like the alligator," he said, as he took his shoes off by loosening the tape that held them in place and stashed them beside a tree. "It brings me strength." Nervously, he played with the bracelet he strung together from twigs the previous day. He had a habit of humming to himself. The brothers who had been selected as the watchmen for this mission made their way down to get a count of the guards, taking caution to place their feet on rocky patches and avoid crunching the leaves underfoot. When they returned to whisper their findings, Moneba could not hide his disappointment. The guards were on both sides of the border that night. The brotherhood would have to carry their ladders to the other end of the fence—a greater distance from the detention centers—and Moneba decided at the last minute to split the group. Pulling Bambino and others with him, he instructed the remaining boys to return to the camp. "I can't risk losing everyone."

Beginning in 2015, the global media turned attention to a migrant and refugee "crisis" unfolding in Europe, and the numbers were powerful. According to the United Nations (UN), nearly 1.3 million people arrived desperately seeking refuge on European shores in the year 2015. Like Bambino, more than 25 percent of them were under the age of 18 and traveling alone. Thousands of unnamed others lost their lives in attempted crossings in the years that followed. As the number of people fleeing the ongoing war in Syria slowly declined, the number fleeing political and economic instability in other countries across the Middle East and Africa began to rise. They traveled the same well-grooved routes toward Greece, Italy, and Spain. The Mediterranean Sea quickly became one of the most trafficked and deadliest migratory routes in the world, as it remains to this day. The lesser-told stories of migration that can be found in hidden camps on the other side of the European border in Morocco reveal an unfolding crisis of equally grave proportion. While headlines direct attention elsewhere, the EU has been molding North African countries into final destinations for African migrants, refugees, and asylum seekers attempting to make their way north and setting a precedent for a new era of mass border externalization.

According to the Universal Declaration of Human Rights, all men, women, and children are guaranteed a number of fundamental rights by birth, regardless of their country of birth. Most central among these is the individual's right to seek asylum in another country if they are no longer safe in their own. These laws were originally created so that every individual, whether fleeing the war-torn landscapes of Bambino's home country or the poverty-stricken cities that he encountered in his long journey across West Africa, would have the chance to seek a better tomorrow. Yet the conditions under which a country should be declared unsafe and an asylum seeker should be granted official refugee status have been contested since the declaration was signed in 1948. Refugee status is not unlimited. The number of people given status every year is determined by quotas that host countries set, which means that asylum seekers must not only "prove" that their claim is valid, they must prove that they are more deserving of refuge than all of the others who will be heard by their caseworker on that given day. While quotas should, in theory, move in tandem with global humanitarian crises and the needs of those who are forced to flee their homes, a clearer correlation can be found with the needs of host countries to bolster their own economies through cheap sources of labor or with the political persuasion of the current administrations in power. The United States, for instance, granted status to the highest number of refugees—over 200,000—under President Jimmy Carter in 1980 and had the lowest refugee resettlement quota to date—granting status to only 21,292 refugees—under President Donald Trump. This latter figure is despite the fact that Trump's presidency began in the midst of the largest human displacement crisis since World War II. According to the United Nations Refugee Agency (also known as the UN High Commissioner for Refugees or the UNHCR), a record 68.5 million people around the world have now been forced from their homes. This amounts to nearly 1 in every 100 people in the world today.

Like the United States, European nations publicly claim that they are overwhelmed by the number of people fleeing conflict and poverty in their home countries, and bolstered by these claims, they have started pushing back. The stories of Bambino, Moneba, and hundreds of thousands of others like them who remain trapped across North Africa reveal how the Guardia Civil has routinized the process of pushing migrants back across the border before they have a chance to apply for asylum. Officials operating on Moroccan soil are then free to carry out abuses that would be punishable under European and international law—improperly repatriating, beating, and even killing those who dare to make a second attempt at crossing, not to mention denying them the right to seek asylum. It is important to remember that our international human rights laws were established in recent history. They were created to address the large number of Jewish families who had been displaced from their homes during World War II and no longer felt safe returning. They were never intended to address displacement on a global scale, nor were they expected to last as long as they have. The legal categories of "refugee" and "asylum seeker" served the political climate of post-World War II Europe, and as Europe stands in the midst of a new "crisis" today, they continue to be a reflection of political ambitions. The current media frenzy surrounding migration, whether in the EU, the United States, or elsewhere, similarly emphasizes the urgency of the situation. The imagined state of emergency that has been created is central to the development and legitimization of violent border regimes.

In reality, all of those setting out on journeys like Bambino's are migrants until their claims for asylum have been reviewed and a foreign government has officially granted them the coveted status of "refugee."

One way to deal with a growing refugee "crisis" is to keep people from ever becoming refugees in the first place by stripping them of their most fundamental human rights. This is being done through a process that I term "border externalization." In the EU, billions are being spent every year to keep Africans—the world's largest population of displaced persons—out of Europe, so that they never have the chance to claim asylum there. But this practice of creating a buffer zone by pushing back the borders of one country into another less developed country on the periphery is not found in Europe alone. In fact, Australia's radical border security model, which was established in 2001, has influenced the border policies of other nations around the world. Australia set a precedent for "offshoring" asylum when it began sending migrants and asylum seekers who were being detained in private centers throughout the mainland to two new detention centers constructed on the small South Pacific island nations of Nauru and Manus in Papua New Guinea. A decade later, in 2013, Australia's new model for border security gained international attention for its novel use of media in trying to deter new migrants and asylum seekers before their journeys to Australia began. The multibillion dollar campaign included commercials, a feature-length film, and a graphic novel depicting asylum seekers suffering from extreme physical and mental health issues in an offshore detention center in the Pacific Islands. The campaign was translated into 18 different languages.

In 2018, the United States announced that it would begin requiring all migrants arriving at the southern border to claim asylum to return to Mexico until a final court ruling on their cases was announced. The policy, following on the heels of Australia's "success," was an unprecedented step toward outsourcing the United States' asylum processing by an administration still bent on constructing a wall between the United States and Mexico. Like those trapped in North African countries or on the islands of Nauru and Manus, asylum seekers who are forcibly returned to Mexico are left without the basic social services guaranteed to them under international law: rights to interpreters, legal counsel, emergency medical assistance, and state-sponsored accommodation in a safe location while their cases are under review.

Border externalization works through political agreements in which countries like Australia, the United States, and those across Europe pay countries just beyond their borders. In exchange for these payments, the countries are expected to act as permanent holding cells for migrants fleeing political or economic instability. As Bambino's narrative illustrates, it can be difficult to draw a line between one driver for migration and another. More commonly, multiple complicating factors of conflict, poverty, persecution, and lack of educational or work opportunities at home drive movement across international borders. It is no coincidence that the holding cells that Australia, the United States, and countries across Europe have supported are not only located in significantly poorer countries, they are often in places where foreign media is tightly controlled. In Morocco, Libya, and Algeria, gaining clearance to conduct research as an academic, journalist, or filmmaker can be challenging. Gaining clearance for research that may expose human rights violations is not possible. From the beginning, I knew this project would require periods of work undercover and that the risks would mount along with the stories that were uncovered.

Human rights violations have grown more pervasive in migrant-dominated spaces throughout North Africa, and I have watched as major international aid organizations that were once on the ground serving the most vulnerable, like Doctors Without Borders (also known as *Médecins Sans Frontières* [MSF]), have also been stripped of their rights to work. Operating on foreign soil far from the gaze of researchers and aid workers means little to no accountability for officials guarding North African borders and policing the unofficial migrant camps and official detention centers there. With both populist movements and human displacement on the rise around the world, one of the greatest challenges we will face as a global community is ensuring the fundamental human rights of those who have been forced to flee their homes and no longer have a country to defend them. At the very least, it is our global responsibility to ensure that migration journeys do not trap individuals in places as dangerous as—or even more than—those they are fleeing.

As an anthropologist, I believe that in order to tell someone's story well, you have to live it. I spent more than three years living alongside the individuals whose stories bring this book and my related documentary film project, *The Burning*, to life. Beginning in their home countries of the Democratic Republic of the Congo, Sierra Leone, and Mali, we traveled over 9,000 miles in all, as they moved closer to the promise of a better tomorrow. The majority of my research for both projects ended up being rooted in Libya, Algeria, and Morocco, where the individuals I traveled with found themselves trapped for years on end—in detention centers and hidden forest camps like the one Bambino calls home. My own journey to bring these projects to life meant days spent traversing deserts by foot, weeks spent packed in the back of smugglers' trucks, and months spent sleeping on the forest floor, where food, water, and shelter are always scarce. When weekly police raids decimated what little the brotherhoods had amassed and officers detained those who were captured, I was not immune. My journey has also meant my own imprisonment, torture, and the repeated loss of my research. It has meant starting over again and again. But in the end, it has meant forging the deepest of bonds with those who have trusted me to share their stories with you. I will not stop until their voices have been heard.

As the first light touched the sky, I remember Moneba walking back up the rocky path to their camp. He had a boy thrown over his shoulder. The boy's clothing was wet with blood, his eyes beaten shut. Moneba eased him down on the ground, and we all gathered around to see a broken femur bone piercing through the boy's skin. He was the most critically injured in the group, but he was not the only one. Those who avoided beatings by the guards showed the ravages of razor wire on flesh. Bambino, who had been placed in the third round of stormers despite his protests, was only midway up the second fence when he and his brothers received orders to turn back. The guards were too many, the stormers were too few, and it was clear that none of them would be able to run to safety that night. The first of the watchmen had already been handcuffed and forced to board a bus that would "deport" them to the Sahara Desert. Moneba, not wanting to lose more brothers in a single mission, instructed them to throw their ladders in the opposite direction and run—this time, back up into the forest where they would patch their wounds and wait. Morale was surprisingly high among the brotherhood, a group well accustomed to disappointment. "Any crossing that we all escape alive," Moneba said, "is a small success."

"*Hrig*," the Moroccan Arabic term for "illegal immigration," translates to "burning." It signifies the literal burning of one's identification papers in order to avoid repatriation if arrested by authorities on the long journey to Europe. But it signifies more than just that. It is the symbolic burning of one's past in hopes of finding a better future abroad. The burning, like a sacrificial rite, is a desperate offering of old lives in exchange for a chance at survival. Morocco is now overflowing with *"harragas,"* or African migrants who have burned all that they had to their names for this chance. Lacking the resources to retrace the thousands of miles that now separate them from their home countries and beaten back at every European border, they camp, they train, and they wait, dreaming of escape. "You could call this place purgatory," Bambino said, as he pressed a small bundle of burning leaves on his friend's leg to quiet the bleeding. "But we call it hell. We're all trapped here waiting in hell."

Burning at Europe's Borders

....

CHAPTER 1

The Question of Ethnography

No one leaves home
unless home is the mouth of a shark.

—Warsan Shire
[excerpt from "Home"]

....

Introduction

In one of my first anthropology courses as an undergraduate student at New York University, I remember Professor Thomas Beidelman instructing us: "There is no better study of a man than what he chooses to study." I would amend this to include women and the things *she* chooses to study, but at the root of Beidelman's statement lies an important point about the underlying questions that all anthropologists carry into "the field" with us. These are not our research questions, but the questions that led us to our research in the first place—the *why*. In the decade that followed, it became increasingly clear to me that the places and people, the issues and questions we choose to study are in every way a reflection of us. Emplacement, a noun, means "to put in a place or a position." For me, the process of emplacing myself as a researcher in a region of the world that is not my own has been two-fold. It required me to continually clarify my *why* to respondents throughout my fieldwork, and it requires me to now clarify my position in the field to readers of my research.

I believe it is important for anthropologists to be transparent about their positions in the field and for readers to remain aware of the limitations and unique possibilities that are created by each position. The same fieldwork that led to the pages before you, had it been conducted by a researcher who identifies as black, male, or Moroccan, would most certainly have led to a different book. My position as a young, white, female, American researcher in Morocco[1] shaped my access to the places that informed my research and the information that people revealed to or concealed from me in those places. Yet, before I first arrived in Morocco's capital city of Rabat in 2007, my desire to ask the questions I set out to ask had been shaped by my own life experiences.

To the men and women who became not only my primary respondents, but my close friends, I explained that I was a researcher specializing in international human rights. I was asking questions to fuel my study of the rapidly changing migration patterns across Africa, I was completing a large-scale research project on the externalization of borders from Europe to Africa, and I was hopeful that my work would have some impact on the lives of migrants trapped across North Africa.[2] But as I realized just how little these words explained, I began reaching further back, searching not for *what* I was doing but *why* I was doing it. It was not to answer questions about human migration. Not to write a book about a new era of border control. Not even to bring fundamental human rights to those whose rights were being denied. I began explaining instead that a transient childhood left me with a deep curiosity about how individual and group identities are constructed in the face of change. It left me with an interest in the unique struggles of migrant communities, and especially those of migrant youth who grow up feeling like their feet are firmly planted in two different worlds.

Throughout college, my experiences influenced my research on the integration of migrant youth in public schools and the exploitation of migrant labor in the service industry—the United States' largest private-sector workforce and the single largest employer of foreign-born workers. In the following years, while studying film at the Spéos Institute in France, my experiences shaped my desire to document the growing socioeconomic divide between Maghrebi and French populations in the Parisian *banlieues*. (Please see the Glossary for definitions of terms such as *banlieues*.) As riots exploded on the outskirts of Paris, it propelled my move farther south to explore how the countries that France's expanding Maghrebi population had once called home were impacted by the loss of nearly 10 percent of their population to immigration. In Morocco, my experiences set me on a path to asking how identity is constructed by migrants, neither in their countries of origin nor in the migrant-populated suburbs where they struggle to build new communities, but in the spaces that lie in between. For the rapidly expanding population of African migrants trapped in Morocco, I wanted to understand what it means to be neither here nor there. What does it mean to exist for an indefinite period of time in a space between an old home and a new one that is only miles away on the other side of the Mediterranean Sea and yet perpetually out of reach?

Today, 12 years after I first set foot in Morocco, I can finally explain that I was seeking a deeper understanding of the human need for identity and the complicated ways in which we construct, deconstruct, and reconstruct it. Migrants' states of liminality between two homes expose this basic human need, and spaces of migrant resettlement and "un-settlement" are therefore a locus for key anthropological questions about how individual, group, and national identities can be shaped by the imaginary lines of borders. Before returning to school to begin a doctorate in anthropology, I spent several years living in North Africa, where my work centered on reforming migrant detention systems and researching the multilateral immigration policies that were leading to the rapid expansion of a new migrant class in Libya, Algeria, and Morocco. Morocco's migrant population comes from across the African continent—the vast majority of them fleeing West and Central Africa. Regardless of their country of origin, they view Morocco as a temporary stop en route to political stability, freedom from persecution, or greater economic and educational opportunities in Europe and beyond. Yet, the externalization of Europe's borders has made their final crossings increasingly difficult and has trapped hundreds of thousands under deplorable conditions in detention centers and hidden forest camps.

In my first months of fieldwork in 2013, I struggled to clarify to this population trapped in North Africa what exactly I hoped to leave with. As anthropologists, we are not simply visitors to a place, perched on the borders of a community. We do more than watch and listen. We live deeply entrenched in the workings of a place and in the lives of a people for extended periods of time. Anthropologists arrive, we take, and we leave. I think it is safe to assume that the majority of us leave with the hope of giving something back, whether through the direct impact of our continued involvement in the community or the indirect impact of our research. Some of the ethnographers among us believe there is a gift to be found in revealing stories that often go untold or voices that often go unheard by wider audiences. There is a gift in lifting individual experiences to the global stage to be seen, recorded, and remembered. But we must reconcile the fact that before we give, we take. And so I told the communities and brotherhoods, the families and individuals who opened their doors or led me to their camps, *As-salaam alaikum*—may peace be upon you. I am an anthropologist. I am interested in you, in the stories that you have to tell, and in the journey that brought you here. I am driven by a desire to bring global attention to the struggles of those trapped at Europe's borders and what I believe is a growing humanitarian crisis in North Africa. But I am also driven by my own passion for drawing connections across diverse human experience, for understanding what unites you—across time and space—with others whose lives have been shaped by the imaginary lines around them, and for the lost art of storytelling. I am here to take a gift, which you are so generously giving to me.

I left for fieldwork without knowing that my greatest challenge would lie not in analyzing mountains of survey data or following competing accounts of migration across media outlets in the Maghreb. It would lie not even in securing interviews with high-ranking governmental officials or gaining access to migrant detainees. My greatest challenge would lie in building close friendships. When working with vulnerable populations, building a researcher–respondent relationship is never enough. Being gifted with the words of those whose stories can be their greatest risk comes only after building trust, understanding, and mutual respect—and what is that but friendship? I knew that between the past and the future, between one home and the next, there is a space of uncertainty that we have all experienced at one time or another in our lives. It is a space where fear and possibility live side by side. I had witnessed how, when confronted with the most extreme forms of uncertainty, there is a human tendency to deny the present state through a constant remembering of the past and a reimagining of the future. By not fully existing in the present, one can survive what seems insurmountable. I knew that in this space, a new form of individual and group identity emerges, but it was only through the close friendships I slowly built with respondents that I was able to explore my larger questions: What are the new forms of identity that emerge in liminality, and how long can the liminal state last?

New Forms of Riutal

Throughout my analysis, I apply the key anthropological concept of liminality by viewing migration as a transformational ritual. I argue that around the world, border externalization is leading to new forms of migration from the global south to the global south and leaving populations trapped in liminal states between their home countries and intended destinations for undefined periods of time. The concept of liminality was first developed in the early twentieth century by ethnographer Arnold van Gennep (1909) and later advanced through anthropologist Victor Turner's research on ritual rites of passage (1969). Van Gennep distinguished between three different types of ritual activity: those that mark the transition of an individual, those that mark the transition of a group, and those that mark the passage of time. However, his ethnographic attention was centered on what he termed "*rites de passage*," or "rituals marking, helping, or celebrating individual or collective passages through the cycle of life" (van Gennep 1909; Szakolczai 2009: 141). Most importantly, he isolated three distinct phases of the *rite de passage*, or liminal rites, which Turner would later term the preliminal, liminal, and postliminal phases. These three distinct phases mark the passage of an individual or group from one culturally defined status within an established social structure to another status within that same social structure. Through an initiation ceremony, for instance, the child transitions to an adult; through a graduation ceremony, the student of law transitions to an attorney at law; through a marriage ceremony, the single man and woman transition to a married husband and wife; and through a citizenship ceremony, a group of immigrants transition to citizens of a new country. Liminal rites continue to be central to the structure of modern societies.

The first phase, or *rite of separation*, requires a metaphorical "death." It is here that I highlight the first parallel between an initiate's experience of transition from one social status to another and a migrant's experience of "burning" one home for another. Van Gennep argued that all liminal rites require the establishment of a "*tabula rasa*" by breaking with one's previous social status. In this phase, both the initiate and the migrant must break with what was known before. Children, for instance, are separated from their home and family and moved to a new space where their initiation ceremony will take place. By physically burning whatever documentation they have to certify their name, history, and very existence—birth certificate, passport, diplomas, health records, bank cards—migrants are breaking with their known social status as citizens of their home country and establishing a clean slate.

In the middle phase, or *rite of liminality*, the initiand and the migrant stand at the threshold between what was known before and what still lies ahead. It is here, in liminality, that they are seen as both vulnerable and threatening to the established social structure. Initiands standing between two social statuses do not have the protection of either, and yet their temporary placement between the two threatens to upset the social structure by creating something that falls outside of accepted categories of identification. What is an individual who is neither child nor adult; neither student nor professional; neither single nor married; neither immigrant nor citizen of the state? In the middle phase, the migrant's vulnerability stems from a lack of protection by both their home country and the intended destination country. But existing without documentation, they are paperless and unaccounted for, which also makes them difficult to police. They are seen as a threat to their temporary homes, where citizens commonly voice concerns about migrants draining resources and bringing disease, crime, terrorism, or economic instability with them.

In the final phase, or *rite of incorporation*, the initiand is reincorporated into the established social structure under a new status. Children, for instance, having completed their ceremony, return to their home and family as adults. For migrants who remain in liminality for undefined periods of time, this phase never arrives. Examining the tripartite structure of liminal rites through a contemporary anthropological lens, they can be viewed as overtly destructive—ties to self and community must be broken or burned—but they can also be viewed as constructive. It is the destructive nature of the first phase that allows a new identity to be constructed, as the initiand and migrant move closer to the final phase of the ritual. How then do we understand the experiences of those who endure a preliminal breaking or burning without ever progressing into postliminal reincorporation? According to van Gennep's earliest theorizations, the liminal phase commonly involves acts of pain or suffering meant to prove one's preparation for the transition that lies ahead. Living outside of the known social structure forces those in liminality to question the self. As time passes, those who are trapped there begin to feel "nameless, spatiotemporally dislocated, and socially unstructured" (Thomassen 2006: 322). This, I argue, is the subject position occupied by migrants trapped in the liminal space of Morocco.

Most research suggests that because antistructure always tends toward structure in the end, liminality is rarely permanent and those in states of transition will eventually be subsumed back into the social structure from which they broke. However, Turner finds that a liminal period can become "fixed" in times when "the suspended character of social life takes on a more permanent character" (Thomassen 2009: 16; Szakolczai 2000).³ Under sustained periods of liminality, the liminal community can create its own distinct social structure termed "normative *communitas*" (Turner 1969), or "schismogenesis" (Bateson 1935).⁴ I continue to question how liminality functions as an anthropological concept today—one that has been linked to borders and disputed territories (e.g., Krasniqi 2019; Horst & Grabska 2015); to migrants and refugees (e.g., Agier 2002; Bauman 2004); and even to the subject position of anthropologists in the field, "separated from [their] culture yet not incorporated into the host culture" (e.g., Stoller 2008; Robben & Sluka

FIGURE 1.1 Map of Primary Migratory Routes between Africa and Southern Europe.
Source: Image is based on a 2012 version of MTM i-Map (imap-migration.org).

2007: 76). Paul Stoller's work examines how it is the anthropologist's fate to always be between things—countries, languages, cultures, even realities. He highlights the creative power of the between, showing how it can transform us, changing our conceptions of who we are, what we know, and how we live in the world (2008). What remains to be explored are the new forms of identity and *communitas* that are emerging under sustained experiences of liminality at our world's most critical borders.

If experiences of migration can in fact function to move individuals between distinct ritual phases and categories of identification without formally established systems or ceremonies, these are not rituals as van Gennep and Turner first envisioned them. There is a new form of ritual at play. In this new form of ritual, there is no expectation of reincorporation. Migrants like Bambino and Moneba burn their pasts for the chance at a future. They are actively choosing to burn their material identities and step into the liminal phase, knowing the pain that will come with it and the low statistical likelihood of their success in the end. Van Gennep and Turner never envisioned children stepping into initiation ceremonies with the knowledge that only a small number of them would emerge from the ritual as adults. Yet this is a step that migrants like Bambino and Moneba are willing to take in exchange for the hope that they may someday emerge on the other side, feet on European soil, occupying the new social status of refugee.

Mapping Morocco

When I designed the multisited research plan for this project, I was committed to following the journeys of three groups of migrants—each one beginning at a different point on the continent in the Democratic Republic of the Congo, Sierra Leone, and Mali. I did not know that just as each of their journeys would be stalled for many years at Europe's southernmost borders in Morocco, the majority of my own research would end up rooted there.[5] In Morocco, I was based out of three cities of varying size: Oujda, the border city where most migrants first enter the country by way of Algeria and where many will later be deported by officers to some of the region's most barren landscapes; Tangier, the bustling port city where migration has become a cut-throat business for smugglers and where hundreds await their chance at crossing over the rough waters of the Mediterranean Sea every night; and Rabat, the comparatively quiet capital city, home to governmental offices, foreign

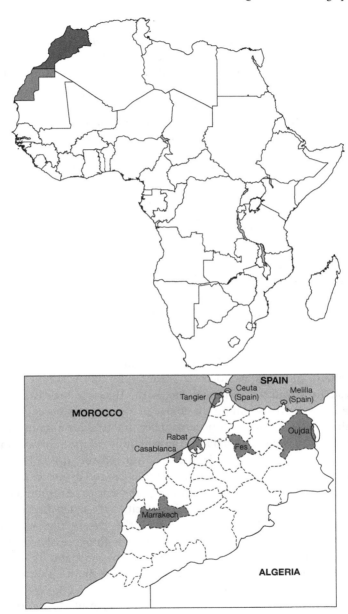

FIGURE 1.2 Map of Africa with Morocco and Primary Research Sites Highlighted.

aid organizations, and a substantial number of African migrants who are entangled with these offices or organizations. Other places central to my research included the Spanish enclaves of Ceuta and Melilla and the migrant-populated camps and slums that encircle both. In the field, it is easy to feel overwhelmed by data—to feel like every morning *adhan*,[6] every conversation, every blanket of wares spread out for sale on the sidewalk should be recorded for future analysis. In the barrage of sights and sounds to be notated and photographed, I took refuge in routine. My routine was established in large part by categorizing my research and my life into the distinct cities and communities that shaped it. Rabat was my home base, and Rabat's central train station was the place where I regularly boarded the four-hour train north to Tangier or began the long journey east to Oujda—a far-flung point on the map that required a combination of winding bus rides and the generosity of passing cars along the final stretch of the trip.

In order to contextualize Morocco's capital city, my home away from home, one must first have a basic understanding of the country's diverse topography and the unique character of the other major cities that are scattered throughout. Morocco is a long, thin slice of land curving around the corner of northern Africa—only 225 miles across at its narrowest point and less than 625 miles long when measured from Tangier to the top of the Western Sahara's disputed territory.[7] Slightly larger than California, Morocco is bordered by the Atlantic Ocean to the west, the Mediterranean Sea to the north, Algeria to the east, and the Sahara Desert to the south. In the course of one day, my bus could leave the balmy shores of the Atlantic, cross over the Atlas Mountains, snow-capped in all seasons, and arrive in the arid dunes of the Sahara—waves of sand stretching to the horizon like a vast red sea. It is a beautiful landscape, and I was fortunate to travel it again and again on my own journeys from north to south and through the stories of respondents.

Moving between Morocco's different cities often felt like moving between countries. I came to associate the desert region, which regularly reaches above 110°F in the summer, with oppressive heat, the unquenchable thirst of your throat rubbed raw by sand, and the dangers that open spaces and high visibility presented to the migrants I traveled with—but also with the peace that accompanies complete silence. If the desert presents migrants with a broad range of natural threats, then Tangier presents them with an equally broad range of human ones. Tangier, located on the northern coast where the Mediterranean Sea meets the Atlantic Ocean and Spain is visible just beyond the shore, has long attracted foreign artists and writers to its dirty, sprawling streets, and maintains its reputation as a melting pot of European and Islamic culture. It is the crossing point from which many migrants attempt their final escape and the epicenter of the country's smuggling activity. In Tangier, the daily rhythms of life revolve around critical exchanges—a community's savings for a seat on a boat, a boy's limb for a chance at the fences, bodies routinely exchanged for handfuls of sweaty cash.

Traveling south from Tangier, you pass through Ouezzane and reach Fès, often called "the Moroccan's Morocco." Fès was the long-standing capital city until French colonial powers restructured the nation in the early 1900s, and there remains a certain authenticity to it. The city is known for its artisans and traditional leather tanneries. Walking the streets day or night, the acidic smell of dying baths hangs heavy in the air, and the red-hued fog let off by drying carcasses clouds your vision. It always feels to me as if the maze of the central *medina*,[8] begging you to duck and squeeze through low, narrow passageways, is intent on keeping those who do not belong there perpetually lost.

If you continue your inland journey south, you will eventually hit Marrakech, a city that thrives on foreign tourism and boasts the world's largest outdoor marketplace. *Jamaa el-fna*, meaning "Assembly of the Dead," is the central square, famously home to snake charmers and fortune tellers, pickpockets and street performers, child beggars and prostitutes. Located on a flat plateau in central Morocco, Marrakech is surrounded by the peaks of the High Atlas range, and even in the winter months, the sun burns and the slightest breeze stirs up the desert sand underfoot. There are gritty hostels alongside lavish hotels, and there are street hawkers accosting you at every turn. Vendor after vendor sell the same strings of dried figs and rugs spun in vibrant hues. Despite periods of national economic recession, real estate development continues in Marrakech, where much of the city's money funnels in from foreign accounts. It feels like Disney World's version of Morocco, packaged and sold to throngs of Europeans who crowd the *medina's* old streets in their running shoes and tank tops, faces freckled from mornings spent lounging by hotel pools and hands painted red with henna.

On the western coast of the country is Casablanca, the largest city in Morocco and the fifth largest city in Africa, with a population of 3.5 million. Although it is only 50 miles down the Atlantic coast from the country's capital, Casablanca is the primary port of entry and the center of economic and commercial activity. It serves as home base to most international corporations operating in Morocco and houses the nation's primary industrial facilities. Lacking the crumbling *medina* walls that dominate the infrastructure of other Moroccan cities, Casablanca can appear uniform and colorless from the outside—a city built for business with colonial remains and skyscrapers in place of *riads*.

Rabat, or *ar-Ribaat*, meaning "a fortified place," is only the fourth largest city in Morocco, but as the country's capital, it is home to the parliamentary building and the crown jewel of the king's many palaces. It is also home to the national university and foreign embassies, making it the center of academic and governmental activity. The walls that once protected the small Atlantic port city from outside invaders still stand around the *medina*. The Bou Regreg River runs alongside these crumbling walls, dividing Rabat from Salé, a smaller city, which now serves as a lower-income bedroom community for those working in Rabat. Together with Temara, a middle-income bedroom community on the other side of Rabat, the population is 1.8 million and growing.[9] While Rabat's role as a port of entry has diminished, it remains a stronghold for the textile, agricultural, and construction industries. The labor demanded by these industries and the promise of aid through nongovernmental organizations (NGOs) draw many African migrants to the city as a "temporary" home.

Morocco's capital was relocated from Fès to Rabat by the country's colonial-era French administrator, General Hubert Lyautey. Following this decision, Sultan Moulay Youssef moved his official residence to Rabat, and in 1913, General Lyautey hired a French architect to redesign the city and establish an official administrative quarter. This large-scale reconstruction project resulted in what is now referred to as the "*ville nouvelle.*" When Morocco gained independence from French rule in 1956, King Mohammed V, then leader of the nation, chose to leave the capital in Rabat and reclaimed the newly developed *ville nouvelle* as home for the monarchy's governmental offices, where they remain to this day. The buildings are grand and imposing, lining both sides of the main thoroughfare, *Avenue Mohammed V*, with columned fronts, wrought iron gates, and guards standing in full military regalia, loaded assault weapons ready at their sides. At first glance, it could be any number of postcolonial cities, but beneath the influence of French architecture are the etchings of Islamic stars and red and green national flags. In Rabat, as in other Moroccan cities, the *ville nouvelle* is reserved for commercial activity, while the sprawling suburbs are home to Moroccans and a rapidly expanding population of migrants from across the African continent.

Conducting ethnographic research on migrants' daily lives in and around Rabat, I returned often to the notion of emplacement, thinking about my own experiences as a foreigner in Morocco and how they converged with, and then so radically diverged from, respondents' experiences of being foreign in a foreign place. I alternated between the "slums"[10] where they lived and the marketplaces where many worked as "hawkers"[11] at one point or another. The heart of Rabat is divided between the *ville nouvelle* and the *medina*, and this divide continues to serve as a stark contrast between the pre- and postcolonial periods—marking old and new, Arab and European, struggling and elite.

Rabat's *medina* is a labyrinth of crumbling white and blue buildings. They are one, two, or three stories at most, and hollowed out in the center where the homeowner's courtyard would have been. Most buildings still have their original doors, hand-carved works of art that require you to shrink down as you pass through them under the *hand of Fatima*. Window glass is uncommon, but lower-level window openings are protected by iron bars and occasionally covered with hanging sheets or towels for privacy. Rarely, you will see a door fashioned with a modern touch like a lock, doorbell, or house number for mail delivery. Along the main thoroughfares, each building now serves multiple purposes, housing large families on the upper levels and restaurants, shops, or small factories on the lower levels.

Within one block, you can pass black-market DVD stands, rolling fruit carts, and a modern storefront selling organically produced argan oil products to tourists—one bottle marketed for healthy cooking, another for a smoother face. But there is an order to the madness. Along *Avenue Mohammed V*, you find peddlers of used clothing from dusk until the evening *adhan* and used cookware only in the mornings. A walk along *Avenue Souika* is much like a walk through a local grocery store, only there, vendors are packed onto both sides of the street for as far as the eye can see. Some sell vegetables, the familiar colors of peppers, onions, and tomatoes sprinkled before them. Others sell fruits—boxes of oranges, bananas, and prickly pears stacked one on top of the other, with large metal scales and weights sitting at the vendors' feet. The produce varies little from one vendor to the next, each displaying the same variety of vegetables or fruits, on the same blue woolen blankets or old wooden crates, stained from years of rotting food. At first, it is difficult to imagine how the more than 100 vendors that I counted along *Avenue Souika* one Thursday evening could survive with such competition, or how one determines from which vendor to buy their tomatoes. But I imagine that most Moroccans make this choice in much the same way that I did—out of an obligation to a vendor who quickly becomes a friend.

Items that fall in and out of season are sold from rolling carts or out of baskets hung over the handlebars of bicycles that vendors peddle up and down *Avenue Souika* in peak shopping hours. In September, you find baskets full of pomegranates and carts overflowing with strawberries, scales and weights tucked inside of the peddlers' backpacks, as they shout "*Anduk! Anduk!*" and watch the crowds part before them. A few specialty shops sell meat, cheese, and eggs, and on every corner, you find a *hanout*—the smaller ones selling soda, candy, chips, and *khobz*, and the larger ones offering other household products ranging from toilet paper to baby formula. In any country, the marketplace can be illustrative of social hierarchies. In Morocco, shifts in the social hierarchy are marked not only through the national origin of the vendors and hawkers seen on the streets, but through the very goods they are allowed to peddle and hawk and the customers who choose to buy from them.

To the east of the *ville nouvelle*, along the shore of the Bou Regreg River, is Youssoufia. It is a lower-income bedroom community and home to the neighborhood of Taqadoum, which is among the most heavily migrant-populated *banlieues* in Morocco and one of my primary research sites. In contrast to the *medina*'s bustling streets, Taqadoum's narrow passageways reveal a dark and quiet corner of the city. The lack of marketplace activity leaves little but dilapidated apartment buildings, and I am always struck by how still the rooftops are in contrast to those that are crowded with clotheslines, television antennas, and clucking livestock. Distinctions between Morocco's residential neighborhoods are marked by the cost and quality of apartment rentals and by the ease of accessibility to Rabat's commercial district. While higher-income neighborhoods are easily accessible on the city's new tramway, lower-income neighborhoods are accessible only by city buses, which are poorly maintained and significantly less reliable. On any given day, I expected to wait at least one hour for a bus that never runs according to schedule. Yet bus fare is cheap, making it an affordable means of transportation—and often the only means of transportation—for those living on the outskirts of the city and working in the marketplace.

City buses are overloaded with passengers at peak travel times, and the combination of standing-room—or squeezing-room—only and the impropriety of women being in such close proximity to unrelated men in the public sphere means that I would commonly find women sitting at the bus stop for several hours, waiting for the end of rush hour and the arrival of a bus with an open seat. Never sitting idle, the women were often huddled over a task as they waited—mending a dress, peeling a large bag of potatoes to be boiled for dinner, or practicing characters on their way to literacy. In fact, the bus stop became one of the places where I was most likely to find lower-class Moroccan women and migrant women who were willing to share a conversation with me. My conversations with local women trended toward the changing social landscape of their city. Waves of new migrants, they claimed with frustration, made an already "difficult" job even more difficult for them. When pressed on statements like this one, they made it clear that the pressures placed on women in Morocco encouraged them to work exclusively in the private sphere (Newcomb 2006). The conflation of race, class, and "illegality," which is on the rise in Morocco, made public spaces not only gendered (male) spaces, but racialized (black) spaces that were now equated with political and economic marginalization. Moroccan women who already felt shame for their work in the public sphere felt doubly stigmatized by the presence of migrant women in similar positions. In much the same way, migrant women from countries like Nigeria and Ghana felt the added pressure of having moved from a society in which women played a key role in the marketplace and commonly occupied the gendered (female) position of "street hawker." In Morocco, they claimed, there was no place for women outside of the home.

Gender identities and expectations, though experienced in the everyday, are not constructed according to local knowledge alone. As other researchers have explored, they are constructed within expanding geographies of "production, trade, and communication" in our globalized world (Ong & Peletz 1995: 8). In the case of mobile subjects like the Nigerian and Ghanian women I spoke with, they can be reconstructed again and again as they move between public and private spheres at home and along their migratory routes. If we understand identity to be shaped by the complex processes of nation building, the restructuring of global economics, and the transnational flows of people across borders, then we must also appreciate how greater mobility leads to more fluid categories of not only gender, but also race, class, and legality. Cutting across national borders, these categories interact with one another to create nuanced subject positions, and with new forms of interconnection, cultural understandings of what it means to be male or female, local or foreign, are becoming harder to define. My bus stop conversations centered on everyday conflicts between the social expectations placed on women in a Muslim society and the economic pressures placed on everyone (women included) in a struggling society. Understanding the lines—real and imaginary—that delineate Rabat's bus routes, tram lines, and many neighborhoods was essential for examining how the city's inhabitants navigate social spaces and the boundaries between them. It raised important questions about how respondents "read" one another's gendered, classed, and racialized performances of foreignness or belonging and how factors such as work, language, and mode of transit have become key markers of liminality in critical border regions like Morocco.

A Rooftop Home Away from Home

For the period of time that I called Rabat home, I lived on the roof of *Riad Art*—an old home turned bed and breakfast that was buried deep in the city's *medina*. There were five small guest rooms surrounding the courtyard and a maid's quarters that I shared with a young Moroccan woman named Hajar. Hajar cleans the rooms in the morning when the guests set out on their sightseeing tours and spends most of her afternoons doing laundry—a laborious task that requires carrying all of the sheets and towels down to the ocean with a washing board and then stringing them up to dry on the rooftop lines beside the bedroom we shared. Hicham, an industrious middle-aged Moroccan man, was hired as a caretaker by the French couple who owns the building. His job requires everything from managing the reservation calendar and repairing leaky faucets to preparing food and translating train schedules from Arabic to one of the other many languages he speaks, all while keeping his wife and two young children from disturbing the guests living around them. Hicham and his family sleep in a makeshift bedroom off the kitchen on the lower level—he and his wife, Majida, alternating their sleeping schedules on the futon and his then six-year-old son and newborn daughter spending their days in the confines of that small space.

Hicham has been a close friend of mine for many years, and when I first returned to Morocco to begin this project, he offered me a place to sleep. Knowing I would only be able to pay him in the form of *dirhams* occasionally hidden in his pockets and the rare gifts he would request (swimming trunks for himself, whitening cream for his wife, English books for his son, and "American" pacifiers for his newborn), I agreed to the arrangement only if he first agreed to give me a job. Hicham finally conceded that I could take over the role of preparing breakfast for the guests, which would allow him to return to his long-honored tradition of morning soccer matches on the beach. While I prepared a traditional breakfast of *msemen* with cheese and honey, soft-boiled eggs, and the guest's choice of coffee, orange juice, or Moroccan tea, Hicham and a ragtag team of men from the neighborhood chased worn soccer balls up and down the tightly packed sand of Rabat *plage* in a series of games that led to a big tournament every *Ramadan*. The coffee making was left to me, because as an American, I was assumed to be a connoisseur. But no matter how many times I insisted that I had mastered the art of preparing Moroccan tea—I knew to add the sugar cubes before the mint and to "release the mint" by slapping the stalks against the countertop before pulling the leaves off, crushing them, and adding them to the now sugared and steaming black tea—Hicham refused to leave without making a large pot of it to perfection. After several weeks in the *riad*, he finally entrusted me with serving it. I poured each small cup to the brim, then emptied the tea back into the kettle, and repeated the cycle five times with higher and higher pours each time—a process believed to steep the tea leaves and evenly distribute the flavor before serving.

Orange juice making is a task similarly relegated to the experts. From my room on the roof, I could hear the clicking of crutches on cobblestone every morning just after the first *adhan*. I ordered a liter or two, depending on the number of *riad* guests, and watched as Hadi, an old Moroccan man with an open, toothless smile, went to work. He seamlessly peeled the oranges one by one with a rusted knife, placed them in his metal press, and held a plastic water bottle collected from the trash in the spout below. He tossed the seeds and pulp to the battalions of stray cats that were always gathered at his feet as the juice began to flow. Hadi was a man of few words, and I took great pleasure in each one he shared with me, our morning conversations growing longer as he came to expect me with the same regularity of the neighborhood strays.

The bedroom I shared with Hajar was small and simple. It had windowless clay walls on four sides and an opening where a door could have been but was not. The clay floor was covered with a tattered wool rug and two straw-stuffed cushions that served as beds. In the corner, we stacked old crates salvaged from *Avenue Souika* to store our collections of personal belongings. In place of a bathroom, there was a bucket placed beside the spigot that Hicham uses to water the plants in the courtyard below. Compared to the forest camps where I had lived for several months before arriving in Rabat, the space felt large, private, and luxurious. The rooftops in the *medina* bleed into one another, and you can walk from housetop to housetop just as you might stroll down the street in another city. Throughout the months that I called *Riad Art* home, I kept everything I owned in that small, doorless, rooftop room: a stack of clothing (mostly large scarves that could be wrapped as dresses or skirts, shirts or hijab), a bag of toiletries, a camera, a laptop, and piles of books, notebooks, and collected photographs. Crime, while certainly present in Morocco, does not loom in the ways that one might expect. The sense of community structured by the tight living quarters of the *medina*—the shared ovens and bathhouses, the open windows and doors—ensures a feeling of material safety, and nothing I owned was ever disturbed, except by curious neighborhood children who occasionally riffled through the *Amreekia's* crates for fun.

On my second night at *Riad Art*, Hajar (who cleans every day but Friday) and her younger sister, Kaoutar (who cleans on Hajar's day off), invited me to join them in one of their central neighborhood rituals—the *hammam*. Like the mosque, the *hammam*, or Moroccan bathhouse, is a cornerstone of most lower-income neighborhoods, and one can be found in every five-to-ten block radius of Rabat's *medina*. Yet despite their prevalence (or perhaps because of it), *hammams* maintain the intimacy of bathing in your own home, and they are not generally open to passing tourists. I had met Hajar and Kaoutar only a time or two before when visiting Hicham at his workplace and was surprised by their invitation. Our interactions had been limited, in part because they did not speak French, English, or standard Arabic, and my lack of Berber language limited our communication, so we laughed as they struggled to explain through a series of gestures what I would need to wear and bring to be properly outfitted for my bath.

In the *medina*, men and women go to community bathhouses every week to bathe. Each *hammam* has a schedule posted on the front door, noting which hours it is open to women and which hours it is open to men. You pay your *dirhams* at the door, enter the changing room, remove all of your clothing, and head to the bathing room with your *hammam* kit in hand. A proper kit, I learned, includes a plastic bucket, a plastic cup, a small scrubbing stone made of clay, and a plastic bag full of traditional soap, which has the consistency of pudding and the color of charcoal. The bathing room is tiled from top to bottom with nothing but a faucet on one wall. Between one and three dozen women of all ages, shapes, and sizes are spread out across the floor before you, as you walk to fill your bucket with steaming hot water at the faucet and stake out a space between the other bathers. First dipping your cup into the bucket, you lather your body with the pudding soap, and let your skin "soften" for a few minutes. You then wash the lather off and proceed to scrub yourself from head to toe with your stone. The whole process takes anywhere between one and three hours, depending on how much gossiping is taking place between you and your fellow bathers. If your body does not turn pink from the scrubbing, if layers of dead skin are not sloughing off onto the floor beneath you, if you do not have at least one spot bleeding from overscrubbing, then those around you will encourage you—"Scrub harder!" "You're here to get clean!" "Scrub your week off!" In *centre ville*, there are women working in the *hammams* who do your scrubbing for you (for a modest fee), but in the *medina*, women scrub themselves, occasionally asking a friend, mother-in-law, or daughter to get the hard-to-reach spots on their backs.

Through our few shared words and many shared gestures, Hajar and Kaoutar walked me through my first journey in their *hammam*. Kaoutar pulled my hair back for me (as I shamefully walked into the bathing room with it down), Hajar filled my bucket, took my cup, and poured the hot water over my head. She made sure I was adequately soaped and instructed me to "*patientez*" until I softened. She then took my stone in her hand and proceeded to scrub me, as the women who work in the nicer *hammams* would do for a customer. I sat cross-legged in the middle of the room, as she scrubbed one arm and then the other, taking her time on every last finger. She then gestured for me to lie down, so she could scrub my stomach, chest, and legs, before rolling me over to scrub my backside.

As I lay on the steaming hot tile floor, trying to enjoy what was, in one sense, a decadent massage, I could not help but feel uncomfortable. Not uncomfortable that I was lying naked in a room full of strangers where the visiting *Amreekia* was the main attraction, but uncomfortable that two women whom I barely knew were in service to me. It took a moment of reflection on my part to see the event not as a Moroccan serving an American but, looking beyond the barriers of nationality and even class between us, to see what is was that united us. They laughed as I winced at the harshness of the stone on my tender spots, contorted myself to cover my (shamefully) shaven body, and made my own attempt to scrub them as they had taught me to do. We laughed together about the frequent flirtations of the *riad* owner's son and the strange couple staying in Room #4. It was a moment of new friendship across cultural and linguistic boundaries, a moment defining of the shared experience of womanhood. It was startlingly and refreshingly intimate. For me, it was an introduction into a new field site and one of the friendships that would shape my period of research there. As I complete this book many years later, I am reminded of the beginnings of these relationships that have grown deeper with time and continue to call me home to the Maghreb every year.

There are many spaces, like the *hammam*, that I have been privileged to observe throughout my time in Morocco, and a number of them are closed to Hajar, who speaks openly about the limitations she feels, born in a country where the public sphere is reserved for her brothers and father and largely unknown to her. She asks me what it is like to have the freedom to move. This question has taken on different meanings over the years, as we discuss my movement in her native country, where doors are often open to me, and my still greater freedom of movement at home in the United States. I began to see how her experiences of restricted movement on a micro scale (restrictions from riding the bus or walking to the market to buy vegetables alone) reflect the macro issues of restricted mobility that I was exploring. The female/male distinction in the country parallels migrant/citizen distinctions in the region, both rooted in notions of private versus public space and contestations over who has the right to belong where. Although many doors are closed to Hajar, as they are to the migrants who became my primary respondents, it was only through her that I was invited into an exclusively female space in our neighborhood and the unique relationships that exist there.

It is a particular form of friendship that can arise between foreigners in a foreign place—between *Amreekia* and local women in a local bathhouse, between researcher and migrants in a hidden camp, between migrant group and migrant group trapped together in between an old home and the promise of something new. Migrants from distinct regions of the continent form strong bonds across cultural and linguistic boundaries in Morocco, as they commonly find themselves crammed together in apartment buildings and camps or competing for the same customers in the marketplaces where they hawk used goods in exchange for coins. These relationships can only be produced in the diasporic context, where old identities are forced to give way to new understandings of the self, the other, and the convergences and divergences between the two.

A Place at the Table

The place I occupy as a foreigner in Moroccan society is an odd one—with one facet of my identity often closing the door that another has just opened. My nationality routinely grants me privileges that my gender denies. My age strips me of status that my skin color ensures. My relative wealth provides me with opportunities my status as non-Muslim forbids. In my first months of fieldwork, I closely observed how I was "read," depending on who was doing the reading and where the reading was taking place. I studied how my dress (my decision to cover my head or not, to wear "Western" clothing or not), my bodily comportment (my decision to avoid eye contact or not, to offer a handshake or not), and my speech (my decision to *"tutoyer"* or *"vouvoyer,"*[12] to respond in English, French, *Fusha* or *Derija*[13]) all impacted who I was "read" to be. I took note of how I could manipulate these readings in order to gain the access my research would require.

It was not until years later, when I began analyzing reams of collected data, that I noticed striking similarities between my own consciousness of self-presentation in Morocco's public sphere and that of the migrants who navigated similar experiences of being "read" on their journeys through North Africa. Ousmane, a Senegalese exchange student completing his degree at Morocco's national university who identifies as black, spoke to me about the code-switching and shape-shifting tactics he adopted to combat the fact that his racial identity leads to him being read as a migrant of lower-class status in Morocco. He makes an effort to speak English on his cell phone (even when there is no one on the other end listening) and to dress well "like I'm going to out to *drag,*" he told me (a Moroccan play on the French verb *draguer,* meaning "to pick up women"). In my analysis, I strive to honor the agency of migrants as they manipulate their own speech, dress, and bodily comportment and to acknowledge the greater fluidity that foreigners who identify as white have. Like Ousmane, I was constantly aware of being read, but unlike him, I had a broad range of privileged categories on which I could draw to counterbalance the less privileged place reserved for women in the Maghreb. This highlights critical distinctions between mutable and immutable categories of identification and the ability of presumably mutable characteristics like speech and dress to become deeply imbued with racial and gendered dimensions in the face of shifting social landscapes.

In co-gendered migrant and Moroccan homes alike, it is common for two tables to be set—one for women and another for men. If the space allows, the women's table is often placed in the kitchen and the men's in the *salon*. I found it notable that across the diversity of homes I dined in throughout my fieldwork, I was consistently seated at the men's table. I never missed a chance to inquire about this seating assignment, raising the obvious question of why I (someone who identifies as a woman and was clearly the only woman in the group of men seated cross-legged around the table) was assigned that seat. The answers became as predictable as the seat itself. I was seated at the men's table because I was not Moroccan, because I was educated, or because I was American. Given the logic behind the explanations, the points were synonymous. Being a foreign, educated, American woman, I would be "bored" by the conversation at the women's table, which the men always presumed centered on "neighborhood gossip," and I would, in turn, be "stimulated" by the conversation at the men's table, which they liked to believe centered on "important debates" about religion, politics, and global affairs. There was a micro/macro, private/public, female/male distinction being made, and my status as a foreigner consistently outweighed my status as a woman, placing me in the macro/public/male realm of the household. However, my status never denied me the ability to move on to the women's table as the meal and the conversation progressed.

I found this scenario, which unfolded many times at the tables of friends and respondents, significant in illustrating the ambiguous place that I occupy in Moroccan society, and it is important to highlight how my ambiguity made this research possible. My dual outsider status granted me unique access to the dinner tables, social spaces (private and public), and conversations of men *and* women that a foreign male or a Moroccan citizen (male or female) would not have been privy to. Just as a foreign male would have been relegated to exclusively male spaces, a Moroccan researcher would have been limited to uncovering the inner worlds of their own gender group. Gender was central to my interactions with Moroccan men and women, much in the same way that

FIGURE **1.3 Author and a Guinean brotherhood share their one daily meal of rice in the hidden forest camp they call home.**
Source: Photograph courtesy of *The Burning*.

nationality was central to my gaining access to and establishing trust with migrant and citizen groups in Morocco. My government-issued research clearance and foreign passport eased my access to governmental offices, state-run detention centers, and the officials working within them. And while many of the questions I posed to migrants would have been seen as threatening if coming from a Moroccan or European researcher, my status as an American removed me from the immediate political crisis at hand and allowed me to establish trust with greater ease. In later chapters, I examine how my status as a young woman in male-dominated migrant slums and camps further influenced the relationships that formed and the stories that were exchanged.

A Note on Chapter Structure

Because migrants' embodied, remembered, and imagined experiences are determined by their simultaneous interactions with other migrant subjects, citizen subjects, and state powers, studying contemporary experiences of displacement requires a multitiered approach. The data analyzed in the following chapters centers on three points: (1) migrants' embodied experiences of daily life in Morocco, (2) migrants' remembered and imagined experiences of home in their countries of origin and desired destinations, and (3) migrants' shifting experiences of mobility and detention in spaces where borders have been externalized. The competing levels of analysis can be categorized as (1) migrant subject to migrant subject (i.e., migrants' interactions with one another in their "temporary" homes and communities in Morocco); (2) citizen subject to migrant subject (i.e., migrants' interactions with Moroccan citizens in the neighborhoods where they live and the marketplaces where the majority of them find informal work); and (3) state structure to migrant subject (i.e., migrants' experiences of mobility and detention as they move across international borders). Rather than devote one chapter to the literature that informed my research, I have situated foundational literature throughout the book. This structure is more reflective of my actual research process, as the writers who most informed and challenged my arguments have grounded and propelled me from my earliest stages of fieldwork all the way through my final stages of writing. This structure also allows me to weave together theory and narrative, privileging the voices and experiences of respondents alongside those of "experts" from a diversity of fields. I have organized the following chapters accordingly.

Chapter Two opens with a case study of a transnational Moroccan family network, exploring what migration means in social and economic terms in modern-day Morocco. I provide readers with two brief historical overviews that will be essential to later analysis—one on the development of migration studies as a key interdisciplinary field in the social sciences, and a second on the development of Morocco as a key crossroads in the study of human migration. The first of these overviews is informed by the foundational theories of migration studies, drawing on scholars from a range of disciplinary backgrounds. Arguing for a move beyond static or linear models, I consider the role of individual experience in shaping desires for mobility and the agency of individual migrants relative to historic shifts in the Maghrebi region, as the mobile subject slowly transitioned from "slave" to "soldier" to "migrant laborer." The second overview draws on a lineage of Maghrebi scholarship to analyze the construction of social differentiation during distinct periods of Moroccan history, including the Islamic conquest of the Maghreb, the trans-Saharan slave trade, and the French-Spanish colonization of Morocco. I close by examining the postcolonization migration boom, which transformed Morocco into one of the world's top emigrant-sending countries by the year 2000, and the nation's more recent transition into a permanent holding cell for African migrants seeking entry into the European Union (EU).

Chapter Three opens with a case study of recent news reports on the growing tide of violent racism against blacks in Morocco, juxtaposing the accounts of a Moroccan university student and a Nigerian migrant of the same age. Their accounts reveal how new conceptualizations of individual and national identity are molded by both Morocco's colonial history and the rapid demographic shifts brought on by changing patterns of migration in Africa. I draw on contemporary scholars of the Maghreb to provide a brief historical overview of the rulers of the Moroccan political state, from King Mohammed V, who led the nation out of French control, to reigning King Mohammed VI. An examination of widespread human rights violations during King Hassan II's "Years of Lead" highlights Mohammed VI's democratic shift in policy, but also raises important questions about the possibility for reformation when a nation remains in the hands of the same monarchy. Narrative accounts of the brutal treatment of African migrants by both Spanish and Moroccan officials reveal the EU's current role in creating Morocco's nascent immigration and asylum policies and how new policies of border externalization are shaping practices on the ground.

Chapter Four opens with a case study of one of Morocco's largest migrant-populated slums, examining the impacts of migration and sustained liminality on notions of home, family, community, and traditional gender roles. The experiences of two migrants challenge readers to consider new kinds of Muslim masculinity that are emerging in migrant spaces and the influence of migrant women on Morocco's traditionally male sphere of public labor. I inform my analysis with contemporary anthropological work by migration scholars from different world regions, arguing that new patterns of migration at Europe's southern borders in Africa are indicative of larger global shifts and require a reevaluation of the very terms and theories applied in studies of transnationalism. In particular, I contend that there is an increasingly problematic distinction between the "migrant" and the "refugee." An overview of contemporary studies of migration reveals the tendency for researchers to situate their work in migrants' receiving communities, sending communities, or "the webs" that span the two (Glick Schiller et al. 1992), and underscores the lack of anthropological research on populations that find themselves trapped in liminal states between two homes.

Chapter Five introduces a new methodological approach that I term "visual life history collection." Just as Chapter Four calls for the need to revise the terms applied, this chapter contends that new methods will better engage with contemporary transnational populations. Presenting two examples from my fieldwork with Sierra Leonean and Congolese migrants, I reveal how visual life histories can open up new realms of experience and articulation in interviews with those who have been displaced. I argue for a rethinking of transnational subjects not as interconnected between sending and receiving countries, past and future lives, but rather as largely disconnected from both, and I explore the possibility for visual and material culture to better access memories of the past and imaginaries of the future. This chapter addresses some of the methodological challenges of working in liminal spaces and urges other researchers to consider the use of photo-elicitation in conjunction with oral history and what I term "oral *future*" collection to access critical processes of memory-making and remaking.

Chapter Six opens with the case study of a Senegalese university student in Morocco, considering the impact of the "other" blacks—international students who make up a small but prominent class of Africans in Morocco—on local conceptions of race, class, and belonging. This case study is juxtaposed with one of a lower-income Moroccan family that identifies as black and raises questions about the syncretization of race, economic marginalization, and assumed political vulnerability in the Maghreb. I examine how the social segregation of those racially identified as "illegal" has concrete impacts on both foreigners and Moroccan citizens whose places of work or habitation leave them in what I term "zones of illegality." While emphasizing that "migrant" and "citizen" should be viewed as emergent forms of racialization that are structuring inequality on a global scale, I inform my analysis with contemporary work by critical race scholars from different world regions. I draw on two competing ethnographic case studies of migrant populations to develop connections between racialization and legalization, situating Morocco within the study of borderlands and highlighting the border as an ideal space for constructing and deconstructing new forms of difference.

In my concluding chapter, I return to the importance of liminality as a guiding framework and move my ethnographic attention to the other side of the Moroccan border as I continue to follow the journeys of Bambino, Moneba, and their Guinean brotherhood. I outline Morocco's newest immigration policies, the human rights conventions that are under violation, and the failure of both European and Moroccan officials to provide detained migrants with access to basic social services. I draw on interviews with governmental officials and my close following of popular media sources across the region to examine how the EU has skillfully exerted pressure on Morocco to amend its immigration policies, strengthen its own borders, and sign agreements leading to the illicit "repatriation" of thousands of African migrants with burned papers to the Maghreb every year. The chapter concludes with one migrant's interpretation of the ritual of "*hrig*" and a call for us all, as members of the global community, to speak out in the defense of fundamental human rights.

My work has been influenced by the approach of person-based ethnography and its long tradition in Morocco and the Muslim world more broadly.[14] The writing of feminist scholars like Lila Abu-Lughod, whose *Writing Women's Worlds* (1993) includes stories, songs, and poems by the women she studied, challenges all ethnographers, or "second tellers of stories," to question the power and limitations of anthropology to accurately portray the lives of others. Abu-Lughod pushed us to privilege the voices of respondents in our writing (1993), while Unni Wikan pushed us even further to challenge the validity of posing research questions in the first place (1991). When I first began constructing an outline for this book from the hundreds of interview transcripts, books of scribbled notations, and years of text, email, and messenger app correspondence with respondents, I struggled to find a way to best capture the emotion, the humor, and the brutality in the words that were shared with me. How could I translate them into a standard form of textual analysis without losing so much of what made them human? It was, after all, the cadence of his speech or her choice of colloquialism, it was the braying of the sheep on the roof above us or the smell of rosemary wafting in from the community oven below, that had brought the people, the places, and, ultimately, the stories of my research to life.

My early attempts showed me just how much can be lost by restructuring narratives—pulling out the most powerful quotes and removing the people from the places where their stories were shared—so I left a space at the opening of each chapter for a less traditional form of analytical writing. It is my intention that these opening case studies emplace you as the reader in the locations that were most central to the development of each chapter. By using the words of respondents to do this, it is also my hope that these introductions put you in direct conversation with the individuals who gave life to the detention centers, marketplaces, slums, and camps that I describe. These people and places created a strong foundation from which I engaged with foundational literature and used my position as ethnographer to pose, to problematize, and, in some cases, *insha'Allah*,[15] to offer answers to the broader questions of this book. Each story I chose to share is reflective of the individual storyteller's life experience, but the more I wrote, the more I began to see the common threads running through them all. I began to see them as windows into a particular time and place and the experiences of those who remain trapped there. My fieldwork experience was an exercise in learning to listen deeply. It was driven by my desire to redefine the art of storytelling and to justify the truth in it without losing any of the beauty.

I want to go home
but my home is the mouth of a shark.
my home is the barrel of the gun.

—Warsan Shire [excerpt from "Home"]

Notes

1. In this book, Morocco, officially "the Kingdom of Morocco," is also referred to by its Arabic name المغرب ("al-Maghrib"), its French name "*le Maroc*," or its position in the Maghreb region. In the Arab-Islamic world, Morocco is most commonly referred to by its full Arabic name *al-Mamlakah al-Maghribiyah*, meaning "The Western Kingdom." In Morocco, it is most commonly referred to as *al-Maghrib*, meaning simply "The West."

2. Unless referring specifically to immigration law, I choose to use the term "migrant," regardless of an individual's point on their migration journey or documented or undocumented political status. Unlike the terms "immigrant" and "emigrant," "migrant" retains a sense of movement, or what Nicholas de Genova calls the "consequent irresolution of social processes of migration" (2005: 3). I find that in the context of contemporary African migrations, applying the term "migrant" to both those of documented status—asylum seekers and refugees—and undocumented status is most reflective of the population's common experiences of marginalization, regardless of political status.

3. Szakolczai (2009) argues that there are three types of permanent liminality, each one closely related to one of the three phases of liminal rites, and provides examples of each: *monasticism* (with monks endlessly preparing for their separation) represents the first phase; *court society* (with individuals endlessly performing their roles in a cyclical and ceremonial game) represents the second phase; and *Bolshevism* (exemplifying a society with individuals endlessly trapped at the end of a ritual) represents the third stage (Szakolczai 2000; Thomassen 2009: 23).

4. The term "schismogenesis," developed by anthropologist Gregory Bateson in the 1930s, has been used to describe situations of permanent liminality (1935). He differentiates between a *symmetrical* form of schismogenesis built on a competitive relationship between categorical equals and a *complementary* form of schismogenesis built on a hierarchical relationship between categorical unequals. With regard to the role of liminality in ritual, he theorizes that there are concrete ritual behaviors that are either inhibited or stimulated by the schismogenic relationship in its various forms.

5. The research for this book included 24 months of cumulative ethnographic research conducted between 2013 and 2015 and an additional 12 months of research conducted between 2016 and 2018. My methodology can be broken down into six distinct phases, although multiple phases were often carried out in tandem with one another:
   - A combined interview/participant observation phase beginning in the Democratic Republic of the Congo, Sierra Leone, and Mali and moving north along primary migratory routes toward the EU
   - A demographic survey phase in Morocco's most heavily migrant-populated neighborhoods and forest camps
   - A combined interview/participant observation phase with core respondents in migrant-populated neighborhoods, forest camps, and marketplaces, where a large number of migrants work in the informal economy
   - A visual life history collection phase with select respondents
   - Ongoing participant observation as a resident in migrant-populated neighborhoods and forest camps and a volunteer caseworker at one of Morocco's largest migrant aid organization, *Le Centre de Droits des Migrants* (CDM)
   - Ongoing review of European and Maghrebi media centered on issues of migration and EU–Morocco relations

6. The *adhan*, or call to prayer, is heard five times a day and structures the rhythms of daily life in Morocco, as in other Muslim countries.

7. The Western Sahara, which was occupied by Spain in the late nineteenth century, has been on the United Nations list of non-self-governing territories since 1963. It is the largest and most populous territory on this list. In 1965, the UN adopted its first resolution on the Western Sahara, formally requesting that Spain decolonize the territory. In 1975, Spain relinquished their administrative control of the Western Sahara to a joint administration lead by Morocco, which has formally claimed the territory since 1957.

8. *Medina* translates to "the original Arab or non-European quarter of a North African town," making reference to the restructuring of the Maghreb's cityscapes during the colonial period. The word *medina* is now used by Moroccans to denote the old part of a city, in contrast to the "*ville nouvelle.*"

9. Rabat has an estimated urban population of 620,000 and a total metropolitan population of 1.2 million.

10. "Slums," known in Arabic as "*hay alfuqara,*" can be defined by the makeshift structure of the housing that is present, but colloquially, they can also be defined by the presence of a large population of migrant squatters.

11. "Hawkers," or informal sidewalk merchants, can be found working in Morocco's outdoor marketplaces at all hours of the day and night. They sell an eclectic mix of goods ranging from fresh fruit to counterfeit clothing, and the lack of storefront allows them to easily move from one corner to another when hassled by police for working without a formal permit.

12. "*Tu*" is a form of speech reserved for addressing friends and family or children and people of "lower social rank." "*Vous*" denotes greater respect or unfamiliarity. While these distinctions are more fluid in francophone countries across Africa than in France, there remains a choice to be made when meeting new people and weighing your comparative place on the social hierarchy before first addressing them (i.e., He is younger than me but male).

13. *Fusha*, or modern standard Arabic, is often referred to as "pure" Arabic, even by Moroccans. However, mastering the language requires a level of education that is uncommon in lower and middle-income households. *Derija*, or the form of Arabic spoken in Morocco, was born from the nation's placement near West Africa and colonial history, and it is set apart by a more rhythmic speech pattern and a sprinkling of French and Spanish phrases. *Derija* is a spoken language, and while it lacks the standardization of *Fusha*, speaking it signals a level of cultural belonging or insiderness that *Fusha* does not.

14. D. Dwyer 1978; Crapanzano 1985; K. K. Dwyer 1982; Wikan 1991; Abu-Lughod 1993; Fisher & Abedi 2002.

15. A popular Arabic phrase meaning literally "if God wills it" and used in place of "hopefully."

CHAPTER 2

At the Crossroads: Africa on the Map of Human Migrations

Introductory Case Study: a Transnational Moroccan Family Network

What does it mean to be Moroccan when your roots are spread across three continents? What does it mean to be from the red soil of Aïn el-Aouda when your mother lives above the Egyptian bakery in Queens, your uncle cleans litter from the stadium floor after Falcons games, and your brother works for a Dutch company in Spain?

> *Yes, that's right, it's the bakery that's known for its harsha. No, they don't let the janitors in till all the fans have left the Dome. My brother thinks Spanish will serve his children well, but last Ramadan, they couldn't tell their own grandfather what they'd been learning in school!*
>
> *I remember my brother saying to him, "Arabic is an old language, Baba."*
>
> *"Yes, it's the language of our family, it's the language of our people! How can you tell me that I won't speak to my own grandchildren?" my father replied.*
>
> *"But it's old, Baba. Old in the sense that it brings no use anymore. What good will Arabic do my children in Europe? It will mark them as outsiders? As Muslims? As terrorists! Their Spanish*

*is beautiful, Baba. I wish you could hear it. English is where they
need to focus their studies next."*

*I laugh now when I remember our childhood dreams. "To
France!" "To Italy!" "To Amreeka!" my brother and I would say.
We spoke with television clips of beautiful homes and beautiful
women in our heads. In reality, we knew nothing about the places
we spoke. How was I to know the kind of work that was waiting for men like us in America? How was I to know that I could
work for many years and never afford a home half as nice as the
one my father grew up in? How was I to know that Moroccans
live like poor men in these rich men's countries? The Spain that
taunted me with Paz Vega and drop-top Renaults was not the
immigrant's Spain.*

—Hicham,[1] M, 38, Moroccan, service industry worker

When I first arrived in Morocco in 2007, it was difficult to meet
anyone whose life had not been directly impacted by migration. In
the years following the nation's independence from France in 1956,[2]
it quickly evolved into one of the world's top emigrant-sending
countries—a position it held until the turn of the century. Being one
of eight children—six sons and two daughters—it was almost without
question that my friend Hicham has siblings scattered across the European continent. He is the youngest, and as is often the case with the
last-born male, he inherited the unspoken obligation of staying home to
shoulder the burdens of his family in Morocco. He is the one expected
to keep up the home that he and his siblings were raised in, handle the
paperwork of his large and increasingly transnational family, and welcome them all back every year when *Ramadan* arrives on the Muslim
calendar. Hicham's experience taught me about the constant stressors
and occasional bursts of pride that come with being the one to carry
your family's name in the community. Through the stories that he and
his siblings shared with me over countless meals together, I pieced
together the meaning of migration for one modern-day Moroccan
family—a family that, like so many others, has become a network of
migrant laborers connected by the soil of their homeland, their shared
ambitions for prosperity abroad, and their desire to someday return to
the place they had all been so desperate to leave.

On Fridays ("a day for rest, for family, and for giving thanks to
Allah"), when Moroccans gather around the table to share a traditional

meal of couscous, Hicham would often take me with him to his family home in Aïn el-Aouda. "You can't eat couscous alone," he would say to me on the occasional Friday when the stack of interviews to be translated and coded loomed heavily in front of me. "If we see a homeless person on the street, we must invite them in to share the meal. It's our duty to see that everyone eats well on Friday and that our meals are always shared." Aïn el-Aouda, a middle-income *banlieue* on the outskirts of Rabat, is accessible only by public bus, and Hicham's home is reached only after a long walk from the town bus stop. Like many of Rabat's newer bedroom communities, it was built in the 1990s when rural-to-urban migration was on the rise. This, coupled with the first spikes in African migrant settlement in Morocco's urban centers, was causing cities like Rabat to burst at their seams. Apartment prices in the then middle-income neighborhoods within the city limits skyrocketed, along with an increasing demand from foreigners moving to Rabat for work or retirement. The city's lower-income neighborhoods, on the other hand, quickly declined, with more and more migrants cramming into one-room rentals. The city became a place accessible to only the richest or the poorest. Middle-income Moroccans were pushed out of their apartments by wealthy families wanting to buy and restore old buildings into their original single-family home structures. Since the majority of recently displaced middle-income Moroccans wanted to disassociate from the city's growing migrant class, moving into lower-income neighborhoods was not an option. No one wanted to be the first to gentrify spaces that had been termed "the Senegalese block," "the Congolese building," or "the Nigerian sleeping rooms."

Working-class families like Hicham's were drawn to the refrigerators and window glass advertised on billboards for new apartment complexes going up further and further outside of the city limits, and they were less concerned with the added commute time. Their jobs abroad, which failed to provide them with social status in the United States or Spain, could afford the small luxuries that were beginning to define an emerging Moroccan middle class—a class built largely on foreign remittances and a consumer culture fed through growing access to Western media. I was interested in exploring one of these new developments from the inside and contrasting it to the *riad* that Hicham and I temporarily called home in Rabat's *medina*—a place similar to what families like his were moving away from.

The Homes Remittances Buy

The bus dropped us off on Aïn el-Aouda's main street, but it was strangely empty for a Friday afternoon. No vendors hawking *khobz*, oil, and sweets for the midday meal. No children begging *dirhams* from the passing *motos*. In fact, there were no streams of traffic passing by us at all. I realized that outside of Rabat's central avenue (which paves the way to the king's palace), I had never seen streets so well maintained. The roads in Aïn el-Aouda are wide, paved in cement, and even have yellow lines denoting crossing zones for motorists. There are cement block sidewalks on either side, lined with evenly spaced street lights and palm trees. In central Rabat, where every inch of space is built on, it is easy to forget that sandy red soil lies underfoot, but here, with so much open space, the air is heavy with it, and every parked car and building entry is coated with a dusting of that deep Moroccan red.

We approached a building four stories high with a linoleum-floored staircase in the middle where a courtyard would have been. It was built to hold three apartments on each level. Hicham's family apartment is three stories up—a location often lamented by his sisters when walking up and down the narrow, winding stairs, arms overloaded with children and shopping bags. Inside, their apartment is laid out much like the other working-class Moroccan homes I had visited, but everything appeared newer and more intricately designed. Two white columns stand in the middle of the *salon,* and traditional sofas run the length of the walls on three sides. The thick cushions are covered in bright, shimmering fabrics—one half of the room upholstered in purple and the other in orange. There are two chandeliers in gold and pink that hang from the ceiling. The walls are covered with memorabilia—old family photographs, framed pages from the Qur'an, and a photograph of the ruling monarch, which is expected in every Moroccan home.[3] Three doors lead to the smaller, closed spaces surrounding the *salon*—the kitchen, the bathroom, and another room where the children play or visiting family members are invited to rest. As is typical, the *salon* doubles as the main "bedroom" at night when everyone sleeps on the sofas, head to feet and feet to head.

At first glance, Hicham's family home appears lavish by Moroccan standards, and were it located in the city center, it would likely belong to a member of Rabat's small but growing elite class. However, new developers are skilled at mass-producing inexpensive finishes that once denoted high class. With a closer look, you can see the "gold" paint already chipping at the corners of the chandeliers and the linoleum squares of "marble" already buckling on the bathroom floors. The intricate moldings were clearly etched from plastic, a "made in China" sticker half expected in the corner of the room. Yet the design indicates Hicham's family's status in a new emerging class. The trinkets brought back by his siblings on their annual *Ramadan* trips home clutter the space with material reminders of their transnationality.

Hicham's older sisters, Soukaina and Fatima Zahra, now live in Italy with their husbands and young children. Their marriages to Moroccan men who were already living abroad were arranged in ways so commonplace they are beginning to supersede traditional practices of matchmaking. Soukaina explained to me how her husband, Mehdi, emailed his mother saying, "I'm ready to put my head on straight," a translation of the *Derija* phrase for, "I'm ready to marry." Mehdi's mother quickly got to work evaluating the eligible young women in their community. After negotiating with Hicham's parents, she told her son she had found someone for him to marry on his next trip home. Soukaina and Mehdi, having only ever seen a passport-sized photograph of one another, were married in a traditional ceremony a few weeks after his arrival, and the two of them moved back to Rome together, husband and wife, three days after being wed. Soukaina said, "You no longer ask about the job a man has, you ask about the country he lives in. Many of us, our families wouldn't consider our marriage to a man in Morocco—this has become low class." Like recent research by Dinah Hannaford on migration and new forms of marriage in Senegal (2017), Soukaina's narrative exposes how the lack of economic stability—much less social mobility—accessible to lower- and middle-class families in Morocco is driving the search for partners beyond the borders of their own country.

A man's placement in the global labor force has become a better indicator of his ability to provide social status and material wealth than his standing in the local community. In Senegal, Hannaford's work reveals a contemporary space in which middle-class women are seeking marriage arrangements with lower-class men—a transgression that would be difficult to imagine if not for the elevated status that lower-class men occupy once they successfully reach European soil. Despite being separated by continents with no immediate plans for reunification, this form of "long-distance" marriage allows male migrants to continue investing in their social life at home and gives the women they marry access to the same material markers of mobility and success—foreign clothing, housewares, and even food products—that Soukaina mentioned many times in our conversations. The Senegalese women who reach outside of the country in an attempt to build successful social lives within Senegal share a common goal with Soukaina and her parents, who sought to increase their status through the ability to access and afford desirable foreign goods (Hannaford 2017).

Hicham's other sister explained how the parents of her husband, Abdul Rahim, found her on the popular marriage site *arabmatchmaking. com*. While this approach may at first appear to give greater agency to the couple in their selection of a partner, it operates in much the same way as Mehdi's mother evaluating the eligible women around her. The only major difference with digital matchmaking, in addition to significantly increasing the pool of women, is that the power of selection falls equally between both set of parents. Just as Mehdi's mother had selected Soukaina from the options in their community, Abdul Rahim's mother selected Fatima Zahra's profile. Yet Hicham's mother was the one who created (along with the help of her more technologically savvy son) a profile for her daughter, and she was as critical in assessing the inquiries sent to Fatima Zahra as Abdul Rahim's mother was in assessing the eligible women online. Over one meal together, Fatima Zahra showed me the website where "my mother found me love," and together with her sister, we scrolled through the profiles, as I asked questions about what they considered desirable in a partner. We laughed about the many things that are universal in the complexities of attraction, love, and family.

There were multiple times when our conversations were accompanied by Friday couscous, and as is always the case, the couscous was brought to the table in a large clay *tagine* and the accompaniments served with it were an illustration of the family's social status. At the tables of university professors, governmental officials, and other elites, the lavish display featured a generous cut of lamb garnished with raisins, almonds, and olives. One step down on the social ladder, the cut of lamb would be replaced with a whole chicken, and below that, part of a chicken that had been divided among neighbors. In the outskirts of Rabat, where I ate the majority of my meals with families like Hicham's, I was more likely to be offered a generous serving of root vegetables over couscous. In migrants' homes and camps, plain rice was the staple food served on Fridays and every other day of the week. Regardless of the accompaniments, both couscous and rice are served with a smaller bowl of oil. I learned from watching those around me that one must first dip the fingers of the right hand (never the left hand, which is dirty) into the oil and then take a mound of couscous or rice, slowly rolling it around in your hand until it becomes a solid ball. Despite countless attempts, my ball-rolling technique never ceased to be a spectacle for migrants, high-ranking officials, and friends alike. As Hicham and I strolled back to the bus stop along the newly poured cement streets of Aïn el-Aouda that Friday, he told me, "To be a Moroccan today means to be a migrant—if you're not a migrant, then you're dreaming of being one. If you are a migrant, then you're dreaming of returning home. But all of us, we're dreaming of a place where we are not." It is a common goal among migrants, whether Senegalese in Morocco or Moroccan in Spain, to work toward the goal of building a "dream house" in their home country, yet it is uncommon for them to visit more than once a year (McMurray 2001). The status that last-born males, like Hicham, hold within transnational family networks asserts one of the central struggles of contemporary migration. It renders return emigrants money-rich but status-poor. Hicham therefore carries the weight of maintaining a physical home for his family and building a social network for them in their absence.

Despite the more than four million Moroccans who are settled in diasporic communities[4] outside of the country today, Morocco is transitioning from one of the world's top immigrant–senders into a net immigrant–receiver. This is a rare transition in the postcolonial world and a first-time transition on the African continent. I argue that it is also evidence of a growing trend in migration patterns from the global south to the global south, as traditional destination countries externalize their border controls to other nations. My research began with the premise that border regions, located at the cultural and geographical intersection of nation-states, offer an ideal site for questioning the construction of new individual and national identities. Morocco's placement only miles from an internally borderless EU is producing new geographies of liminality and legality, as political status becomes an increasingly important marker of identity around the world.

Who Has the Right?

Migration is universal, and it is not unique to humans. It is the seasonal movement of animals from one region to another. It is the movement of cells inside an organism. And for as far back as we can trace our own history, migration has also been a part of the human condition (Cameron 2013; Nelson 2018). Transnational migration as we know it today is the result of a simple and socially constructed binary—legal and illegal. These labels fundamentally organize how all humans experience daily life. They determine who has the right to access space and who has the right to move within that space. Although they are socially constructed, these labels are assigned at birth and are not easily amended. I was born in the United States to parents who were both full citizens at the time of my birth and because of this, I was gifted certain inalienable rights—the right to life, liberty, and the pursuit of happiness, including the right to move to 171 (or 100%) of the 171 nations that were independently recognized in the year that I was born. Mohammed, a friend and colleague of mine also pursuing a PhD in the Social Sciences during my period of fieldwork in Morocco, was born in the same year, in a small town outside of Rabat, to parents of Moroccan nationality. His birthright includes the right to move to 48 (or 24%) of the 195 nations that are recognized in our world today. All of these nations are located in Africa, with a few exceptions, and together, they represent a selection of some of the poorest economies in the world. Outside of the African continent, Mohammed can move to Myanmar, Tajikistan, Iran, Jordan, Turkey, Bolivia, Nicaragua, Ecuador, Brazil, or one of three Caribbean islands (Grenada, Dominica, or Saint Vincent and the Grenadines). With the exception of Mali, Senegal, Guinea, and the Democratic Republic of the Congo, Mohammed's visa would be limited to between 3 and 90 days, and applying for it would require showing upward of $20,000 (USD) in his personal bank account.

But Mohammed's options seem generous if we compare them to those of Najia, a respondent who became a close friend of mine. "No one dreams of becoming a criminal," I remember her saying to me in one of our first conversations. Najia is tall and willowy, with a wide scar across her left check and the kind of beauty that makes heads turn. She walks with confidence, like someone who has been told since she was young that she was something special—that someday, she would make her family proud. Her hair is long and plaited in the Nigerian way, but in Morocco, she wears it twisted in a bun and tied under a brightly colored headscarf. "Back home," she told me as we wound through the *medina* streets side by side, "I saw big men whose families were building homes with the money they sent. I saw big men who were sending their children—even their daughters—to the good school in town. They were bringing gifts back for everyone in the village when they visited. Clothes and little chocolates with tin foil wrapping on every one. So, I thought, why can't I be a big woman someday?"

Najia was born to Nigerian parents in Lagos in 1988. She grew up doing the things that good daughters in Nigeria do. "I cleaned the house, prepared the dinner, carried our vegetables to the market where Yumma sold them," she explained, referring to her mother. "I always looked after my brothers, so they didn't get into too much foolishness and Yumma didn't worry too much about them when she was gone." And she was not only a good daughter—she was a good student, too. "She was so smart, that one, they couldn't send her home to become a woman, even if they tried! She kept moving up in the grades," explained an elder from her community. It was around the time Najia's oldest brother was killed in Libya on his own attempted migration to Europe that she started to dream bigger. Hearing the stories his friends carried home to her family—how her brother had been beaten so badly in detention that they did not want to carry his body home—could have influenced her to stay. But instead, it was the impetus for her movement. As the next eldest, she felt it was her obligation to finish the journey her brother had started. "I had this image in my mind of my mother in a house with a real floor. It was so motivating for me," she said. She set her sights on being the first in her village to go to college and find a good job, the kind of job that would eventually lift her family from their poverty. But that was before Najia knew how the world worked and how all of the borders in it are closed to women like her.

According to the Universal Declaration of Human Rights, all citizens of the world have the right to live, work, and travel freely within their home country. We are all guaranteed this basic right to mobility at birth. Every individual also has the right to travel from and return to their home country, without the loss of citizenship. But the reality is that a person's right to move beyond the borders they were born behind has long been constrained. "It was hard for me," Najia remembered, "realizing the only way I would ever help my family would be by breaking the law." She had always played by the rules. Yet with time, the money she was saving for college became the money she was saving for a smuggler who knew the way.

Like Najia, many of us have been raised to believe that good begets good. We believe that hard work, good grades, and high test scores will lead to greater educational opportunities—that exceptional students will be rewarded in the end. But what if you were born in a country that offered you no chance to pursue a higher education, despite your exceptional performance in school? What if you had learned that no matter how hard you work, you will never know if your family will have enough food on the table at the end of the week? What if the only chance you had for greater educational or economic opportunity lay beyond the borders of your country?

The disheartening truth is that those who have little reason to leave their home countries are among the very few born with the freedom to move. Those whose only opportunities for a stable future lie beyond the borders they were born behind are the ones who discover that they are trapped. This correlation between opportunities for social and economic mobility within one's own country and rights to physical mobility is found around the world. Born in the United States, I am statistically among the least likely to migrate in search of economic or educational opportunities, and yet I am among the small population of global citizens for whom the world's borders are open. Born in a country that continues to suffer from a history of colonial exploitation, political instability, and economic depression, Najia grew up dreaming of escape. Yet with the exception of Barbados, Dominica, or Fiji, she was born without the right to leave the African continent. When I include all the African nations to which she can apply for a temporary visa, still only 10 percent of the world's borders are open to her.

"I knew my parents would worry," she explained. "Even before my brother was killed, we'd heard stories about all of the dangers of migration—the theft, the beatings, the rape—so I didn't tell them I was leaving. I was scared. At first, I thought about turning back almost every day. But the longer you travel, the harder it is to turn back, and at some point, you realize that you're going to keep going until you make it all the way. How do you go back empty handed to a family that struggles to eat?" Like most migrants who find themselves trapped in Morocco, Najia's days are long and hard. Hawking goods on the streets, she is regularly shooed by the brooms of Moroccan shop owners and assaulted by the officers patrolling the streets. "My mother's feet," she said, "they're still dusty. I just wanted her to have better."

The experiences of Mohammed and Najia are suggestive of larger shifts in global migration trends that are unfolding at Morocco's borders and beyond. It is in their lifetimes (and in mine) that traditional immigrant-receiving countries, like the United States and those across

Europe, have reached new saturation points and begun pushing their border controls further south. Morocco is among the first to be affected by this "pushing back." As such, it is at risk of setting a new standard for effective border externalization policies and leading the way for other former emigrant-sending countries to be transformed into permanent holding cells for labor flows from the global south.

Refugee "Crises" in the Headlines

In my first months back in the United States, media attention turned to the Syrian refugee "crisis" that was just reaching European shores, and I was frequently approached to give talks and write opinion pieces on the issue. I thought about the challenges I faced in my earliest years of research when I was trying to convince colleagues or granting institutions to expand the lens of migration studies from the critical border between the United States and Mexico and look for a moment to Europe's radical border reformations. This was no longer difficult to do. At academic conferences and across major news networks, Europe was taking center stage. Suddenly, by way of my history of work with migrants arriving to Europe's borders from a completely different world region, my assumed "expertise" had been expanded to include those fleeing Syria. I was poised to make an argument for the commonality between the two—to argue how, in reality, the majority of those fleeing Africa *and* Syria are not official refugees but undocumented migrants who pay smugglers to help them "illegally" cross borders with the hope of reaching Europe where they can apply for refugee status. I could then argue how new policies of border externalization and the biased review of asylum cases have created an unequal distribution of human rights at Europe's borders. It is behind these borders that the majority of those fleeing war and poverty across Africa remain trapped. While it is on the other side of Europe's borders that the stories of those who have fled war and poverty in Syria are being told. I used the widespread interest in the refugee "crisis" to begin conversations about the role of race in determining political status, and for the first time on a public stage, I contended that the mass criminalization of blackness has rendered it virtually impossible for certain populations to assert their vulnerability under international law.[5]

As migration studies become an increasingly important subfield across the social sciences, the literature is in a state of transition, and scholars are questioning the extent to which movement can still be linked to distinct push and pull factors. Instead, some are beginning to conceptualize movement as propelled by a combination of external (or society-level "push" and "pull") factors and internal (or individual-level) factors that act simultaneously on migrants.[6] This reconceptualization requires a shift in focus from global to local stages, as well as a theoretical shift, assigning greater agency to each migrant, even those who travel the well-grooved paths between major labor-supply and labor-demand regions of the world. Viewing migration as an individual experience allows for a deeper kind of study, giving names and narratives to numbers and maps.

In the case of new patterns of movement between Africa and Europe, I questioned how often migration is the result of the EU's shifting labor markets and how often the stronger "pull" comes from a migrant's individual aspirations and desires. My conversations with one migrant named Bouboucar pushed me to ask, for instance, was his movement molded most by the job advertisements he had seen for factory workers in Germany or by his desire to be the first in his family to educate his daughter? "Not everyone thinks you should spend money on your daughters, but my daughter will be a great success!" he told me. To what degree was his decision to leave home shaped by his own desires or by his son's pleading desire to have a new pair of headphones he calls "Beats"? "I want the red, 'Fight AIDS' ones, Baba! All of the other boys have them!" How often is migration from the Democratic Republic of the Congo the result of Kabila's ascension to power and decades of civil unrest, and how often does the stronger "push" come from personal stories of material success on the other side? My conversations with another migrant named Mariam raised similar questions about how one individual's movement can be molded by competing scales of influence. She shared with me her fear of forced marriage to her father's cousin. "He's old enough to have twelve cows and the gray hair to prove it!" And also her interest in her sister's stories about working as a maid in southern France. "Her boyfriend is very handsome, and when she visits home, she brings silk scarves for the whole family!" Migrants like Bouboucar and Mariam serve as links between the global and the local, and understanding their individual experiences is critical in connecting larger social and political shifts to the most intimate details of everyday life.

The task of the ethnographer is moving from the study of *migration* (population level) to the study of *migrants* (individual level) and drawing lines between the macro and the micro, which together motivate movement. As the work of scholars like Abu-Lughod (1993) and Behar (2003) illustrates, the practice of person-centered ethnography requires that the listener becomes the second teller of the stories that are shared, and it is in this process of conversion from listener/observer to teller/analyzer that connections can be drawn. As individuals, we are not always conscious of the social and political influences underlying our seemingly unique desires and actions. As a researcher, I have questioned to what extent I, standing decidedly outside of respondents' processes of migration, can claim that Bouboucar was in fact pulled by the labor demand in emerging European economies and not by the sight of his neighbor's daughter dressed in the starched uniform of Dakar's *Muslim School for Girls*. Similarly, to what extent can I claim that Mariam was pushed by the political fervor of the Congo's new leader and not by photographs of her sister's apartment, complete with a washing machine and a vase of red silk flowers on the kitchen counter?

Morocco is situated at a critical border, negotiating between two economically and culturally distinct regions of our increasingly globalized world. Like its fellow "labor frontier" country, Mexico, it plays various roles, aiding in both the movement and the detention of migrants (Ferrer-Gallardo 2008; De Haas & Vezzoli 2012; Baldwin-Edwards 2006). However, unlike the United States' southern neighbor, Morocco's role in mediating the flows of migrants has been overlooked by popular media. Exploring the evolution of migration patterns in North Africa allows me to illuminate how movement across borders has never been determined by demographic factors alone. Just as the individual movement of migrants like Bouboucar and Mariam is shaped by their personal aspirations and desires, shifts in movement on the national level are shaped by the unique geopolitical context of the region.

From Early Models to Contemporary Studies of Human Migration

Migration studies have long attracted researchers from across disciplines, and contemporary research draws on the work of not only anthropologists and sociologists, but also historians, political scientists, geographers, and economists. The vast body of research available means that I have been pushed to focus and narrow my informing literature, and so I have pulled together the strings that seem most relevant for research at Europe's borders, overlooking equally important literature that might better inform studies in other world regions. This section offers a brief history of migration studies, moving from Wilbur Zelinsky's earliest attempts to set human migration to an equation that would predict the future state of mobility (1971) to the most recent attempts to study human migration through global network analysis.

Morocco's precolonial history exemplifies the importance of societal mobility long before the influences of modernization and serves as a strong counterargument for early theories that posited migration as a step toward "development." Theories that equate migration with processes of societal development or "westernization" overlook the historic precedents of movement between state structures (Lucassen & Lucassen 2009). In fact, scholars of migration from a range of disciplinary backgrounds now critique the notion that migratory movement increased dramatically with the rise of nineteenth-century modernization. This follows even earlier critiques of the notion that time periods predating the modern era were defined by static populations that lived in isolated communities (Gupta & Ferguson 1992). Humans, it turns out, have always been on the move.

The Trouble with the Mobility Transition Model

Geographer Wilbur Zelinsky is best known for introducing the notion of human migration as linked to economic development. His seminal article, "The Hypothesis of the Mobility Transition," formulated the first concrete theory for tracking past and predicting future movements of human populations across regional, national, and transitional boundaries (1971). Zelinsky is an important forefather for cross-disciplinary scholars of migration, and although most research no longer supports linear models of development theory, his models of inter- and intracontinental migration remain relevant.

"In a pre-modern traditional society," Zelinsky claims, "the life patterns of all but a few privileged or exceptional persons were preordained by circumstances of birth" (Zelinsky 1971: 224). His hypothesis[7] was predicated on the assumption that "options of activities were rigidly constrained by gender and inherited by class, caste, occupation, religion, and location" (Zelinsky: 224). Therefore, barring disaster, the orbit of one's physical movement was circumscribed from a young age, the range of information and ideas that were available to one was narrow and stagnant, and these conditions changed almost imperceptibly from one generation to the next. The widely accepted notion that, except for the most elite classes, one's potential movement came about only as a result of crises (war or natural disaster) indicates why so much of the early literature on human migration focuses on groups that we now define as "refugees," or those who were physically displaced from their homes (Lucassen & Lucassen 2009).

The crux of Zelinsky's argument is that each of the five distinct phases of development—ranging from the "premodern traditional society" to the "future super-advanced society"—is linked to a distinct form of mobility. These forms of mobility are ever evolving along a linear path in a process termed "the mobility transition." This theory broadened the existing concept of demographic transitions, or high population growth, which had previously been seen as *the* cause of migration, by linking migration to a combination of demographic transition, economic growth, and increased options for transportation and communication that accompany modernization. What Zelinsky terms the "vital transition" is, in fact, what we would now call "development." He claims that the onset of modernization brings with it "a great shaking loose of migrants from the countryside," or high rates of rural-to-urban migration (Zelinsky 1971: 236). The rapid growth of urban centers and the expansion of industrial and commercial opportunities in periods of modernization have historically attracted and absorbed outpourings of laborers from rural surroundings.

Shortly after the publication of Zelinsky's hypothesis (1971), scholars across disciplines sought to counter his model by uncovering earlier and earlier tracked movements of human populations. Most notable among the movements that were discovered are the sixteenth-century processes of proletarianization (Tilly 1978); the seventeenth-century slave trade across the Indian Ocean (Vink 2003); and the steadily rising demand for seasonal laborers, soldiers, and sailors across supposedly "static" boundaries in the following decades (Lucassen 2004). We now know that, counter to Zelinsky's model, all of these large-scale human migrations took place before the onset of modernization. However, the data sets that would be needed for a complete analysis of changing rates of migration between pre- and post-Industrial Revolution periods is complicated by the historically poor documentation of migratory movement. One major challenge in confronting and improving models of linear development like Zelinsky's is the lack of comprehensive and comparable data that is available on human migrations, past and present. The fact that migratory routes have long been designed to avoid legal documentation and official border crossings has made the study of migration challenging for centuries. Whether due to the state's desire to obscure the forced movement of enslaved populations or the efforts of individual migrants who take the same paths that have been maintained to control the movement of undocumented and exploitable laborers, numbers are rarely tracked and migrants' papers are commonly forged, burned, or lost in transit. In their article, "The Mobility Transition Revisited," historians Jan and Leo Lucassen make a first attempt at analyzing the existing data on human migrations, focusing on movement into and out of the Asian-European continent in the years leading up to the Industrial Revolution, or what they claim to be the onset of modernization (2009). While their conclusions follow the trend of proving the premodernization mobility of human populations, they also conclude that Zelinsky's theory falls in line with the available data.

Attempts to reconstruct migration rates for Europe in the period 1500–1900 have shed new light on the linear modeling of a "mobility transition." It is clear that any causal relationship between the Industrial Revolution and mobility must assume that early modern Europe was a sedentary society, an assumption that historians have convincingly dismissed. However, researchers' concentration on relatively short periods of time and small parts of Europe means there is no data available to refute claims of a sharp jump in the number of migrations after 1850. Was movement the result of the rise of free market economies and the modern state? Or was movement the result or "side effect" of modernization—mass commercialization, mass consumption, and what is now referred to as the "westernization" (or even the "Americanization") of the "developing" world (Hochstadt 1999)? The availability of cheaper and faster transport dramatically increased migrants' chances of finding permanent or temporary work farther and farther away from home and resulted in a significant change. The change was not to the structural causes of migration but rather to the scale of it. A migrant's likelihood of moving across boundaries between cities, states, and continents has always been a factor of their distance from those borders, but the orbit of one's physical movement was expanding.

The Tiered Development Model

Although scholars are increasingly aware of the movement of individuals and groups across territorial boundaries in the pre-Industrial Revolution period, the mobility transition theory holds up when applied to

larger scale transcontinental migrations, which emerged in the twentieth century and were rare in centuries past. In fact, the transcontinental
migration of large populations has only been documented in four cases
throughout earlier time periods.[8] Most relevant among these four cases
is the earliest phase of the West African slave trade, which was responsible for the movement of large populations from the Muslim world,
formerly stretching across North Africa. Throughout the sixteenth
and seventeenth centuries, approximately half a million Muslims, predominantly from North Africa, were enslaved and taken to Italy (Davis
2003), along with hundreds of thousands of West African slaves, who
were brought by the Portuguese to Iberia and Italy between the 1440s
and 1640s (Almeida Mendes 2008). These populations made a significant demographic impact in cities across Europe, such as Lisbon, where
in the mid-1500s, black Muslim slaves accounted for 10 percent of the
population (10,000 individuals) (Davis 2003). The trans-Saharan slave
trade[9] was also prominent throughout this time period, bringing West
African slaves to North Africa, and specifically to Morocco, where one
of the region's largest slave markets stood in Marrakech (Ennaji 1994).
In later chapters, I address how this period is critical for understanding
the origins of blackness as a racialized social category in the Maghreb.

Early transcontinental migrations, while documented, are still
notable exceptions, and Zelinsky's hypothesis that small-scale, rural-
to-urban migrations serve as a precedent for larger-scale migrations
across national borders remains true. Geographer Ronald Skeldon built
on Zelinsky's work by expanding its Eurocentric view and establishing
lines of comparison between nations in all regions of the world that
have experienced similar transitions from net emigrant-sending to net
immigrant-receiving countries. He posits migration as being integral to
modernization—a process that is both spurred by economic development and serves as a catalyst for further economic development. Like
Zelinsky's five phases, Skeldon's model distinguishes between five distinct "development tiers":

> (1) The old core (e.g. Western Europe), (2) The new core (e.g. North
> America, Japan), (3) The expanding core (e.g. China, South Africa,
> Eastern Europe), (4) The labor frontier (e.g. Morocco, Egypt, Turkey,
> Mexico, the Philippines, and until recently, Spain and Portugal), and
> (5) The resource niche (e.g. large parts of sub-Saharan Africa, central
> Asia, and Latin America) (Skeldon 1997: 65).

Simplifying Skeldon's tiered development model, we are left with a foundational inverse relationship: where economic development and state formation are high, more complex systems of transnational migration are present. Conversely, where economic development and state formation are low, migratory movement is confined within the borders of a nation. Spain presents a model case study for the tiered development model, and many have argued that Morocco is following a similar path to becoming a net immigrant-receiving country (De Haas 2005, 2012). Yet, I would contend that these arguments fail to account for the influence of European policies on North African borders and the new era of border externalization.

If you can imagine the eight-mile stretch that separates Spain from Morocco as the narrowest part of an hourglass, then the Spanish side of the hourglass opens into the internally borderless states of the EU above, while the Moroccan side opens into the African continent below. Morocco's northern borders with Spain are the narrowest part of the hourglass through which all of Africa's migrants must pass. Spain is situated on the side with expanding labor markets and a rising demand for exploitable labor, while Morocco is situated on the other side. Spain's rapid ascension from "labor frontier" country to "expanding core" country was aided by its prime placement within the EU, while arguments that Morocco will soon follow fail to account for some of the realities of being situated on the side with struggling labors markets and a rising demand for escape. As bolstered security measures across southern Europe and North Africa reroute the movement of formerly colonized African citizens not toward a metropole, but instead toward another former colony, a unique form of movement from the global south to the global south is on the rise.

A New Migration Hump

Economists Edward Taylor and Phillip Martin's joint research moved the field beyond linear modeling through their introduction of the "migration hump theory," which many researchers still apply to explain the transition of "labor frontier" countries like Morocco and Mexico into net immigrant-receiving countries in relatively short periods of time. They argue that temporary increases in transnational migration—or a so-called migration hump—is a standard part of the process of economic development and an indication of a nation's progress along linear models of development (Martin 1993; Martin & Taylor 1996).

In the middle stages of development, an initial increase in per capita GDP leads to a spike in mobility because a certain threshold of wealth is needed for citizens to manage the costs of migration across borders. At later stages of development, an increase in the overall wealth of a nation and the job opportunities available there transform the country from net exporter to net importer of labor. Not only are there enough desirable job opportunities to deter immigration from the country, but expanding industrial and commercial sectors demand the cheap and exploitable sources of labor provided by immigration to the country.

Most recently, Hein De Haas, a geographer whose research is deeply rooted in the history of human migrations to, through, and from Morocco, presented his own model, which challenges scholars to account for "historical-regional" and "time-spatial" variation (2008). Most importantly, he calls for a transnational perspective that views the relationship between development stages and specific types of migratory movement as "indirect and probabilistic," rather than direct or deterministic (De Haas 2008). His work highlights the fact that a decreasing relative development level also holds the possibility of transforming a net emigrant-sending country into a net immigrant-receiving country, moving in the opposite direction along linear models of development. When tracking indicators of development, it is important to weigh not only economic and demographic variables, but also sociocultural variables, which play an increasingly important role in the development–migration nexus. As De Haas claims, increased wealth, transportation, and communication aside, sociocultural variables, such as education, internet availability (or access to information more generally), and social capital are responsible for shifting an individual's aspirations, desires, and probability of migration. I find that combining De Haas's approach with "hump" theories of development allows for a more complete study of contemporary transnational migration and broadens our view of development. If we take mobility as a fact, the important question for researchers becomes not *when* did populations begin migrating, but *how* have human migrations changed over time and *what* is the connection between larger social structures and individual agency?

Slave, Soldier, "Seasonal" Laborer

Migrant laborers have historically been assumed to be four things: young, single, male, and members of a low socioeconomic class (Lucassen & Lucassen 2009). They migrate with the hopes of earning enough money to establish themselves as "independent producers" or "economically attractive marriage partners" (Lucassen & Lucassen 2009: 363–364). While they have traditionally been categorized as "seamen, soldiers, domestics, and tramping artisans," historical studies of migration make little distinction between these four occupational categories, and the category of slave is notably absent. (Lucassen & Lucassen 2009). The analysis of early transcontinental migrations, including the West African slave trade and later exchanges of labor between colonial and colonized states, highlights the important connection between African states and colonial powers' demands for labor (whether sailor, soldier, or domestic laborer). I add a new dimension to the analysis by arguing for the fluid transition that migrants have been forced to make between the categories of slave (or forced migrant), sailor/soldier (or conscripted migrant), and domestic laborer (or "illegal," irregular, or seasonal migrant).

Rather than focusing on the Industrial Revolution as a point of transformation, I turn attention to the metamorphosis that migrants have been forced to make from slave to soldier to modern-day migrant laborer, and ask, could the so-called military revolution not instead be a turning point in the history of human migrations? From the early sixteenth century on, the military revolution can be characterized by a new use of firepower and expanding fortification of the state, substantially increasing the size of armies and changing the structure of state boundaries (Parker 1988). Rather than a "pull" factor that had once been confined to periods of war, the standing army became a constant draw for migrants—a "military mouth which needed to be fed at all times" (Parker 1988: 59). "Soldier" therefore became an accessible track to professionalization, and young single men from low socioeconomic classes left their homes in pursuit of the title, spawning the large-scale rural-to-urban migration of soldiers and later, the temporary transnational migration of armies. The "fiscal-military state," an expression borrowed by Charles Tilly, fell in line, quickly converting taxpayers' money into military salaries and facilitating the mobilization of new forms of wage labor and the increasing spatial mobility that it afforded.

The historical data compiled by Lucassen and Lucassen can be applied to illustrate how the fiscal–military state had a significant impact on movement in the Maghreb and across the Mediterranean. Most notably, men were needed to bolster France's colonial troops, commonly called "*La Coloniale*," which were composed exclusively of North African (Morocco, Algeria, and Tunisia) soldiers. From the 1830s, new soldiers were recruited from mainland France and its broader empire, playing a substantial role from World War I through the Algerian War of Independence (Munholland 1964), and setting the stage for a tradition of labor exchange between the colonies and the metropole. This period mobilized large parts of Europe's population in intercontinental flows, while simultaneously mobilizing the postcolonial world in intracontinental flows that would soon transition from a forced exodus of conscripted migrants to an arguably more agentic exodus of migrant laborers. It was not the migratory routes that changed, but the occupational titles of those traveling them.

Despite growing interest in the study of migration and the new data-tracking and storing technologies available to researchers, there are shockingly few comprehensive data sets on the movement of people between countries. A comparison of nineteenth-century rates of African-European migration and the burgeoning rates of migration across those same borders today is impeded by the lack of comparable data. Contemporary researchers still have little to draw on but national censuses (where available and when dependable) and numbers collected by the UN Refugee Agency (UNHCR)[10] and the International Organization for Migration (IOM),[11] which lack data on irregular migrations. The system used to quantify premodern migration was even more problematic than the census statistics that researchers find themselves struggling with today, as it lacked comparable state data on all fronts and was only recently formalized through the efforts of the Lucassens (2009). The fact that tracking the current movement of migrants across Moroccan borders is even remotely comparable to the difficulties historians encountered in tracking the sixteenth-century proletarianization of Europe speaks volumes to the efforts that migrants, smugglers, and states have historically made to obscure borders and those crossing them.

Measuring Migrations: How Far Or How Strange Is the Destination?

In an attempt to organize the various types of movement that are commonly grouped under the broad category of "migration" today, researchers have made distinctions between movement that is regional or transitional, temporary or permanent, forced or voluntary, and inter- or intracontinental. Despite the historical focus on inter- versus intracontinental migration, new studies of migrant communities support the argument that the distance traveled is actually much less important in marking the experience of migration than the "cultural" or "political" borders that are crossed (Manning 2005). Looking to modern-day Morocco as a case study, we could suppose that migrants coming from Muslim-majority Senegal, Mali, or Niger would have an easier journey than migrants coming from countries with substantial Christian populations like Togo, Ghana, or the Democratic Republic of the Congo (DRC). The argument supposes that it is the cultural dissonance and not the distance between countries that is most important. However, the argument requires that one category of identification be privileged above others. In this case, privileging religion overlooks the role of race and language in creating cultural dissonance or unexpected synergies between Moroccan and West African populations. Morocco, after all, was linked to non-Muslim African countries through the trans-Saharan trade and to other French colonies throughout the long period of French colonization across the continent.[12]

The recognition of cultural and political borders as real (though socially constructed) is a necessary step in giving voice to the experiences of migrants, but I contend that the argument be pushed further. Cultural dissonance operates on multiple levels. Cultural and political borders, like physical borders, still exist outside of the individual migrant and can fail to account for other factors that are uniquely defining of each individual's journey. Moving from the study of "migration" to the study of "migrants," it is important to consider not only the cultural and political markers that all migrants from a particular country carry with them, but also the individual markers of gender, race, and class that vary within the population and are largely defining of lived experience. These individual markers can transcend nationality and define how two individuals from the same sending country or religious background experience borders differently. In one instance, Ousmane, a Muslim Senegalese male with a high socioeconomic position, finds that his higher level of education offers him tools for manipulating cultural borders when in conversation. These tools are especially useful when he is occupying the marginalized position of a migrant in Morocco. However, even when manipulating his self-presentation to obscure his religion or nationality in a foreign country, he remains racially marked as "other." He carries his race with him across borders. A Muslim Moroccan female from a low socioeconomic position who has migrated to Spain may lack the tools for skillfully manipulating her self-presentation as non-Muslim or nonforeigner across cultural borders, but she is read as nonblack before she ever enters a conversation. She, too, carries her race with her across borders. Cultural belonging can be both seen and heard, but it is important to remember that rarely is an individual given the chance to be heard before they have already been seen.

According to historian Patrick Manning's migration typology, a "cross-community migration" demarcates any movement in which migrants feel the "cultural impact" of their journey, regardless of the distance traveled (2005). Migrants, he claims, are most likely to "gain new insights" when moving across cultural, often linguistic, borders, and this type of migration speeds the spread of innovation in the receiving country, too. When first reading it, I thought of Hicham and his transnational family network, many of whom described to me the challenges of managing their "Moroccan-ness" with their foreignness. His sisters, Soukaina and Fatima Zahra, who both live in Italy with their Moroccan husbands and foreign-born children, were especially open about the conflicting expectations that had been placed on them. The proper role of women in Morocco was at odds with the public lives they were expected to lead in their new, secular communities, where they held part-time jobs outside of the home.

"I learned that I can't give my daughter a *hijab* and then tell her that she's Italian," said Fatima Zahra. Wanting the best for their children, but also wanting to impart their deeply-held cultural and religious beliefs, Hicham's siblings struggled over the most basic decisions, like which language to speak at home or what kind of clothing to wear. During my time in Morocco, I saw the reverse impact of transnational migration in everything from the changing material desires of Moroccans whose family members lived abroad to the impact of Western media on those who remained at home. "How can you give Moroccan youth Arab MTV and then tell them not to dance?" Soukaina asked, voicing the frustrations of many. "You cannot show us how the rest of the world is living and then expect us not to dance, not to drink, not to have sex. Of course, we are going to want to experience freedom for ourselves, too." Their family's experience of cross-cultural exchange shows that they have certainly "gain[ed] new insights." But I contend that it is in the sending countries, not the receiving countries, that the impact of cultural change is most underappreciated. Hicham explained it best when he said, "The process of migration changes the individual, not the system. It's the individuals who will eventually change the system when they return home with new beliefs, new priorities, new ways of doing things." He went on to use Morocco as an example. "It's not that Moroccans are unproductive, it's that the Moroccan system doesn't allow for productivity. Place a Moroccan in a functioning system, and he becomes a productive worker. It's the return of these workers from the EU who will one by one make Morocco a more productive place. Then, we won't need to leave our homes to find work." The rhetoric of cultural changes brought on by expanding Muslim migrant populations in Europe may be widespread in popular media, but the changes felt in the *banlieues* of Paris are minimal when compared to the changing attitudes in Moroccan cities.

Morocco's Critical Place at the Crossroads

The Sahara Desert is often portrayed as a barrier—difficult at best and insurmountable at worst—that separates one world from another. However, recent work by scholars of the region have taken historian Fernand Braudel's description of the Sahara as "the second face of the Mediterranean" and used it as the starting point for reexamining the region not as a barrier but as a crossroads (1949). It connects, not separates, Africa and the Mediterranean. The countries of the Maghreb are deeply involved with, not isolated from, their neighbors on either side of the Saharan "coastlines" (McDougall & Scheele 2012). The Sahara, McDougall and Scheele argue, is best seen as an interdependent network that spans the desert's vast expanses. It is the heartbeat of the region, sustaining complex systems of trade, migration, conflict, and cooperation.

From Berber to Muslim: The Islamic Conquest of the Maghreb (647–709)

In Morocco, one's chosen speech, whether French, Berber, modern standard Arabic (*Fusha*), or Moroccan Arabic (*Derija*), hints at multiple facets of identity from socioeconomic status to political status. In my research in migrant-populated communities in Morocco, I saw how language can establish allegiances between communities, bringing together migrants from the same linguistic background in "brotherhoods," and can set boundaries between others. It became one of the primary ways in which I heard, recorded, and questioned new forms of racial and political discrimination across the country, and with time, I noted that more and more of the words I was hearing in the public sphere were racially charged. "*Haratin*," a term historically used to mark one as a "freed slave," is one example of language that is being used to set boundaries between those who belong and those who do not. However, the origins of the term are still debated. In his research on slavery in Morocco, Maghrebi scholar Chouki el Hamel suggests that the term is derived from one of three possible roots: the Berber word "*ahardan*," meaning "dark color" (black or reddish); the Arabic words "*hurr*" and "*thani*," meaning literally "the second free man" or possibly "a second-class free person"; or the Arabic verb "*haratha*" meaning "to cultivate" (2002: 38). The deconstruction of its etymology mimics what el Hamel calls an ongoing "difficulty in defining the identity of blacks in Morocco" (2002: 39).

In one of my first conversations with Dr. Mohammed Benjelloun, a professor of Islamic Studies at Morocco's national university, I raised a series of questions related to the role of race in Islam. I wanted to know: Does the Qur'an make note of different racial groups, and if so, is one group marked as superior or inferior to another? How do Islamic teachings inform race relations in the Muslim world today? Dr. Benjelloun was adamant that neither the Qur'an nor the Hadith[13] make any note of racial difference. "Racism is not a part of Islam. It never has been, and it never will be. In the eyes of Allah, all men are equal." In fact, according to the words of the Qur'an, "We have created you from a male and a female, and made you into nations and tribes, that you might get to know one another. The noblest of you in God's sight is he who is most righteous" (43:13). Dr. Benjelloun's discussion of modern-day differentiation in the Islamic world was structured along lines of religious and not racial difference, just as it would be when he later justified distinctions that had been made between the free (Muslim) and the enslaved (non-Muslim). I took a special interest in his mention of the "Curse of Ham," which scholars from different faiths have suggested is a common misnomer for the curse upon Canaan, imposed by the biblical patriarch Noah (Goldenberg 2003). While most conclude that the story's original objective was to justify the subjection of the Canaanites to the Israelites, the narrative is interpreted by some Jews, Christians, and Muslims—including *imam* Fouad al-Hajji, whom I later interviewed—as an explanation for black skin and a justification for slavery in later centuries (Goldenberg 2003, Brett 2000). One of the earliest Arabic writers to address race, renowned religious scholar Ibn Qutayba (828–889 CE), also commented on the Curse of Ham and used the narrative to explain the racial differences between the Arab world and the rest of the African continent. "Ham was a white man having a beautiful face and form. But Allah (to Him belongs glory and power) changed his color and the color of his descendants because of his father's curse. Ham went off, followed by his children.... They are the Sudan" (Muhammad 1981: 15). More than simply linking racial difference to geographic placement, his interpretation links the darker-skinned descendants of Ham to a legacy of wrongdoing and punishment.

Yet it was the even more problematic writings of famous Arabic travel writer, Ibn Battuta (1304–1369) on which Dr. Benjelloun built his argument. As he explained, "Battuta opened the eyes of people who could not travel. He showed them that we do not just look different from our brothers in Africa, we *are* different." Famous for his travel accounts compiled in the *Rihla* ("The Journey"), Battuta wrote about racial differences found throughout Asia, the Middle East, and Africa, drawing correlative relationships between race, culture, and behavior. In his 1353 *Adventures in West Africa*, he remarked on people's "feeble intellect" and the "pagan attitudes," evidenced by "bare breasts, sexual freedom, polygamy, and bad manners" (el Hamel 2002: 41). Ibn Khaldun (1332–1406), a Tunisian scholar who followed in the footsteps of Ibn Battuta, is regarded by Muslim scholars today as one of the founding fathers of modern sociology. For me, he will always be renowned as the one to rewrite much of the misguided thinking about race, culture, and behavior. He wrote against the existing scholarship that claimed the people of the Sudan were descendants of Ham, cursed with their dark skin, and he also negated the notion that skin color could be linked to distinct or undesirable personal traits. Challenging accepted notions, he claimed that "the peoples of the Sudan [are] black-skinned because of the intense heat of the climate in which they live.... Furthermore, the strange practices and customs of these peoples [can] be attributed to their climates and [are] not genetic in origin" (el Hamel 2002: 42). The rich history of trade linking Morocco to the rest of the African continent means that blacks interacted with Berbers even before the advent of Islam. Ibn Khaldun's writings point to racial stereotypes that were present before religion became a point of differentiation between the two groups.

In Africa, Islam traveled along migratory routes, and conversion occurred primarily through trade rather than through conquering, as was prevalent across the Middle East (Hall 2011). Berbers were forced to move farther south into the Sahara region after successive invasions by the Vandals, Romans, and Byzantines, beginning when the Vandals first crossed to Africa in 429. Citing Berbers as "technologically superior, thanks to their contact with different cultures [through trade] and the use of the camel," el Hamel claims that they likely conquered local black populations in the Sahara and "assumed for themselves a superior status" (2002: 43). From this point, a racial binary developed between the two groups. Blacks living in what became Berber territory were forced into roles of servitude (servant, slave) or roles of interdependence (intermarriage, trade partner) (Hall 2002). When Islam finally reached the Berbers with the first Arabian military expeditions into the Maghreb between 642 and 669, blacks were further subjugated. Just as Berbers became Muslims, blacks (or non-Muslims) became infidels, making them the only population religiously sanctioned to be slaves. The borders with Sudan became a primary point for importing enslaved populations into an expanding Islamic empire throughout the seventh century, cementing a distinction between Arabs (Muslims) and blacks (servants/ slaves) on the grounds of both racial and religious differentiation.

The Arab Slave Trade (650–1900s) and Morocco's Black Army (1672–1727)

Slaves serving the Mediterranean world throughout the thirteenth century were predominantly Arab Muslims,[14] and those serving the Maghreb were brought from the sub-Saharan region. What resulted was a map of movement not unlike that of present-day labor migrations in which the vast majority of Moroccans now end up in western European labor markets and the vast majority of journeys beginning in sub-Saharan Africa either end in or return migrants to the Maghreb. The Arab slave trade, which began in 650 and was not officially abolished until 1970, predates the European slave trade by over 700 years. Estimates of the slave population differ widely, with historians believing that between 8 million (Luiz Felipe de Alencastro) and 25 million (Paul Bairoch) enslaved Africans were taken across the Red Sea, Indian Ocean, and Sahara Desert during this period to serve as soldiers, servants, laborers, concubines, and eunuchs in the Muslim world, which spanned three continents at its peak (Bairoch 1994; De Alencastro 2017). Those settling in Morocco were concentrated in wealthier, urban enclaves and came primarily from East Africa (Nubians and Zanj). Scholars of the region have since drawn on art, journals, and legal documents to examine how notions of racial identity and social stratification were shaped by the large numbers of slaves living in Morocco at the height of the trade.[15]

To this day, Morocco, Algeria, Tunisia, and Libya remain united by the slogan: "One Islam, one nation" (*al-maghrib al-'arabi*). In his research on the history of slavery in the Maghreb, el Hamel expands the meaning of this slogan beyond the nations' shared history and religious solidarity (2002). He claims that it is, in fact, a unification over "one culture, one language, and a silence" (2002: 29). The cultural tradition of silence el Hamel references is the Maghreb's "refusal to engage in discussions on slavery and race" (2002: 29). His research is based largely on historical readings of the Islamic legal texts that address the practices of slavery and the social status of slaves in society. Drawing a distinction between skin color and racial categorization, he argues that Morocco's period of slavery set the foundation for the racial biases that are found throughout the country today.

Fouad al-Hajji,[16] a self-described "progressive" *imam*, was introduced to me by a friend who had studied with him in university, and he eagerly agreed to answer some of my questions about the role of religion in contemporary race relations. However, al-Hajji wanted to start from the beginning. "In Morocco, you can't talk about race without talking about slavery." Despite my then daily conversations with respondents on the subject of race, I was surprised by his response. He was the first to broach the subject of slavery with me, and he wanted to pose the questions. "So why don't you ask me? Did the Qur'an play any role in instituting slavery?" According to the *imam* and others to whom I would pose similar questions over the course of my fieldwork, the answer is not a simple yes or no. "All [four] legal schools of Sunni and the school of Shi'a sanctioned the enslavement of non-Muslims, regardless of their skin color.[17] Slavery has always been an issue of religion, and not of race, you see?" Al-Hajji was quick to assert that even the Prophet, "*Sallah Allah 'alaihi wa sallam* (peace be upon him)," owned slaves.

Mohammed Ennaji was one of a few Moroccan scholars to tackle the issue of slavery in the Maghreb before el Hamel (Ennaji 1994), and he is noted for challenging the assumption of many Western scholars that a common religion overshadowed the racial hierarchies that emerged between black and Arab Muslims. As one nineteenth-century British historian mistakenly claimed, "They [the Muslims] divide Mankind into Believers and Unbelievers and this division cuts across every difference of Physical Race" (Toynbee 1934: 226). Historian Bernard Lewis later refuted such theorizations as an "imagined construct," asserting that across the Maghreb, race relations were structured by the notion that blacks (both Muslim and non-Muslim) were "of an inferior and lesser breed," a notion substantiated by the fact that they were "almost entirely missing from the positions of wealth, power, and privilege" (el Hamel 2002: 33, Lewis 1990: 20). While Morocco's history of enslaving black Muslims is rarely discussed in popular debate, the mass enslavement of previously freed slaves, or *"haratin,"* during the reign of Sultan Moulay Ismail ibn Sharif (1672–1727) serves as one prominent and troubling example of the practice.

Moulay Ismail ibn Sharif sought to create a black royal army (*jaysh 'abid al-bukhari*) to defend the Muslim world, leading to a public outcry not so much about "defending a group of people from being enslaved," but rather about "defending the Islamic tenet that makes it illegal to enslave a fellow Muslim" (el Hamel 2002: 44). As thousands upon thousands of formerly freed slaves were forced into uniform by his *fatwa*, skin color became the key marker by which groups were divided—no longer "Muslim" and "non-Muslim," but "Arab" and *"haratin,"* "white" and "black." In contrast to free men (Arabs and Berbers) who the Sultan defined in his writings as "irresponsible, lazy, weak, envious, and opportunistic," the Sultan found black men to be "loyal, professional, strong, servile, content, satisfied, patient, and strong" (el Hamel 2002). However, legal documents from the same time period make note of *haratin* as "restless thieves and rebels." This indicates, as el Hamel highlights, that their good qualities were thought to be subject to their status as slaves and that, once freed, their natural qualities would make them a threat to society (2002).[18]

Moulay Ismail ibn Sharif is remembered for being hugely "successful" in his mission, eventually establishing a standing army of over 150,000 formerly freed slaves that defended and expanded the royal kingdom throughout his reign (Abum-Nasr 1987). Despite this "success," the Sultan's army was dissolved shortly following his death. Each *haratin* soldier was replaced by an Arab soldier, and the Arab soldiers were given the right to enslave the black soldiers they were replacing for their personal use, collecting all of their personal belongings, including wives and children, as their own. El Hamel argues that this period of reenslavement was critical in merging three of the accepted social and racialized categories present in Morocco at the time—*"labd"* (slave), *"aswad"* (black), and *"hartani"* (freed slave) (2002: 49). Equally important to note is how irrelevant the religious category of "Muslim" was in distinguishing between free and enslaved populations. I argue that a common religion continues to be irrelevant in distinguishing between legally included and excluded populations today, despite the continued rhetoric of Islamic inclusiveness and a Moroccan racial consciousness that many claim is colorblind. In my final meeting with Fouad al-Hajji and the more elite members of his mosque, we sat cross-legged around a table drinking mint tea, and I listened to them debate the role of race in Islam. "In Morocco, there is no race, only religion," proclaimed the *imam*, to which one of the younger men replied, "But we don't see religion, we see race."

The French and Spanish Colonization of Morocco (1860–1956)

Prior to the colonial period, Morocco remained a country that was divided racially (between Arabs and blacks), religiously (between Muslims and a small population of Jews[19]), and linguistically (between primarily Arabic and Berber speakers). Even among Arab Muslims, numerous divisions existed between followers of the Sufi[20] orders; the *shurafa* (or direct descendants of the Prophet Muhammad), who enjoyed certain privileges; and the *ulama* (authorities on *Shari'a* law) and *Sheikh* (Sufi masters), who occupied an even more privileged status. Socioeconomic divisions also existed between the various forms of labor, including pastoralists, nomads, agriculturists, merchants, artisans, a landed quasi-aristocracy, and an emergent population of slaves and *haratin* (el Hamel 2002). Moroccan scholars have drawn on legal documents to illustrate how physical characteristics, especially skin color, were central in demarcating *haratin*, or freed slaves, from other populations. The group was recognized not only by their legal status as freed, but by their skin color as "*aswad*," or black. The French colonization of Algeria marked the beginning of a sociopolitical restructuring of the region, in which distinct categories of religious and linguistic identification were integrated under the common categories of "Muslim" and "Moroccan." But the same cannot be argued for the racial categories of "Arab" and "black," which remain distinct to this day.

At the turn of the twentieth century, France and Spain established protectorates over Morocco, ceding France majority control, and giving Spain the Western Sahara and northern Rif Mountains, where the Spanish enclaves of Ceuta and Melilla still exist. The colonial division of Morocco and the rest of the African continent following the Berlin Conference of 1884 is highlighted in Figure 2.1. After the conquest of Algeria (1830) and the establishment of a protectorate over Tunisia (1881), France took control of Morocco with the Treaty of Fez on March 30, 1912. A second treaty signed by France and Spain later that year granted

FIGURE 2.1 Map of Colonial Era Africa following the Berlin Conference of 1884.

Spain a "Zone of Influence" in northern and southern Morocco. The Tangier Protocol, signed by France, Spain, and the United Kingdom in 1923, gave Tangier special status as an international zone, and it remained a multilateral trading hub for decades to come. From a legal perspective, the treaties established did not strip Morocco of its status as a sovereign state. France used Tunisia as the example for how to structure a successful protectorate, and sought instead to strip the Sultan of all power and rule the nation through a colonial government. According to General Hubert Lyautey:

> In Morocco, there is only one government, the *sharifian* government, protected by the French. . . .[We] offend no tradition, change no custom, and remind ourselves that in all human societies there is

a ruling class, born to rule, without which nothing can be done. . . .
[We] enlist the ruling class in our service . . . and the country will be
pacified, and at far less cost and with greater certainty than by all the
military expeditions we could send there.[21]

But Morocco's thousand-year tradition of independence, France's
late conquest of the country, and Morocco's proximity to Spain have
all been cited as reasons behind the unique relationship that developed
between France and its newest colony (Segalla 2009). Morocco's French
rulers attempted to use urban planning and colonial education to prevent "cultural mixing" and maintain the traditional society. They pro-
moted economic development through the exploitation of Morocco's
mineral wealth, restructuring of its cityscapes, implementation of new
transportation systems, and expansion of an agricultural system that
would meet the demands of the French market. This period forcibly
integrated the autonomous tribes of rural Morocco with urban centers
under one "modern" state and marked the beginning of new forms of
labor exchange between North Africa and Europe (Hart 2000; de Haas
2005). During the 1914–1918 period, more than 30,000 Moroccans im-
migrated to France, foreshadowing a mass importation of migrant labor
from the colony (Hammoudi 1997; Bourqia & Miller 1999).

The Postcolonization Migration Boom (1956–2005)
and Morocco's Transition into a "Destination" (2005–present)

The Maghreb is a space in which colonial dynamics continue to shape the
present day, and as other scholars have examined, the making of "natives"
and "Europeans" was based on assumptions of radical racial and cultural
differences, many of which persist today (Da Silva 2007; Pierre 2012).
Compared to Algeria in the infamously bloody Algerian War of Independence (1952–1964), Morocco made a smoother transition out of the
colonial period. King Mohammed V negotiated the gradual restoration
of a free Morocco within a framework of French-Moroccan interdependence. In February 1956, he agreed to transform Morocco into a constitutional monarchy with a parliamentary democracy in exchange for
acquiring limited home rule. Further negotiations for full independence
ended with the French-Moroccan Agreement signed on March 2, 1956.
France officially lifted its protectorate over Morocco, and the internation-
alized city of Tangier was reintegrated with the signing of the Tangier
Protocol. The lifting of the Spanish protectorate was finalized later that
year, although Spain has yet to relinquish control of Ceuta and Melilla.

The decades that followed Morocco's independence brought drastic changes in migration. With the "great migration boom" of 1963, the number of Moroccan migrants in France rose from 30,000 to 300,000 in only 10 years (Bonnet & Bossard 1973). By 2004, the number of Moroccans abroad rose to a record high of over 3 million (more than 10% of the current population of 31.9 million), with 2.6 million residing in western European countries alone (Sadiqi 2004). Since then, rates of emigration from Morocco to Europe have been declining as the rate of immigration to Morocco from other African countries continues to grow.

Despite the rich history of trade linking Morocco to the rest of the African continent, the Maghreb continues to be an outlier in African studies. New patterns of movement and detention are serving to solidify the region as an island between Saharan shorelines, rather than diversify it, and applying the trope of "island-ness" provides a lens into why this may be the case (Baldacchino 2004). In my first months of research, I noted the ubiquity with which the terms "Arab" and "Moroccan" were used interchangeably, often in direct opposition to the terms "black," "African," or, most commonly, "sub-Saharan." The term "sub-Saharan"—one that both Moroccan citizens and migrants use to group together those whose journeys began in East, West, or Central Africa—brings a number of issues to the surface.

An Island Surrounded by Land

The UN Development Program currently lists 46 of Africa's 54 recognized countries as part of the "sub-Saharan" region, excluding only Algeria, Djibouti, Egypt, Libya, Morocco, Somalia, Sudan, and Tunisia. If this term were truly meant to divide the continent based on one geographic feature—the Sahara Desert—then Mauritania, the majority of which is located in the Sahara, would not be considered a part of the sub-Saharan region. In fact, four of the countries excluded from the sub-Saharan region are located in the Sahara, and Eritrea is deemed "sub," while its southern neighbor Djibouti is not. On examination, it seems inescapable that the term "sub" is meant to connote not only below but also lesser than. The lexical trick of dividing Africa into what is "sub" and "above" an imagined line is rooted in a division of the continent that has long been based on racial difference and not geography. The term "sub-Saharan" has become, as critical race theorist Tatenda Chinondidyachii Mashanda claims, "a way of saying 'Black Africa' and talking about 'black Africans' without sounding overtly racist" (de Haldevang 2016).

With the implementation of "sub-Saharan" as the nouveau "Black Africa," the Maghreb remains a space just white enough to be distinct from the continent, but not white enough to be European. Yet in both regions, "sub" and "above" the racial divide, there is a failure to recognize the degree of variation that exists. One is glossed over as "sub-Saharan" and the other as a subset of the Middle East North Africa (MENA) block, regardless of the vast differences between countries like South Africa and Sudan, Morocco and Iran. This failure is most glaring in the "sub" region, where thousands of distinct languages and cultures are found. After extended discussions with respondents who identify as both citizens and migrants in Morocco, I have, in some cases, chosen to group subsets of Morocco's migrant population under the term "sub-Saharan" in order to reflect the ways in which both groups consistently identified themselves to me and are identified in Morocco's public sphere. Although more than one dozen nationalities are represented in the group of foreign exchange students who were involved in my research, and even more are represented among the larger population of migrants, the lack of space allowed for either group to establish an identity beyond their race—to acknowledge, for instance, the importance of nationality, ethnicity, or class in shaping their identity—highlights the role that race has long played in distinguishing the Maghreb from the African continent. My decision to use the term "sub-Saharan" is therefore made with an awareness of the tendency to lump Africa and the contemporary experiences of Africans into one ahistorical clump.

While "island-ness" is often theorized in terms of isolation, Brunhes (1920) encouraged researchers to think of it in terms of location and identity instead. "An island's signature is its obvious optic: it is a geographically finite, total, discrete, sharply precise physical entity which accentuates clear and holistic notions of location and identity" (Brunhes 1920 in Baldacchino 2004: 272). Brunhes describes an island that exists naturally with a clearly defined boundary around its physical space and an equally clear understanding of who belongs as a citizen of the space. Morocco, a crossroads of human migration, does not exist as a natural island. Rather, it has constructed its "island-ness" in spite of its location, requiring an even stricter boundary to be drawn and policed around identity. As the population of sub-Saharans living in the Maghreb grows and diversifies, the Moroccan identity is being challenged. I argue that the same ideology used to group the sub-Saharan region of Africa on a macro level is operating on a micro scale within the Moroccan state, where race is determining lines of belonging.

Migration has long been an integral part of Moroccan identity, and as Hicham is quoted in the opening of this chapter, "To be a Moroccan today means to be a migrant." The following chapters contribute to a rich history of research aimed at understanding how migration engenders new forms of racial identification and stratification.[22] The transition from slave to soldier to migrant laborer was structured by societal-level shifts, but it leaves unanswered questions about where the lines of agency can be drawn. Knowing the stories that will fit within the UN-sanctioned definition of a refugee, some African migrants are now working to afford fake documents that will make them Congolese or Sudanese in origin. Less than one decade ago, they would have been working toward an identity as Côte D'Ivoirian or Sierra Leonean instead. Along the same lines, Moroccans are now adopting new strategies in their attempts to impersonate Syrian asylum seekers when crossing to Europe, as other groups will likely do in the coming years. As I examine how new political categories of inclusion and exclusion are reshaping postcolonial identities of "black" and "Arab," "Muslim" and "Christian," "Moroccan" and "African," the role of the individual migrant in creating, manipulating, and resisting these categories is revealed. If being a Moroccan means being a migrant, then what does it mean when being a migrant now means being black?

Notes

1. Names and other identifying details have been changed to protect the privacy of research respondents.
2. The French–Spanish protectorate over Morocco was established in 1912, and the nation was not freed from French control until 1956. The Spanish remain in control of parts of Morocco to this day.
3. While every Moroccan is expected to have a framed photograph of the reigning King Mohammed VI visible in the main room of their home or business, there is no photograph that has been standardized for this purpose. Therefore, the choice of image—a formal portrait of the king in his full military regalia or a candid shot of him on his jet ski? A recent image or one of him as a younger man? A solitary moment or one of him with his wife and two children?—can be an interesting point of discussion.
4. The Moroccan diaspora is estimated at 4.5 million and consists of immigrants from Morocco and their descendants. Approximately two-thirds of the Moroccan diaspora is currently living in Europe (Eurostat).
5. Throughout my analysis, I consider race as a social construction that is real in its multiple manifestations in individual lives and group experiences.

One of the most notable features of race as a social construction is the status of whiteness as an "unmarked" category standing in opposition to other marked categories of racial identity. While it is unmarked, it enables the sociopolitical visibility of whiteness across the globe. Conversely, the mark of otherness leaves people of color sociopolitically invisible. From a Foucauldian perspective, I consider whiteness as a "tool of power" used to strip people of color of the agency to define themselves (Foucault 1980: 162), making one either white or other.

6. See Castles 2000; Levitt 2001; Olwig 2007.

7. Zelinsky succinctly lays out his hypothesis of the mobility transition: "There are definite, patterned regularities in the growth of personal mobility through space-time during recent history, and these regularities comprise an essential component of the modernization process" (1971: 221–222). Like Rostow's *The Stages of Economic Growth* (1960), Zelinsky distinguishes five phases: (1) The premodern traditional society (high fertility and mortality; low population growth, if any); (2) the early transitional society (rapid decline in mortality; rapid increase in population growth); (3) the late transitional society (rapid decline in fertility; significant but decreasing population growth); (4) the advanced society (fertility and mortality stabilized at low levels; low population growth, if any); and (5) the future "super-advanced" society (sustained low fertility and mortality). Zelinsky's foundational contribution argues as follows: premodern societies (phase A) are characterized mainly by limited circular migration. In the early stages of the "vital transition" (phase B), all forms of mobility increase (circular, rural colonization frontiers, internal rural-to-urban, international). In phase C, international migration decreases rapidly, rural-to-urban internal migration slackens but remains at high levels, and circular movements further increase and grow in structural complexity. At the end of phase C, the rural exodus significantly decreases, as the number of those employed in agricultural production approaches the minimum level associated with optimum economic return. In phase D, residential mobility, urban-to-urban, and circular migration become more important, and countries transform themselves from net emigration to net immigration countries because of the mounting immigration of unskilled and semiskilled workers from developing countries. In phase E, most internal migration is urban-to-urban and residential, while immigration of laborers continues (1971: 230–231).

8. First among these, at the beginning of the sixteenth century, approximately 50,000 migrants from the Ottoman Empire colonized the Balkans, and the Turkish tribes settled in Bulgaria (Todorov 1983). Second, in the early seventeenth century, approximately 270,000 Kalmyks migrated from

western Mongolia to the borders of the Caspian Sea in European Russia (Hellie 2008). Third and fourth are outlined in the text above.

9. The trans-Saharan trade more generally denotes any movement of peoples or goods requiring travel across the Sahara Desert to reach sub-Saharan Africa from North Africa, Europe, or the Middle East. While existing from prehistoric times and still transporting caravans today, the trade was at its peak from the eighth to the early seventeenth century.

10. The office of the United Nations High Commissioner for Refugees (UNHCR), also known as the UN Refugee Agency, was established in 1950 to assist the millions of Europeans who fled or lost their homes during World War II. It continues to be the principal international organization tasked with protecting refugees, or those who have been displaced from their homes around the world. According to the official mandate, "The UNHCR works to provide international protection to refugees and to seek permanent solutions for them." Their mandate extends to official refugees, forcibly displaced communities, and stateless people, and they seek "permanent solutions" primarily through voluntary repatriation, local integration, or resettlement to a safe third country.

11. The International Organization for Migration (IOM), originally called the Intergovernmental Committee for European Migration, was established in 1951 to assist in the resettlement of people following World War II. In 2016, it became a related organization of the United Nations. It continues to be the principal international organization tasked with protecting migrants. According to the official mandate, "The IOM works to ensure the orderly and humane management of migration, to promote international cooperation on migration issues, to assist in the search for practical solutions to migration problems, and to provide humanitarian assistance to migrants in need."

12. Beginning with Senegal in 1677, France colonized large portions of modern-day North Africa (including Morocco, Algeria, Egypt, and Tunisia); West Africa (including Côte d'Ivoire, Benin, Mali, Niger, Guinea, Mauritania, Senegal, Burkina Faso, Togo, Nigeria, and Gambia); Central Africa (including Chad, Central African Republic, Republic of the Congo, Gabon, and Cameroon); and East Africa (including Eritrea, Madagascar, and Dijbouti), where francophone traditions still persist.

13. The Hadith, derived from the Arabic word for "report," are a collection of stories claiming to report the exact words of the Prophet Muhammad. They are second only to the Qur'an in developing Islamic jurisprudence and are regarded as important tools for interpreting the Qur'an today. Unlike the Qur'an, which was compiled under the direction of the early Islamic State in Medina, the Hadith were not compiled by a central authority. They were

based on stories in circulation after the death of Muhammad and gathered throughout the 8th and 9th centuries. Each Hadith is based on two parts—a chain of narrators reporting the Hadith (*isnad*) and the text itself (*matn*). While individual Hadith are classified by Muslim clerics and jurists as "*sahih*" (authentic), "*hasan*" (good), or "*da'if*" (weak), there is no unanimous agreement, and groups may disagree on the classification.

14. Spanish slavery has been noted for being "nondiscriminatory," with slaves being a mix of "white," "black," or "olive." However, records show that those taken to modern-day western Europe were almost exclusively individuals who would be considered Arab by today's standards of ethnic and racial classification (Phillips 1985).

15. Lewis 1979; Khatibi 1983; Laroui 1983; el Hamel 2002.

16. The name given to those who have completed the *Hajj*, which replaces the Arabic equivalent of "Mr."

17. Islam asserts that the basic human condition is freedom, but with the codification of Islamic law in the ninth century, the religion formally recognized the category of slaves. In addition to being non-Muslim, slaves must be born to a slave parent, captured in a war, or purchased from the previous slave-owner.

18. El Hamel's research is based, in part, on his close reading of "The Registers of the Slaves of Sultan Mawlay Isma'il" (or "*Daftar Mamalik as-Sultan*") dated 1710 and conserved in good condition in the *Bibliothèque Générale* in Rabat, Morocco. In this document, close to 1,000 black slaves who were present in Morocco at the beginning of the eighteenth century are listed with biographical data, including "their names, slave labels or categories, and descriptions of their physical characteristics (tall, fat, thick bearded, dark skinned, etc.)" (2014: 177).

19. Before the founding of Israel in 1948, there were between 250,000 and 350,000 Arabic-speaking Jews in Morocco, making it the largest Jewish community in the Muslim world (Hirschberg 1974). It is estimated that fewer than 2,500 remain today, and most are concentrated in Casablanca or their original communities in northern Morocco.

20. Sufism, also called *Tasawwuf*, is the inner mystical dimension of Islam. Practitioners of the religion, or Sufis, belong to different orders (*turuq*) that are formed around a grand master (*Mawla*), who must maintain a direct chain of teachers back to the Prophet Muhammad. Sufis regard Muhammad as their ultimate leader.

21. "French-Moroccan Declaration." *Department of State Bulletin*, 34 (873): 466–467, March 19, 1956 (unofficial translation).

22. Chavez 2008; Willen 2007a; Ngai 2005; Ong 2003, 1996; Khatibi 1983.

CHAPTER 3

Colony, Monarchy, Muslim Democracy: Morocco as the New "Destination" for African Migrants

Introductory Case Study: Two Sides to Every Story

My fieldwork was bookended by murder. On August 12, 2013, a middle-aged Moroccan man stabbed a young Senegalese man to death on a public bus. As news of the violent murder spread throughout Rabat, reactions to it signaled a country that is divided into two camps on the issue of immigration. One side condemned the tragedy, calling out "*Murderer!*" and demanding that the basic human rights of Morocco's rapidly expanding migrant population be defended. The other side chanted approval, even encouraging others to "*Protect our country!*" and "*Send them home!*" I had arrived in a nation taut with tension between citizens and migrants, Arabs and blacks, Moroccans and "Africans." The dividing line lay between those who define themselves by their allegiance to *Jazirat al-Maghrib*,[1] an island distinct from the larger continent, and those who are instead defined by their birthplace beyond Morocco's borders.

The competing accounts given me by Chidiki, a Nigerian migrant, and Amine, a Moroccan graduate student of the same age, reveal not only the national state of division, but the individual tensions in each man's understanding of himself in changing times.

Chidiki began: "*I'll tell you how it happened. A young man boarded a bus from Rabat to Fès. He told the woman who was sitting in his seat that she was in the wrong seat. She refused to move. She pretended like she didn't hear him. Then she refused to let him sit in the open seat beside her. She pretended like she didn't see him and moved her bags to the open seat. The husband of the woman boarded the bus and confronted the young man—'Why are you speaking to my wife?' he demanded. A fight broke out between them as the young man tried to explain. The husband pulled out a knife and killed the young man right there on the crowded bus. No one tried to stop him. He was a military man. The young man was a migrant from Senegal.*"

—Chidiki, M, 22, Nigerian migrant

The two respondents both told me, "*The young man's name was Ismaila Faye.*"

"*You let a migrant tell you the story? He won't tell you right. It's not about race,*" Amine began the story from his perspective.

"*You know, there's a section of the Qur'an that tells us color makes no difference. It's what lies in the heart of a man that matters. There's no racism in Morocco, because the Prophet, sallah Allah 'alaihi wa sallam* [peace be upon him], *told us that every man—white, black, red, yellow—is made the same.*

It's not about race, it's about culture.

Africans have a different language, different traditions, different ways of doing things, so you wouldn't want them living in your neighborhood or marrying your children. I'm not a racist. I have black friends. I even have a black girl who's a friend, but I can't imagine having a black girlfriend. It's not about race. I wouldn't want someone who was obese or wore a hijab everyday as my girlfriend either. Would you judge me if I said I didn't want someone who was deformed or blind? To me, it's just not attractive. And, can you imagine, I would have a black child! I just can't imagine having a black child. In Morocco, the lighter your skin is, the more attractive you are. Everyone would question why a light-skinned Moroccan married a dark-skinned Moroccan. They would think I had lost my mind if I married someone black.

It's not about race, it's about history.

You know, blacks have been in Morocco for a long time, but they started here as slaves, and it's difficult for them to escape that history. It's the same for Moroccans in Spain. No one wants a Muslim as their neighbor there. They worry about the safety of their children. The Spanish don't look down on us because of race. They look down on us because we're different. To them, we look poor and dangerous, like people who should clean their streets. They think we're trying to steal their jobs from them. They think we're all terrorists.

It's not about race, it's about work.

I have a friend who runs a construction company. He pays Africans 20 dirhams an hour and Moroccans 10 dirhams an hour, because he knows Africans work twice as hard. Africans are hard working. If Moroccans worked harder, he would pay them more. They're going to take all of our jobs from us soon.

It's not about race, it's about money.

When you hear someone say they don't want an African to live in their apartment, it's not to protect their neighborhood, it's to protect their wallet. Why would I rent my apartment to someone when I'm not sure if they'll be able to pay me rent next month? You know, I lived in the same building as a Congolese man when I was in school, and our neighbor always called him a goat. The boys from the building would throw rocks at him sometimes when he passed them on the street. He always paid his rent early. He always smiled at me when I passed him. I never heard him speak. At first, I thought there was no racism in Morocco. But when I reflect on it, I start to remember little things like this."

—Amine, M, 22, Moroccan student

The two respondents spoke his name again, *"Ismaila Faye— may Allah grant his soul everlasting Paradise."*

Chidiki concluded, *"The racism in Morocco is brutal. Some Africans may be seen as Muslim brothers inside of the mosque, but outside of it, they are all blacks. Why did no one on that bus call Ismaila Faye his brother?"*

Chidiki and Amine's words are about more than just the murder of Ismaila Faye. Subsequent interviews revealed that their stories are also about how they make sense of themselves in relation to one another. Amine asserted again that hierarchies of racial difference are no different than those of regional difference and that just as many "*Rabatis*" would protest their daughter marrying a "*Marrakechi*," any Moroccan man would protest his daughter's marriage to an African. However, the language of cultural difference cloaks his obsession with race, highlighting deep-rooted racisms that are born, as he says, out of Morocco's long history of slavery (El Hamel 2002, 2014). I could not help but notice the parallels Amine drew between the treatment of Moroccans in Spain—where, as "darker" and presumably "dangerous" Muslims, he believed they are feared for stealing jobs and demoralizing communities—and the treatment of Africans like Chidiki in Morocco—where they, too, are feared for the presumed economic and social threats they represent.

Although Chidiki and Amine gave me conflicting accounts of the same murder, there are a few facts that I know to be true. I know that Ismaila Faye, a 31-year-old migrant from Senegal, was stabbed to death with a knife. I know that he was awaiting departure from Rabat's central bus station, where I traveled to and from on most days. I know that the man who murdered him (whose name was never released, for his own protection) remains uncharged for the crime to this day. It is still debated whether Faye asked the man's wife to move from a seat that had been assigned to him or whether, as some Moroccan sources claim, Faye was already seated when the man's wife arrived and asked him to move so that she did not have to sit beside him. However, all sources agree that the altercation ensued when the man boarded the bus and saw Faye speaking to his wife (al Makhfi 2013). He was stabbed multiple times. In the weeks that followed, public attention turned to a series of protests for the regularization of undocumented or "irregular" migrants in Rabat and to an antiracism media campaign, called "*Ma smeeteesh Azzi*" ("*Je ne m'appelle pas Azzi*" or "My name is not Nigger"), that was launched by European NGOs and went viral in late 2014. A poster from the campaign is pictured in Figure 3.1 below.

"Is it a crime now, being black? Is it punishable by death? Will there be no retribution?"[2] asked Eric Williams, another migrant living in Morocco, when he was interviewed for a local newspaper article on Faye's murder. This question, "Is it a crime now, being black?" struck a chord with the public, being repeated again and again in various clips on the unfolding story. Parliamentary member Mehdi Bensaïd of the Authenticity and Modernity Party (PAM) was the first Moroccan to publicly declare Faye's murder "racist," adding that "when faced with immigration, [Moroccans] behave like members of the *Front National* in

FIGURE **3.1** *Je ne m'appelle pas Azzi"/"Ma smeeteesh Azzi"* **antiracism campaign poster.**
Campaign archives.

France," in a reference to the European party's staunch anti-immigration policies (Bachelet 2014).[3] Despite his statements, the legislative draft for Morocco's first antiracism law, which PAM presented in the following year, still sits on parliamentary shelves.

When a similar story made headlines only 12 months later, reactions had changed. A Moroccan police officer slit the throat of another young Senegalese man, leaving him to bleed to death on a public street. Silent were the voices that had demanded social change, and emboldened were those calling for political change—for stricter immigration policies and tighter border controls. For the first time, I began hearing an open discourse about *"le peril noir."* The headlines were all too familiar. On August 29, 2014, Charles Ndour, a 25-year-old migrant from Senegal, was found dead on the outskirts of Tangier. The Moroccan officer who murdered him (his name unreleased for his protection) remains uncharged.

> According to eyewitnesses, some Moroccans stormed into the apartment where Charles Ndour lived with seven other migrants in Tangier's peripheral neighborhood of Boukhalef. They led the women to the back of the apartment and asked all the men but Charles to stand outside, "as if they wanted to make an example out of him, as if they wanted to show us what they were capable of, really terrorize us," [said one migrant witness]. They slit Charles' throat open with a knife and

pushed him outside to die on the street. He was found face-down in a pool of his own blood. The mishandling of this affair by Moroccan authorities has sparked outrage in Senegalese communities who protest the conditions surrounding his death.[4]

This news report, similar other reports of the incident, ends with a tone of concession: "Though shocking, Ndour's death did not come as a surprise to anyone." Like Chidiki, I wanted to shout, "*Why did no one on that street call Charles Ndour his brother?*" In contrast to the protests and antiracism campaigns launched in Rabat in the wake of Faye's murder, Boukhalef saw a series of xenophobic demonstrations and the organization of a militia calling themselves the "*Syndicat des racistes*," or "Trade Union of Racists" (Bachelet 2014). Many people supported the eventual finding that Ndour's death was the result of an "altercation" and that no one could be blamed. Those who were not in support faulted the slumlords who run schemes around Tangier, escalating tension, which is already high between migrants and Moroccans. Slumlords, or "*marchands de sommeil*," routinely take over the northern Moroccan residences of citizens who are living abroad and rent them to migrants who are awaiting their chance at crossing to Europe over the Mediterranean Sea. What were single-family homes become hostels, holding anywhere between 8 and 30 migrants per room. Serious issues arise every summer when Moroccans return for vacation and thousands of migrants are evicted onto the streets.

Even outside of the slumlord schemes dominating the rental markets in towns like Boukhalef, migrants face significant challenges in finding housing in Morocco, forcing many to retreat to the forest camps hidden around Ceuta and Melilla, where their lives center on training for escape. In Moroccan cities, landlords commonly refuse to rent to migrant tenants. Those who do charge higher rents, require multiple months of payment as a security deposit and are known to take money without providing housing or to evict migrants shortly after they arrive without returning their deposits. Countless times, I heard about similar scenarios unfolding when migrants took jobs from Moroccans and were left with no course of action when they were unpaid. As one Congolese man explained, "I can't go to the police when I'm cheated or attacked. If I present a problem, then I *am* the problem." The largest barrier to "escape" for most migrants in Morocco is money. It takes money to leave, whether to return to one's home country or to travel north toward the promise of a new life in Europe, but the routine exploitation and extortion of migrants in Morocco makes the accumulation of money all but impossible. They are, quite literally, trapped.

"Your landlord can enter your apartment at any time, and he will. He will enter it almost every day and take anything of value you have in there," one woman from Mali explained to me. Although I never witnessed what migrants call "apartment searches" by a landlord, I did frequently witness what police officers call "pat-downs." Like apartment searches, routine pat-downs make it difficult for migrants to accumulate money. They cannot leave money in their homes, and they cannot carry it on their bodies. Even when some creatively cut open their shoes to store bills under their soles or hid money in the bottom of a bag full of rice at home (two tactics I witnessed more than once), they were eventually found out. I saw migrants approached by Moroccan officers in uniform while awaiting buses on crowded street corners, hawking fruit in the marketplace, or walking down the street with their young children in hand. The officers would search their bodies and their belongings, often dumping all of their goods out onto the street before taking everything of value. Many times, I saw a response to this theft (*"Please, brother, no!"*) met with violent assault. I saw migrants bloodied, bruised, and left sprawled out on the street like their belongings as people casually walked by. The visible presence of an ethnographer, a foreigner, did not make these attacks any more or less brutal or commonplace. I was occasionally a target myself, and in several different altercations, I had officers physically aggress me, threaten me, detain me, and confiscate my equipment, simply for standing beside those who were being searched. One of the most difficult parts of my ethnographic work in Morocco has been knowing just how little I can to do to help those who are so immediately and outrageously wronged. Often, it brings to the forefront a question that anthropologist Ruth Behar posed: "If you can't stop the horror, shouldn't you at least be there to document it?" (1996: 2).

In the months that followed Ndour's death, reports of new murders continued to surface. Moussa Seck, a 19-year-old migrant from Senegal, and Cédric Bété, a 23-year-old migrant from Cameroon, were the next to make headlines. The first young man "fell" from the window in his fourth-floor apartment building in Boukhalef during a police raid. The second was chased onto the roof of his four-story building by raiding police officers before also "falling" to his death. Both were deemed "highly suspicious conditions," but no arrests were made following the investigations and the names of the raiding officers were never released (Bachelet 2014). In an interview with the local press, one migrant said, "We feel like the police are trying to chase us out of Tangier."[5] Moroccan activist Boubker el-Khamlichi of *l'Association Marocaine des Droits Humains* (the Moroccan Association for Human Rights) publicly condemned the Moroccan police force's treatment of migrants as "savage" and charged that recent murders were part of a deliberate plan, constructed and backed by the EU, to deter migrants from attempting to make crossings (Rippingale 2014). He was among the first to publicly state a connection between the treatment of African migrants in Morocco and the investment of the EU in externalizing its southern borders. No longer drawing on the historic construction of blacks as slaves, el-Khamlichi's comments suggest that blacks have become inextricably linked to the fear of and desire to control the migrant subject (El Hamel 2014, 2002). When I interviewed him at his office in Casablanca one month later, el-Khamlichi expanded on this subject. "It's a policy really. It's a way of pressuring migrants to leave our country voluntarily before they make it any further north. You had better believe Europe is giving money to Morocco to play the role of their policeman." El-Khamlichi places blame not only with the Moroccan state, but with the neoliberal arm reaching south of its own borders to construct a new class of marginalized subjects across the Maghreb.

Tangier's police chief, Abdellah Belahfid, declined to offer me any response on the deaths of Moussa or Cédric, but he did publicly deny that his force was bowing to European pressure to stop the flow of migrants traveling north (Rippingale 2014). "These raids are a part of our routine police operations," he claimed in my later interview with him. This routine, he said, was established "to fight the migrants responsible for the trafficking of hard drugs" and "to protect our local communities." Tracing his logic backwards, it is clear that the chief links Moussa and Cédric to an assumed nationality simply by way of their blackness, and further links them to an assumed political vulnerability simply by way of their assumed countries of origin. Because they were from countries south of Morocco, they were undocumented migrants. Yet, he was able to navigate his description of the Moroccan police force's routinized brutality against blacks and his duty to protect Moroccan citizens without the mention of race. It has become a question not of racial identity but of rightful belonging.

The War on Migrants, the War on Drugs

In my following of popular media and interviews with policymakers in Morocco, I often heard stories about Morocco's migrant population that differed dramatically from my lived experience with them. Again and again, I heard stories about disease, crime, drugs, and prostitution. I heard the backlash of fear instilled by routine headlines such as "Morocco Is Under Attack." On many occasions, both governmental officials granting research clearances and police officers on the streets told me that my research was being prevented "for my own protection." The populations displaced by conflict and poverty, whose struggles I was attempting to document, were not the ones in need of protection. They were the threat.

Throughout my time spent traveling with families on migratory routes from Central and West Africa, I have witnessed forced prostitution at the hands of smugglers who regularly pluck women and girls from groups as they shuttle them from one border crossing to another. But rarely do their journeys end on the African continent. These women and girls who are forced into prostitution are among the most likely to have "successful" crossings—forced into labor markets where the demand for sex is high and the customers pay well. When they do end up in Morocco, then rarely are the paying customers fellow migrants. In the migrant communities where I lived, prostitution was spoken of as a crime inflicted on them or their sisters—not a crime they were actively engaged in. Mamu, a young man from Niger, explained, "Sex with Moroccan women, prostitutes or not—this does not happen. Sex with black women—where are they? Sex with black prostitutes—this costs money, and so this does not happen either. Black women are for Moroccan men. Moroccan women are for Moroccan men. Even the boys are for Moroccan men!" His friends laughed in agreement, and they went on to explain that drugs, like women, demanded money, and among migrant communities in Morocco, money is always in short supply.

When analyzing the trafficking of people and goods between Africa and the EU, it is difficult to overlook the critical role that Morocco plays in moving illicit goods. Moroccan drug cartels, which have been steadily expanding over the past two decades, are increasingly linked to those across Africa and Latin America (Zemer 2010). While Morocco has undeniably become a central route for trafficking, there is no evidence to suggest that the quantity of drugs brought to Morocco from sub-Saharan African countries is even a fraction of the quantity of cannabis that is produced in and exported directly from Morocco's northern Rif Mountain region. According to the UN Office on Drugs and Crime (UNODC) report, Morocco annually cultivates as much as 47,500 acres for a total production of 38,000 tons of cannabis and 760 tons of cannabis resin—or 21 percent of the world's total production and over 70 percent of the cannabis consumed in Europe in 2012. In fact, Morocco was ranked the world's top producer of cannabis until Afghanistan took the top position following the 2012 report.

Although drugs were officially banned in Morocco following independence, the long-standing tradition of cannabis production in the Rif Mountains, the use of cannabis as a recreational drug preferable to alcohol in the eyes of many Muslims, and the practical need for diversified crop production have all led to recent debates over legalization.[6] The cultivation of cannabis is a vital source of income for more than 800,000 Moroccans, and impoverished regions in northern Morocco are dependent on it.[7] Cannabis, better known as *hashish*[8] in Morocco, was first introduced during the Arab invasions between the seventh and fifteenth centuries. Prior to the expansion of drug-trafficking networks, it was grown on a small scale all across the country. Smoked in a pipe with tobacco or mixed with honey and eaten, it was used in religious rituals and enjoyed recreationally. It was not until growing demand from tourists and traffickers in the 1960s that larger-scale techniques were adopted to replace artisanal ones, and the Rif Mountains became the center of Morocco's cannabis production.[9] Historians suggest that two events led Morocco to be one of the world's top producers—cannabis production privileges were legally granted to several Riffian tribes due to the crop's cultural significance, and the monarchy simultaneously deinvested in the region, propelling many Riffians to leave for Europe in the following decades (Zemer 2010). This migration is thought to serve as the foundation for the "Moroccan network" of cannabis trafficking between North Africa and the EU.

Despite Morocco's critical role in moving illicit goods across international borders today, popular debate on the threat of drugs in the community rarely centers on the state's own production and trade of cannabis. Instead, it is about the increasing threat of drugs bought in by migrants and smuggling rings. As Mamu explained, "No cartel would trust me with drugs! They know I'll be lucky to make it to the other side [of the Algerian-Moroccan border] with my shoes still on my feet, much less anything of value on me." My engagement with the smuggling rings that largely control African migrants' movement through the region indicates that it is the higher ranking among them and not those paying the smuggling fees who are most likely to be found transporting goods, whether they be "illegal" persons or drugs.

Aid from the Other Side

As racially charged violence continues to increase along with the number of migrants living in Morocco, the number of NGOs turning to migrant issues has also expanded. Since the rise of Morocco's post-colonization migration boom, an established group of organizations has been working on issues of Moroccan immigration, ranging from the integration of return migrants to anti-immigration media campaigns that highlight the dangers of traveling along smuggling routes. However, the population of African migrants now settling around urban centers is confronting the nation with a new set of challenges. Some of the smaller European-funded NGOs have expanded their services in recent years to include not only Moroccan return emigrants, but migrants trapped in Morocco on their journeys north. The major Moroccan organizations are still struggling to determine the correct provision of social services between their own citizens, migrants from other African countries, and an emergent population of "invisible" youth that are born to migrant parents in liminal spaces of settlement.

Chidiki, whom I first met at *La Fondation Orient-Occident* (FOO), a Rabat-based Moroccan NGO, was doing translation work for them on days when he could find nothing else. FOO struggles to offer a range of basic services to many more African migrants than their office can accommodate, and like a similar organization where I volunteered while living in Rabat, they are constricted by the lack of legalization processes available to migrants in Morocco. Migrants seeking applications for temporary work visas, temporary student visas, official refugee status, or even protection as unaccompanied minors were frequently given a packet of crackers or a small *Derija* phrasebook as a consolation. Despite this, there continues to be a rhetoric of empowerment and change in these spaces, leaving Chidiki and many others like him feeling frustrated. As he explained:

> The organizers told us, we can change things. But we said, no, we
> cannot. Africans don't believe that change can happen. They've never
> seen it happen. One of the problems is that here [in Morocco] we're
> all immigrants. People don't leave their homes to sit through meet-
> ings, they leave their homes to make money. You don't come here
> to tell your stories in a book, you come here to make money. Some-
> times I think, who wants to hear my voice anyway? It's not my coun-
> try. It's hard to form a community from a group of immigrants. The
> only thing we share is the feeling that we don't belong. Europeans
> feel differently. They feel more comfortable because they're at home
> wherever they go. They have a voice. They haven't had to fight every
> day of their lives just to stay alive. The little money I make, I send it
> home. Like my brothers and sisters, I have nothing left at the end of
> the week. When your life is easy, you have time to fight for justice.
> Our lives are hard, so we have no time. My spirit was tired before the
> fight even began. We don't have the educations we wanted, the jobs
> we wanted. Europeans have had a fortunate life. It's easy for them to
> believe in good. It's not the same for me. Justice is a new idea. I don't
> believe much good is waiting for me anymore. Sometimes people
> don't understand how lucky they were just to be born. I asked the
> organizers, what good is it to know your rights, if there's no one who
> protects them?

In Morocco, the face of Spain persists as both captor and savior. The
vast majority of the few services available to African migrants are provided by European, usually Spanish- or French-run, organizations and
volunteers. As a migrant, it is the European volunteers who offer you
new clothes at church on Sunday mornings, the Italian doctor who
sees your sick child, the French woman who teaches you how to read,
and the Spanish lawyer who informs you of your rights. It is me, the
American researcher, who helps you fill out your asylum application,
sets up a Skype account for you to call home, and brings groceries
to the apartment you share with seven others. There is no question
why visions of Europe as the land of great opportunity—visions of
Spanish streets paved with gold—are easy for migrants to keep alive.
Even on the migratory routes that the EU is so desperately trying to
block, Europeans appear at every turn to lend a hand. For migrants
from North Africa and other regions of the continent, the faces of

oppression—the extorting smugglers and aggressing police officers—are the faces of their own people. It is the sub-Saharan "camels"[10] and the Moroccan police officers who harass them, supporting negative images of the places they are so desperately seeking to escape. Moving from the micro to the macro scale, it becomes clear that it is neither the Nigerian smuggler (not even the Nigerian smuggling ring) nor the Moroccan officers (not even the Moroccan police force) who is constricting movement across North Africa. By traveling across Spanish borders—crossing into Ceuta, Melilla, and over the waters of the Mediterranean—I saw that movement from Africa is constricted primarily by the EU-funded Guardia Civil force. But to see this, you first have to make it to the other side.

The Long Road Home

At night, the 150-mile stretch of road that runs along the Moroccan-Algerian border between Bouarfa and Oujda comes alive. Unlike any border I have seen before, it is a desert border, and so it is always changing. The sand underfoot buries the tracks of those who walk just before you, and the peaks of the dunes rise and fall around you with the wind. This is the stretch of land that is walked by those who have been deported. And it is here, in 2014, that I made a temporary home for myself and began collecting the stories of migrants who had been illicitly "repatriated" by Moroccan officials, not to their countries of origin, but to a desolate stretch of land in the Sahara Desert.

Despite smugglers' instructions to burn all identification papers before leaving home in fear of repatriation and despite repatriation being a mandate of international law, I never witnessed a proper repatriation at the borders between Spain and Morocco. Instead, Morocco's migrant community lives in constant fear of deportation to the Moroccan-Algerian border, where men, women, and even children are dropped by Moroccan officials in a practice informally termed a "push back." From the desert, migrants know they have little choice but to walk back into Morocco and begin the long process of training or saving for their next attempted escape.

On one of my first nights at the border, I encountered a group of two dozen young men and boys walking on the dirt road that runs from the desert to the nearest town. Speaking French heavily accented by their West African roots, they explained how they had been "dropped" from Melilla the previous morning. "You don't want to walk back toward the people who dropped you, but where else can you go?" This question that one of the young men in the group posed to me speaks to the physical lack of options for migrants who have been dropped. Later conversations with him and the others highlighted a second internal struggle that many face in turning away from their dream of reaching the other side of the Mediterranean Sea. If border controls serve as the primary push, then the dream of setting foot in Europe remains an even stronger pull for most migrants. They are trapped not only by the physical and economic constraints that determine their movement, but also by the social systems that supported them in their journeys north and continue to add to the psychological stress of returning home before achieving success. Whether it is the shame they would feel returning home to a community that financially supported their journeys without the money to repay this investment or the desire to offer those left behind with a safer and more secure future, the migrants whom I came to know well have a complicated set of factors shaping their sense of mobility, obligation, and aspiration. As one man explained, maintaining the hope that a better future is still waiting in the distance is all that makes their present state sufferable.

Migrants use Morocco as a launching pad into Europe in one of four ways. Most commonly, as it is the only option that requires no payment to smugglers, it is by scaling the rings of razor-wire fences surrounding the Spanish enclaves of Ceuta and Melilla. Second, those with some resources at hand pool together their savings to purchase an outboard motor and an inflatable raft better known as a *zodiac* or an old wooden fishing boat known as a *patera*. Most often, they pay smugglers a reduced amount for the "route," or the right to pass, and they self-captain their small boats across the rough waters of the Mediterranean to the southern coast of mainland Spain at night. A third option, one for those with some resources at hand, has been to stow away in the trunks, engines, or specially constructed "cages" hidden under cars and trucks crossing into the Spanish enclaves. This method, however, has become less common since 2018, as it is now standard protocol for border guards to attach sonic devices to the hoods of all crossing vehicles, checking for the number of heartbeats inside. Fourth and least commonly, as it is the most expensive option, migrants carry false paperwork across European borders in hopes of applying for official status once they have safely reached the other side. The group I encountered on one of my first nights in Oujda had attempted a fence crossing into Melilla, not alone, but in a mass of hundreds that stormed the fences after nightfall. They explained how they were among the few who had succeeded in scaling all three rings of razor wire surrounding the enclave that night, but while climbing down the last fence, they had been severely beaten with batons by the Guardia Civil. After beating them off the fence, the Guardia Civil officers handcuffed them and handed them back over to the Moroccan officers who were waiting on the other side of the fence.

Abraham, a young man who fled his home in Côte D'Ivoire two years before arriving in Morocco, waved his papers at me as we spoke, showing me that he was an "official refugee," recognized by the UN Refugee Agency (UNHCR). In theory, the papers he held in his hand should have afforded him the basic protections that are guaranteed to all refugees. Yet Abraham and I both knew that in Morocco, there are no refugee camps, and until he reached European soil, he would remain subject to the same abuse as others in his group who lacked any official paperwork. While Morocco is home to a UNHCR bureau, the difficulties that all Africans, regardless of their status as undocumented migrants, asylum seekers, or official refugees, face in accessing housing and work lead many who have not yet received papers to postpone the review of their applications. Being granted status in a country can make it more difficult to leave it.

"We hand out applications," one caseworker at UNHCR's main bureau in Rabat explained to me, "but most migrants prefer to keep their applications in their pockets in the hopes of reaching Europe where they'll file them." Despite a growing population of migrants in Morocco, the number willing to avail themselves of the UNHCR's assistance has actually been dwindling. The vast majority of those who are seeking assistance now come from the relatively small percentage of women or unaccompanied minors who find themselves trapped in the Maghreb. In 2014, Rabat received only 3,927 applications, followed by Fès, which received the second highest number at 1,999. "It's an incredibly frustrating job," the caseworker continued, echoing Chidiki's sentiments. "I want to help, but my hands are tied. There's a real humanitarian crisis unfolding in Morocco. We have all of these women and children trapped in a country where their most basic rights are being denied, and they are in constant danger. I can't give them the safety they deserve."

Abraham was one of the few young men I met who had decided to apply for status in Morocco and whose case had been approved. He explained that after traveling over 3,000 miles on foot, his smuggler had abandoned him and the rest of his group in Algeria. Finally reaching Morocco on his own, he was instructed by the other Côte D'Ivoirians he met at the border that he should continue traveling north toward Melilla. There, he made his first of what would become numerous attempts at crossing, only to be handcuffed and returned to the desert by the Algerian border, which he had just spent the past weeks trying to escape. When he reached Morocco the second time, he turned away from Melilla and instead headed toward Rabat, where he had been told there was some possibility of accessing international aid. It was only after he was granted refugee status and learned it was "still impossible to build a life in Morocco as a black man" that Abraham decided to try crossing into Melilla once again. On his final attempt, I could imagine him proudly waving his papers at the Spanish officers, just as he had done for me—certain they would grant him some protection. But he learned that even with feet on European soil, papers do not always guarantee one's legal rights. When we last spoke, he was not sure how long he would wait until he tried again, but he was sure of one thing, "I'm growing tired of this cycle."

Hussein, one of the young men who had been walking with Abraham on the morning I first met him, told me he had given up after multiple failed attempts at crossing. He had been living and working outside of Boukhalef when a Moroccan officer arrested him and forced him to board a bus with others who had been pulled from the fences around Melilla earlier in the morning. "I was sleeping in my apartment when the police came. They handcuffed me and put me on a bus full of other young men. The bus stopped in Oujda. They pulled us off, and the bus turned around. This is the first time I've been dropped. But some of my friends in Boukhalef, they've been dropped more times than they can remember." It was true that nearly all of the migrants I interviewed over the course of my fieldwork had been "dropped" at some point, many of them multiple times. Whenever I met an individual who had not experienced this form of deportation firsthand, they knew of others who had. "If the police find you," explained Khadija, a woman from Mali, "and they want to do more than just take the money out of your pockets, then they'll threaten to take you to the border." Like others, Khadija was frequently harassed by police when hawking repurposed goods on the streets around Rabat. "They take you to the middle of nowhere, and they drop you. There, any way out is difficult. It's difficult to go back to your own country. It's difficult to come back here. It's difficult to survive the night." Those who do survive, begin their long journey toward Oujda, where they find what little work they can and save up what little money they can for the trip back to Rabat or farther north toward Ceuta and Melilla.

Whether picked up by police in the migrant-populated slums and camps they call home or beaten off the fences surrounding Morocco's Spanish enclaves, the events that followed were always explained to me in the same way. Joseph Shaka, a young man from Nigeria, was working under the table for a small construction company in Casablanca when the police came for him. "I am black. That is why I am supposed to die," he explained to local reporters when questioned about the charges brought against him (Wilkinson 2005 & Hinshaw 2015). He was taken to the desert on a bus with other men and women who had been picked up in surrounding areas and reported that 10 of the women in his group died from exposure on their journey back toward Oujda. Bemba Martin, a young man from the Democratic Republic of the Congo who was in Shaka's group claimed, "This isn't how you fight immigration. This is how you hunt for blacks" (Parkinson & Wilkinson 2005).

For those dropped in the desert, the conditions are perilous. Those who survive the extreme heat, dehydration, and starvation are soon faced with another host of threats. In one week alone, I heard more than one dozen firsthand accounts of attacks on migrants by Moroccan gangs who routinely hide out in the woods surrounding Oujda to beat, rape, and steal from those who are passing through. Many told me how smugglers worked in cooperation with local gangs, notifying them of when and where they would be dropping their next group, in exchange for a percentage of the pillaging. Every one of the migrants who described these assaults to me remembered them not because the violence or theft against them was at all remarkable by that point in their journeys, but because the gangs that hide out in the woods do so with packs of dogs at their sides. "Of all the horrors I'd come to expect by the time we reached that last border, I didn't expect the dogs," said Hussein, as he pulled up his pant-leg to expose a deep and festering wound. "You can ask any of us who crossed there, and we'll tell you how the sound of their barking is hard to forget."

While no official statistics exist, I estimated that 5,000 migrants were gathered in the sprawling encampments just outside of Oujda in the time that I was there. Mostly young men, with a small percentage of women and children among them, the groups were composed of those who had just arrived in Morocco with the dream of reaching Spain, and those who, like Abraham and Hussein, had already scaled the fences or crossed the waters and felt European soil underfoot. The "dropping" of migrants to an uncertain survival in the desert lends a visceral and visual reality of the cycle that so many remain trapped in today. *Board this bus. Empty your pockets. See if you can escape the desert without food or water. See if you can find your way back to the place where you are now. And if you do, then see if you can do it all again.*

Trapped at the Gates of Europe

Global attention first turned to the issue of Morocco's illicit deportation practices in 2005 when the international organization Doctors Without Borders (*Médecins Sans Frontières* or MSF) tracked and rescued a group of more than 500 migrants who had been abandoned by Moroccan officials to fend for themselves in a desert area, far from any food or water. This was the same desert where Abraham and his small group were dropped nearly 10 years later in 2014. MSF's initial rescue efforts targeted the large number of children and women in the group, in addition to the more than 50 men who had sustained serious injuries before being "pushed back." While some of the lacerations and bruises they were found with could have been the result of razor wire, as Moroccan officials claimed, the group presented with other injuries consistent with blunt force trauma, which is routinely caused by baton beatings at the hands of Moroccan and Spanish police. Despite the brutality the migrants had just experienced at the borders to Europe, MSF reported that those who were not under their direct medical attention were eager to set out on the treacherous 400-mile journey across the desert toward the Spanish enclaves again. This, perhaps more than anything, speaks to the desperate situations they were fleeing in their home countries.

In the winter of 2013, as my fieldwork transitioned from Rabat to Oujda, international aid organizations were again shocked by the discovery of 92 bodies, including 32 women and 48 children, who had been abandoned in the Sahara by their "camels," or smugglers tasked with bringing them across Algeria. According to local authorities, "We found their bodies scattered over a large area in small groups. Some were lying under trees, others exposed to the sun. Sometimes, we found mothers huddled over their children. Sometimes, we found children alone." The few who survived and made it to the nearest town on foot explained that their truck had broken down, and many had died of thirst and exposure before they could escape the desert. The survivors also asserted their status as victims of human trafficking who were trying to make it to Europe by way of Morocco. It can be difficult for officials to make a distinction between those who are being trafficked and those who are migrating when it is the same smuggling rings that facilitate the movement of both. In this case, however, the unusually large percentage of women and children in the group led rescuers to assume they were being moved against their will.

Following this incident, MSF again turned global attention to Morocco, releasing a 38-page report titled "Violence, Vulnerability, and Migration: Trapped at the Gates of Europe" (2013). MSF's annual reports, which are widely distributed to national and international governing bodies, select and outline the most critical of global humanitarian crises in the given year. In 2013, it was the crisis of migrants in Morocco that they chose to spotlight.

> Over the last ten years, as the European Union has increasingly externalized its migration policies, Morocco has changed from being a transit country for migrants en route to Europe to being a destination country by default. MSF's experience in country demonstrates that the longer sub-Saharan migrants stay in Morocco, the more vulnerable they become. Their pre-existing vulnerabilities, related to factors such as age and gender, as well as traumas commonly experienced during the migration process, accumulate as they are trapped in Morocco and are subjected to policies and practices that neglect, exclude, and actively discriminate against them. (*Excerpt from introduction*, MSF 2013)

MSF's data illustrates that the main factors influencing the critical medical and psychological needs of migrants in Morocco are their precarious living situations and the widespread institutional and criminal violence against them. Despite the attempts of MSF and other aid organizations to highlight the rising criminality against those trapped in Morocco, the latest report notes that the period since 2011 has seen a sharp increase in violence against African migrants by both Moroccan and Spanish authorities (MSF 2013). Yet the problem extends far beyond these officials. Violence is routine in both human smuggling and trafficking networks, and shocking levels of sexual violence against migrants, including men, women, and children, shape the migration journeys of most.

A great discrepancy exists between European immigration policies and the nascent immigration policies that Morocco has constructed under European influence. While one has historically respected fundamental human rights, the other was built to view migration through a security prism that criminalizes and dehumanizes those who are trapped between two homes. The EU's concern for the rights of asylum seekers and refugees has come to a head with the desire to secure its own borders. By exporting border controls further south and supporting the development of Moroccan policies that detain and illicitly deport, there developed a tacit understanding that just south of the Spanish border, the rules change. There is no longer an obligation to uphold the same standards of treatment, placing Spanish officials operating on Moroccan soil in a position to carry out abuses that would be punishable under European law. But in analyzing Morocco's position at the crossroads between Africa and Europe, there is also an active role to be explored—Morocco as more than a passive receiver of EU aid and intervention (Natter 2013; Collyer et al 2009). According to Emeritus Professor Mohammed Boudoudou, one of Morocco's leading experts on migration, "The European Union wants Morocco to act as its police dog, and Morocco accepted this role because it is still a poor country. It accepted this role in exchange for money, for protection, for the promise of development. It accepted this role with its own dream of being something great." The cost to pursuing this dream of greatness? A vulnerable population hundreds of thousands strong and growing by the day.

A Brief History of the World's Oldest Monarchy

My status as a foreigner in Morocco was never more obvious to me than in the shock that I continued to feel at routine military and police aggressions against those who were racially identified as migrants in the public sphere. The modern Moroccan state and its military police apparatus have been molded by the country's French and Spanish colonial regimes and the long-standing monarchy that survived colonialism and brought citizens from the iron-fisted rule of King Hassan II to the comparatively benevolent rule of King Mohammed VI. The years following Morocco's independence from France in 1956 produced the nation's current political alliances and economic agreements with European states. Understanding the postcolonial period is therefore essential to any analysis of the role that state agencies and officers play in the daily lives of both citizens and migrants in the Maghreb.

Literature on postindependence Morocco commonly centers on social and economic shifts in relation to the rotating seat of the nation's monarchy. Even in daily conversations with Moroccans, I noted how time periods are more often marked with the names of monarchs than with years. The reigns of Hassan II and Mohammed VI signified more than new leaders—they signified new constructions of national identity. If you ask Moroccans, many will define Mohammed VI's rule by the Equity and Reconciliation Commission (*Instance Equité et Réconciliation*—IER) that he launched in 2004. Morocco's IER was the Arab-Islamic world's first attempt at a tribunal predicated on the values of transnational justice, signifying not only a more democratic national identity, but consequent shifts in individual liberties, state transparency, and the observance of international human rights conventions. It brought Mohammed VI's predecessor, Hassan II, under official scrutiny, marking a turn from more authoritative rule and formalizing the recognition of a "citizen-victim." For the first time, individuals had the ability to speak out against those who occupied seats of power.

This period marked by Morocco's attempts at transnational justice is especially relevant to studies of citizenship, "illegality," and the treatment of Morocco's new migrant class, as it propelled the reigning king onto the international stage through his recognition of human rights. Although Morocco's IER closed in 2006, it continues to spark global debate over the ability of the Truth and Reconciliation Commission model[11] to be adapted to diverse contexts (Shaw & Waldorf 2010). Within the region, it fuels conversations about the challenges of integrating Western notions of rule of law with Morocco's longstanding tradition of arguably absolutist monarchic rule. Introducing a new set of legal inclusions, the IER carved out a space for Morocco's citizen-victims, leading some to question whether noncitizen victims would ever be granted the same rights in the eyes of the state. Drawing on literature from the Maghrebi region, I explore the brutal postindependence "Years of Lead," which necessitated Morocco's IER, and the more recent policies of Mohammed VI, which offered the promise of democratic reform in the face of sweeping "Arab Spring" protests.

The Colonization of the Maghreb: The Rise and Fall (and Rise Again) of King Mohammed V (1927–1953, 1957–1961)

In April of 1956, after 44 years under French rule, Morocco regained independence and Mohammed V resumed his position of leadership, crowning himself king of his newly freed people. Prior to his exile by the French colonial regime between 1953 and 1955, Mohammed V had ruled as the sultan of Morocco, beginning in 1927. His rule was characterized by civil unrest in the years leading up to Morocco's independence, but he was largely adored by his people for the role he played in emancipation and his commitment to formalizing systems of education after colonization (Slyomovics 2005).

Despite the nation's return to the monarchy, Maghrebi scholars Abdallah Laroui (1983) and Abdellah Hammoudi (1997) have argued that the years following independence should not be viewed as "the resurgence of a pre-colonial system" (Hammoudi 1997: 133), but rather as the emergence of a new postcolonial structure. As was true in other regions of postcolonial Africa throughout the mid-twentieth century (Mamdani 1996), authoritarianism in the form of monarchic rule had evolved, "drap[ing] itself into a new legitimacy after independence" (Hammoudi 1997: 133). With this evolution came a new nationalist fervor. Among the public, there was a desire to rebuild state institutions in a distinctly Moroccan fashion, (Laroui 1983). Among the rulers, there was a desire to reinstate absolutist control over a population fresh out of popular dissent against the French colonial regime (Hammoudi 1997). Elaine Combs-Schilling (1989) has investigated how authoritarianism was reinstated through performance on the national stage. National celebrations of the Prophet's birthday held in 1593 and 300 years later in 1993 were similarly orchestrated, with the monarch placed as the central figure. Like Sultan Ahmad I al-Mansur in the 1500s, King Mohammed VI was cloaked in symbolism marking him as the moral, religious, and fatherly head of state (Combs-Schilling 1989). In the new postcolonial structure, authoritarianism was bolstered by the monarchy's linking of nationalism to the Maghreb's rich cultural and religious traditions.

The "Years of Lead": King Hassan II Establishes Morocco's Military Police State (1961–1999)

Following the death of King Mohammed V in 1961, his eldest son, Hassan II, was crowned king and remained in power until his own death in 1999. Hassan II's conservative rule, unlike that of his father, is remembered for his consolidation of power and the spread of gross human rights violations against his own people (Slyomovics 2005). This dark period of Moroccan history, beginning with the assassination of political leader Mehdi Ben Barka in 1965,[12] is now openly referred to as the "Years of Lead," named for the iron fist with which Hassan II ruled.

In Morocco's first constitution, written only two years after Hassan II assumed the throne, he affirmed the nation's multiparty system of governance, while granting himself significant power that would later be used to establish control over dissenting citizens (Hammoudi 1997). When the first elections were held in 1965, they were rigged to favor loyalists and resulted in large-scale protests organized by opposition parties (Gilson Miller 2013). One protest led by the most powerful of Hassan II's opposing forces—Mehdi Ben Barka's National Union of People's Forces (*Union Nationale des Forces Populaires*)—led the king to quickly dissolve the nation's parliament. Although he maintained the mechanisms of parliamentary democracy, Hassan II ruled Morocco directly until the end of the Cold War. His reign witnessed a drastic increase in state practices of "imprisonment, torture, killing, and forced disappearance," which were first directed at suspected political dissidents but were later "widespread and arbitrary" (Slyomovics 2005: 34). As one respondent remembered, "If you spoke out once, you were never heard from again." These practices extended beyond those who vocally protested, impacting the lives of all citizens whose line of work (especially academics, journalists, and others assumed to hold "progressive" opinions) could place them in vulnerable positions.

In her research on Fatna el-Bouih, the former political prisoner and current female face of political activism in Morocco, Susan Slyomovics examines Morocco's transition from absolutist to constitutional rule through the control the state exercised over one woman's body (2002; Foucault 1977). In the state's physical confinement and intellectual censorship of el-Bouih, Slyomovics sees the rise and fall of one king's political power. She questions what it took for el-Bouih to speak out against the government once again, nine years after her release from prison. El-Bouih was first arrested in 1974, after becoming active in the National Union of High School Students (*Union Nationale des Élèves du Secondaire*) and leading a protest for the group. Three years later, after a second arrest, she was forcibly disappeared. El-Bouih, along with other notable feminist activists, was placed in *Derb Moulay Cherif,* Casablanca's infamous secret prison and torture center, where she was held without trial for several years. In the end, she was sentenced to five years imprisonment for "conspiring against the security of the state," "membership in the Marxist-Leninist group March 23," and "distributing political paraphernalia" (El Bouih & Slyomovics 2002). El-Bouih's political activism did not begin again until 1991, when she became a member, and soon after, a leader, in a council for Moroccan women's groups (*al-Majlis al-Watani lil-Transiq*), which was fighting to give women equal rights in marriage, polygamy, divorce, inheritance, and child custody.[13]

When I sat down with el-Bouih in her home outside of Casablanca in 2014, I was interested in how her embodiment of state power—her ability to speak out for women under one ruler and her imprisonment for doing so under another—had shaped her feelings toward the nation and king. Is she a nationalist? An activist? Does she believe it is possible to be both? Her neighborhood is reflective of the elite status that she and her husband, Youssef Madad, a well-known journalist in his own right, occupy in Moroccan society. However, once inside her home, it feels more like you have entered a museum devoted to her long fight for a new Morocco. The walls are covered not only with old family photographs, but with framed newspaper clippings and pages torn from academic texts. In each document, lines have been thoughtfully highlighted and underscored. Knowing that a photograph of the king is required in every Moroccan home, I asked her how she chose which one to display. "I like to imagine him as a young boy," she replied. But it was not just King Mohammed VI who graced her walls, it was many in Morocco's long line of leaders from the Alaouite Dynasty, which was founded in 1631 and continues to this day. I discovered that her experience was like those of many former political prisoners who felt, as she said, an "enormous psychological relief with the death of King Hassan II." It was only in the "new era" of Mohammed VI that she felt free to become an active member of society again, stating, "We have to believe that things will get better." What was remarkable to me was that a woman who had lost eight years of her life to wrongful imprisonment and had suffered untold abuses during that time could still speak about her country with such optimism. I questioned whether this was a reflection of el-Bouih's own resilience in the face of oppression, or whether it spoke more broadly to the power of authorities to mandate forgiveness in a nation where the political and religious spheres have been merged into one. Despite an increased acceptance of protest marked by the reign of Mohammed VI, Morocco remains an executive monarchy, and power is concentrated in the hands of one man, who is both the leader of the nation and the leader of the faithful, or *Amir-al-Mu'minin* ("the prince of the believers").

A Modern Monarchy: King Mohammed VI Builds a Bridge between the Muslim World and "the West" (1999–present)

Facing pressure from the international community, King Hassan II took a slow turn toward processes of democratization in the final years leading up to his death, creating the Consultative Committee of Human Rights (*Commission Nationale Consultative des Droits de l'Homme*) in 1990 and finally ratifying the UN's Convention Against Torture and Other Cruel, Inhumane, or Degrading Treatment or Punishment in 1993. But it was not until King Mohammed VI's ascension to power at the turn of the century that this work accelerated. Peter Hazan (2010) and Susan Slyomovics (2005) have argued that it was in the context of Mohammed VI's "carefully managed" process of democratization that Morocco launched the Arab-Islamic world's first Truth and Reconciliation Commission, a political move aimed at garnering positive media attention and solidifying Morocco's image as an "ally" of the West (2010: 94).[14]

In his inaugural speech as leader of the nation, Mohammed VI acknowledged, for the first time, state responsibility for the disappearance of dissidents during Hassan II's reign. He brought forth citizen-victims like el-Bouih to formally address their imprisonment and torture in front of the perpetrators of these crimes against them (Slyomovics 2005). He outlined a national plan centered on "a constitutional monarchy; a multiparty system; economic liberalism; regionalism and decentralization; building the rule of law; safeguarding human rights; and individual and collective liberties" (Lalami 2011a), and he gave many Moroccans hope that their country would emulate post-Franco Spain. Spain was held up as a model for not only economic development, but a peaceful transition to democratic rule. In a final attempt to distance his reign from that of his father, Mohammed VI restructured the top leaders, removing Driss Basri, the public face of political repression under Hassan II, and in 2002, Morocco saw the freest legislative elections the country had ever known.

In 2004, Mohammed VI's Equity and Reconciliation Commission (IER) was announced to the world, with a three-pronged goal to "shed light on all cases of forced disappearance and arbitrary detention; compensate [and] seek to redress all damages suffered by the victims; and establish a report analyzing the violations of human rights [and] recommendations to guarantee the definitive break with practices of the past" (Hazan 2010: 96). Within months, more than 20,000 files were opened—some to obtain information on those who were still missing and others to obtain compensation for years of imprisonment, torture endured, or loved ones who were lost. Morocco's IER differed from the South African, Chilean, and Argentine commissions on which it was modeled by covering the longest period to ever be investigated, beginning with independence in 1956 and ending 43 years later with the death of Hassan II. Unlike other commissions, which had all been created under a period of political change and with public involvement, Morocco's IER was not the product of a new political leader or social movement (Shaw & Waldorf 2010). It was a construction of the state's continuing system of governance and reflective of Mohammed VI's efforts to restore a positive national identity to his "Western Kingdom" on the global stage.

Morocco's IER differed not only in the circumstances of its creation, but also in its internal functioning. They chose not to offer state agents amnesty in exchange for full disclosure of crimes committed, and therefore they had little cooperation from state, police, or military forces in the investigation of files that were opened (Wilson 2001; Hazan 2008). Even more problematic was the IER's decision to forbid any naming in the collection of information from citizen-victims in public trials (Amnesty International 2010). Thus, even if the IER had succeeded in producing an exhaustive account of the crimes perpetrated by the state during Hassan II's reign, and even if it had provided compensation to all of the citizen-victims, it could not have ended the impunity that the perpetrators of past abuses continue to enjoy to this day. The inability to name or prosecute perpetrators led many to question whether reconciliation can be effected through monetary restitutions alone, or if Morocco's model overlooked the deeper values of punishment, political change, and restoration embedded in notions of transnational justice. These questions remain important, as Morocco's adaptation of a Western legal construct to an Islamic state has influenced similar commissions across the Middle East.[15]

The Arab Spring and the Moroccan Exception

In the wake of the recent political revolutions that reshaped North Africa, United States Secretary of State Hilary Clinton launched a new "Strategic Dialogue" with Morocco in which she praised King Mohammed VI and his nation as "a leader and a model" for the region. The double role held by many leaders in Arab-Islamic countries today—a role that posits they are direct descendants of a royal line and direct descendants of the Prophet—is more than symbolic. It shapes citizens' relationships with the state, and as some have argued, it played a critical role in creating what has been termed the Moroccan "exception" (Lalami 2011b). As international media turned to the powerful citizen revolts that came to be known as the Arab Spring, Morocco stood strong, raising the question of how Mohammed VI successfully quieted the revolting masses. Was it the trust he had established with his people through Morocco's truth and justice initiative? Was it the fear of losing an established system of governance without knowing what would replace it? Or was it a deeper reverence for the world's longest-standing religious monarchy? In Morocco, royal authority has been held by a succession of sultan–kings since the early ninth century—a phenomenon unequaled in world history. While a majority of Moroccans now stress the need for "a solely constitutional monarchy," they similarly emphasize the centrality of religious tradition in their daily lives (Cherribi & Pesce 2014). These competing desires pull citizens in opposite directions of the political spectrum, as the king's central role is detrimental to political reform but essential to Islamic tradition.

Morocco, long considered one of the most stable countries in the Arab-Islamic world, was not immune to the waves of protest sweeping North Africa in 2010. With the ousting of Tunisia's Zine el-Abidine Ben Ali and Egypt's Hosni Mubarak, the streets of Rabat erupted in popular protest for "democracy and dignity" (Lalami 2011b). Spurred by protests in neighboring countries, a group of young Moroccan activists calling themselves "Democracy and Freedom Now" (notably without a French translation) drew on social networking technology to begin organizing their own day of protest. In contrast to protesters in other North African countries, those who joined the February 20th movement in Morocco in 2011 did not call for the end of Mohammed VI's reign, but rather for a parliamentary model of government. Moroccan journalist, publisher, and winner of the International Press Freedom Award, Aboubakr Jamaï, questioned whether the protesters went far enough. Among the list of demands presented to Mohammed VI were "constitutional reforms; the dissolution of the present parliament; the creation of a temporary transitional government; an independent judiciary; accountability for elected officials; language rights for Berber speakers; and the release of all political prisoners." In reaction to these demands, Morocco's Minister of Communication publicly explained that the nation had "embarked on an irreversible process of democracy a long time ago" and credited Mohammed VI for this work. Military and police forces, which played a critical role in maintaining peace throughout the series of protests that followed, remained firmly under the control of the king.

Amine, the young Moroccan man who offered his account of racially charged violence at the opening of this chapter, was among those protesting. He explained the frustration that was felt by the majority youth population that had organized the February 20th movement. Morocco is burdened with a high unemployment rate, hovering around 22 percent for Moroccan males aged 15 to 29 and even higher for those like Amine who hold a university degree.[16] As he said, "We want change, but many of us don't have the resources to fight for it. We, too, feel trapped in this country."

The (Il)Legalization of Morocco's Newest Subjects

At the end of 2014, shortly after my return to Rabat from the border city of Oujda, King Mohammed VI launched what would later be called "an exceptional period of regularization," in response to rising police brutality against migrants and media attention to the murders of young men like Ismaila Faye. In the government's first public recognition of Morocco's growing migrant population, the king opened a process of regularization for those who met a series of strict requirements.[17] The following Monday, I saw the long lines of what the newly opened *Aliens' Bureau* (or Foreign Aliens' Office) later claimed were over 5,000 migrants queuing to submit an application in Rabat alone. The bureau reported that in total over 30,000 migrants coming from 116 different countries applied. In the following months, 18,000 applications were approved—the majority of those approved coming from Syria,[18] followed by Senegal, Nigeria, and Côte d'Ivoire. However, the approved migrants whom I spoke to were greatly disappointed to discover that "approval" meant nothing more than legal residency status in the country for one year. There were claims that the entire regularization "scheme" had been instituted to allow Moroccan officials to collect statistics on the number and nationality of migrants that were present, all in the interest of organizing more efficient systems for border control and repatriation. Regardless of the state's intention, when this "exceptional" period closed in December of 2014, migrants were again left with no avenues to legal status, and those who had chosen to submit an application were left with a paper trail linked to their legal names.

In one of our final interviews, Amine and I met at the library of the national university where he is completing a graduate degree in Political

Science. "Our laws and racisms are reflective of a country that hasn't dealt with a population of immigrants before," he said, proceeding to explain the challenges confronting all countries that are managing their transitions into new immigrant "destinations":

> You can't take a child and expect him to run a country. In the same way, you can't take a people who have never been educated and expect them to run a country. Concepts like democracy, racial equality, women's rights, they must be fed slowly to the child, if you want him to digest them. Our education as a people must come before our political reform. Moroccans, we are lacking in good education. Many of our children don't even go to school. How can you expect immigrants to access schools or hospitals in our country when Moroccans themselves cannot? The immigrants' burdens are not ours to carry. We have enough on our own.

Amine encouraged me to think of Africa as one large tapestry. Colonial powers cut the continent—once a single work of art—into pieces and sewed it back together in a patchwork, making the threads weaker than they were before. Following his analogy, I knew that colonialism was not only responsible for "cutting" the continent along arbitrary lines, but that these divides were often made with the intention of forcing together opposing groups in order to lower the risk of citizen cooperation and revolt. Viewing the continent as a patchwork, Amine explained that within each nation, multiple threads of identity exist. The threads that are linked to ethnicity, religion, language, and culture are the older, tattered threads that were present before the colonial powers. These were and still are integral to each citizen's conception of identity. The threads that are linked to nationalism are the newest threads. These were sewn in by the colonizers, serving to restructure the tapestry and differentiate one African nation from another. They created boundaries between those from the same ethnic group and alliances between those from different groups. Nationalism is the one part of the tapestry that was not present in the original design. I extend Amine's analogy to explain that drawing lines to delineate between Morocco's citizens and Morocco's new migrant class similarly gives rise to new forms of national and individual identity. The threads linked to political status are now the newest, sewn in not by the colonizers but by a neocolonial hand reaching south of its own border to engender new forms of difference. These are the threads marking those who have the right to occupy space, to move in space, and to access their basic rights as human beings.

Notes

1. *Jazirat al-Maghrib,* another name for Morocco, can be translated as "North Africa, the island."
2. Jalal al Makhfi, "Morocco's African immigrants fear rising racism tide." September 6, 2013. AFP.
3. The National Front is a socially conservative and nationalist far-right political party in France, best known for its opposition to the European Union.
4. Sebastien Bachelet, "Murder of Senegalese Migrant Overshadows "Radically New" Politics of Migration in Morocco." *All Africa,* September 23, 2014.
5. James Rippingale, "Are Moroccan Gangsters Being Paid to Beat Up Sub-Saharan Migrants?" *Vice,* November 22, 2014.
6. In 2009, leader Fouad Ali el Himma received multipartisan support among Moroccan politicians for his proposal to rebrand cannabis as a traditional Moroccan herbal remedy, rather than an illicit drug. In 2014, the Party of Authenticity and Modernity (PAM) proposed a draft law that would maintain the consumption of recreational cannabis as illegal but license and regulate growers, redirecting their exports to legal medicinal and industrial cannabis products.
7. Cannabis accounts for 3 percent of the gross national product (GNP) of Morocco's agricultural sector (UNODC Report 2012).
8. *Hashish* is an extracted product composed of purified preparations of stalked resin glands from the cannabis plant. It contains the same active ingredients as marijuana—namely, tetrahydrocannabinol (THC)—but often in much higher concentrations than present in the unsifted buds used in the production of marijuana.
9. Suffering from poverty and still plagued by the government's memory of former Riffian leader Abdelkrim al Khattabi, who openly contested the monarchy, the region seized the opportunity to professionalize their production.
10. "Camel," or "*jamal*" in Arabic, is a term commonly used to identify those engaged in the business of human smuggling. It is similar to "coyote," an informal term used for smugglers working along the Mexican-American border.
11. The Truth and Reconciliation Commission model was first popularized in postapartheid South Africa, where citizen-victims were heard and citizen-perpetrators were sentenced by a court-like restorative justice body.
12. Mehdi Ben Barka was a Moroccan politician and head of the National Union of Popular Forces (UNPF). A strong opponent of French Imperialism and King Hassan II, he "disappeared" in Paris in 1965. In 2018, the details of his disappearance were established in the book Rise And Kill First: *The Secret History of Israel's Targeted Assassinations.* Based on interviews with Israeli

intelligence operatives who were involved in the operation, it was concluded that Ben Barka was murdered by Moroccan agents and French police.

13. The family code, known as the *Mudawana* in Moroccan law, concerns issues of marriage, polygamy, divorce, inheritance, and child custody. Originally based on the Maliki school of Sunni Islamic jurisprudence, it was codified after independence in 1956. Fatna el-Bouih and the council for Moroccan women's groups led the fight for the most recent amendments to the law, which were passed by the Parliament in 2004 and have been praised by human rights activists for their measures to address women's rights and gender equality within an Islamic legal framework.

14. Morocco's special relationship with the United States is long standing. Morocco was the first state to recognize the United States' independence in 1777, and it currently holds the longest unbroken treaty relationship with the United States. Although the region became less central to American foreign policy following the Cold War years, the terrorist attacks of 9/11 led the United States to refocus diplomacy on the Middle East and North Africa. This included reinforcing a strong United States–Moroccan partnership centered on shared economic and security interests. Morocco is now a designated major non-NATO ally (one of only 15 globally and 2 on the African continent), as well as a free trade agreement (FTA) partner with the United States.

15. Among those influenced by Morocco's Equity and Reconciliation Commission are Lebanon's Commission on Disappearances and Abductions, Iraq's Special Tribunal, and Afghanistan's Independent Human Rights Commission.

16. "Youth," which is defined here as those between the ages of 15 and 29, account for 30 percent of Morocco's population and 44 percent of those of working age. In this population subset, 22 percent of males and 38 percent of females are unemployed.

17. In order to qualify for regularization during this period, applicants had to meet the following criteria: One must have documentation of having lived in Morocco for at least five continuous years; obtained a two-year work contract signed by a recognized Moroccan company; been legally married to a Moroccan national for at least two years or a foreign resident legally resettled in Morocco for at least four years; or be the documented child (under the age of 16) of a migrant who meets these requirements.

18. The government automatically granted all Syrian applicants temporary legal status in tacit recognition of their refugee status, although the majority of them would have been legally categorized as undocumented migrants at the time.

CHAPTER 4

Vulnerability and the Gendering of Political Status

What are you doing in this neighborhood, girl? Your shoes are worth more than our lives. You should go home!

—KHADIJA, F, 36, Malian migrant

....

Introductory Case Study: A Neighborhood No One Calls Home

Like the vast majority of female migrants temporarily settled in Rabat, Khadija spends her days hawking goods around the *medina*. Shortly after the first *adhan*, she begins the long journey from her neighborhood of Taqadoum to the city center. I often met her at the bus stop, where she sat waiting with a brightly patterned cloth, knotted and slung over her shoulder, holding all of her wares. Some days, her hands would be weighted down with other bags full of food she had prepared the night before—sweets or little rolls stuffed with minced vegetables.

Don't know where you are, girl? You're on the black side of the street now. Those boys are talking to you. Don't you hear them? Don't you talk back!

She always boards the first morning bus, packing herself in tightly among the male passengers and enduring the jostling 45- minute ride to *centre ville*. She is eager to set up before the businessmen and school children begin their days and cares little what the other passengers think of her.

Someone's going to hurt you, white girl. I asked you what you're doing here. Don't you look at those boys. Tell them to leave you alone. Now, find yourself a ride home. Someone's going to steal the scarf off your head!

Exiting the bus, Khadija decides where to start selling her wares. Some days, she heads straight to the bustling *Avenue Souika* to spread her cloth out on the sidewalk in the heart of the *medina*, knowing it will not be long before the first shop owner emerges with his broom, forcing her to move to another open patch of cement.

I told you to go home, little girl. Don't just stand there. If you're going to be asking me all these questions, then you might as well be helping me. Aren't you strong enough? Here, carry this!

Other mornings, she begins her sales in the city center, spreading her wares out on the main avenues that connect the *medina*'s maze of food stalls and black markets to Rabat's formal economic activity. These sidewalks are also crowded with sellers hawking goods, but unlike in the *medina*, where many sellers own small retail spaces on the bottom floors of old *riads*, all sellers in the city center are ambulatory. My days with Khadija taught me that the space is occupied by three distinct types: those who sell goods from a rolling cart; those, like Khadija, who sell goods off of their backs; and those who beg for money (often in exchange for a small good). Although Khadija is free from the brooms of shop owners on the main avenues, she knows that more abundant selling opportunities carry with them greater risks. Most of the buildings alongside the main thoroughfares are patrolled by uniformed military men, who regularly harass the hawkers and beggars gathered there. For migrants, the risk is even higher.

Lay these out in a row. Put the pink ones out first. The kids like the pink ones best. Go on, ask them what they want to buy. Don't you speak their language? Tell them mine are the best. What do they want? I can find it. I can make it. I can sell it for less. Aren't you trying to help me? Smile at that one, he likes you. Tell him what he wants to buy. Aren't you trying to help me make some money today, smart girl?

In the months I spent shadowing Khadija and other migrants and Moroccans hawking goods around Rabat, I developed a keen sense of who would be approached by uniformed men and who would be left at their posts to beg, trade, or sell. Unsurprisingly, it was largely determined by race and assumed political status. Those who were approached never resisted their goods being confiscated along with whatever money they had earned that day. They knew the dangers of working in Morocco's black market economy, and they did what they could to avoid the ultimate risk of deportation to the Moroccan-Algerian border. On most days, I combined a more traditional form of participant observation with semistructured interviewing in a "go-along" style, which allowed me to situate individual experience within the larger socioeconomic sphere.[1] I participated in Khadija's activities as her "assistant" in the marketplace and simultaneously observed her interactions with state actors, Moroccan citizens, and fellow migrants. It was through watching, listening, and raising questions for those who crossed in and out of respondents' daily lives—questions I would often not have known to ask otherwise—that I was able to gain a deeper understanding of their lived experience in liminality or belonging.

The most elite of the ambulatory sellers stroll up and down the avenue with their carts, all of them selling a similar assortment of prepackaged snacks and bottled sodas. The nicer carts have a series of plastic containers mounted on their sides, displaying salted peanuts, sunflower seeds, and raisins waiting to be spooned out into little rolls of newspaper and weighed in the hanging metal scales. I never saw anyone but Moroccan men wheeling these carts, and despite the fact that they, too, lacked proper licensing for selling their goods, I never saw any altercation between them and Moroccan officials. When asked if he ever worried about the illicit nature of his work, Youssef, an older Moroccan hawker with a stern face, told me, "There are too many Africans to worry about me." The growing presence of migrants in the informal economy has actually made work for Moroccans like Youssef safer. This added safety, along with the minimal threat that migrants pose to their profits (as Youssef asserted, "Migrants don't sell anything that Moroccans want to buy"), left me questioning the continued hostility and aggression toward Khadija.

Like sellers with carts, I found the role of "beggar" to be one that is uniquely occupied by Moroccans in the public sphere. These men and women rarely move from corner to corner, but rather, they sit on the pavement, staking out lucrative intersections and gradually laying claim to their territories through their presence day after day. The majority of beggars are women, almost always accompanied by multiple young children. The only men I saw begging on the sidewalk had some form of visible physical impairment—an amputated limb, a disfigured foot, an oozing wound. Some beggars sit empty-handed, imploring the kindness of strangers with the common refrain, "*Sadaka lah yarham lwalidin.*"[2] Others sit with cloths spread before them, like Khadija does, except that the goods displayed on their cloths are not for sale but for the taking— in exchange for a "small kindness." These goods include small packages of stiff paper tissues and individually wrapped pieces of peppermint chewing gum. Occasionally, children sneak gum into your pockets and then run after you begging for payment. I was curious about the large number of beggar women and children congregated around Rabat's central train station every day and the large sums of "small kindnesses" they appeared to accumulate over the course of the day. Shadowing Khadija on the main avenue one morning, I watched as Moroccans, one after the other, leaned down to place coins in the hands and cups of beggars and offer bills in exchange for paper and gum. Rarely did anyone stop by Khadija's cloth. Did she never consider testing this other approach to hawking—did she never consider selling, instead, her own vulnerability in exchange for the kindness of strangers?

In Morocco, as in other Muslim societies, Islam not only structures religious life, it shapes cultural values and daily practices. This was most apparent to me in the kindness, openness, and generosity with which people treat the poor. The Moroccans whom I came to know as friends took their religious (and neighborly) duty to care for those less fortunate than them seriously—from their offerings of coins and Friday couscous to beggars, to the significant donations of food and money they ritually gave at the end of *Ramadan* and the beginning of *Eid al-Fitr* every year.[3] According to the five pillars of Islam, it is essential that every follower practices charity (*Zakāt*), faith (*Shahada*), prayer (*Salat*), fasting (*Sawm*), and, if able, a pilgrimage to Mecca (*Hajj*). Jalal al-Hajji was one of the *imams* whom I saw regularly—the *adhan* from his mosque playing five times a day through the loudspeakers mounted on the top of the minaret by my rooftop room. My friend Hicham, who prayed at Jalal al-Hajji's mosque, arranged for me to ask him some questions about the five pillars, and especially about *Zakāt*. I wanted to learn more about the role of charity and how the "new" Muslims in his community (the large number of migrants living around Rabat) were being included in or excluded from the ritual practice of giving.

"*Zakāt*," he began, "is the principle of knowing that all things belong to Allah. It is our duty to work toward eliminating the inequalities in our community by redistributing Allah's blessings equally." However, the word "community" can be understood in many ways. In Morocco, where Muslims follow the *Mālikī* legal tradition and 98 percent of the population identifies as Sunni, the tenets of inclusiveness can vary from theory to practice. While migrants from Muslim-majority countries across the African continent are certainly a part of the larger Islamic community, they can also be seen as foreigners in the local communities that many Moroccan Muslims feel indebted to serving. In fact, they are viewed by some, like Jalal al-Hajji, as "a strain on the needs of our poor brothers." Khadija, familiar with this sentiment, believed the beggar's post is one that has been constructed in response to the Moroccan Muslim's duty "to Moroccans, not to Muslims."

Al-Hajji elaborated on the "strain" his community was facing by explaining that Africans, when offered work doing manual labor, first ask how much money they will be paid for their time. "They don't accept work because they need work," he said. "They ask, 'is your work worth my time?' And if it is not, they say, 'no, I won't accept that work, I can make 100 *dirhams*[4] a day begging in the street!'" Al-Hajji said that, regardless of race, he has respect for migrants who refuse to beg and work hard at whatever job they are given without questioning the pay. "There is no racism in Morocco, if that is what you're trying to prove here. We have respect for good workers and disrespect for *harragas*. If you show me one who works from 8 in the morning till 8 at night without complaining like a Moroccan, then I will tell you that I respect him, even if he is black." What struck me in this exchange with the imam was his use of the term "*harraga*" and the insinuation that "illegal" migrants are not only synonymous with a particular racial category, but also with qualities of laziness, greediness, and deception. On the walk back from our interview, I pressed Hicham for further interpretation. "Where are the migrant beggars the imam spoke about?" I had spent every day on the streets of Rabat that month and had not seen a single migrant with hands outstretched for coins. After thinking for a while, Hicham admitted that he, too, had seen none. "I guess they stopped begging when we stopped giving them alms."

With a bruised faith in *Zakāt*, Khadija sells whatever she can find. Most days, it is a random assortment of goods discarded by Moroccans and picked out of the trash behind apartment buildings or the heaping mounds of garbage at the dump—soiled clothing and old shoes, broken plastic toys and half-used bottles of cologne. She takes care repairing each one before sale, scrubbing the stains from the clothes and topping the cologne off with water. On her best days, Khadija sells counterfeit designer clothing she buys from a Senegalese migrant who lives in her apartment building. She explained that he would rather not sell to her because the clothing is worth more the farther north that it travels, but they have become friends, and in exchange for his kindness, she occasionally cooks him the foods his mother used to prepare.

Youssef, the man with a rolling cart, was right in asserting that many of the goods salvaged and sold by migrants on the street are in little (if any) demand by passing Moroccans. However, he overlooked the critical role that migrants play in filling the demand for counterfeit goods in Morocco's black market economy. The path of goods traveling north from Senegal to Morocco and on to Europe has existed for as long as human migrations themselves. I remember Khadija's neighbor asking me one day with pride, "Haven't you ever been to London or Paris? Haven't you seen the purses and sunglasses for sale on the street? The Guccis and the Pradas? Haven't you ever seen the Louis shoes that look like the real thing?" He was describing a trade in which his role at the crossroads was central, and the network of counterfeit imports from West Africa is not limited to clothing alone. If you have ever bought a bootleg DVD or a touristy trinket in Europe, there is a good chance that it started its long journey north in Senegal, and there is a fair chance that it spent some time for sale on a Moroccan sidewalk before it made its way to you. Rabat, like London and Paris, is bursting with keychains in the shapes of Big Ben and the Eiffel Tower. While the presence of migrants hawking goods in the public sphere has been criticized in national discourse, with large-scale efforts by Moroccan sellers to disperse them, the counterfeit goods that are sold have become coveted by Moroccans in recent years (Benmehdi 2011). The bootleg American media drives the materialistic desire that the clothing fulfills. Ironically, it is the transnational networks of Moroccan families like Hicham's, with their tastes in everything from fashion to music shaped by their transnationality, that are the primary driver behind the black-market economy, providing a meager livelihood to the migrants living in and around Morocco's urban centers.

Doing "Man's Work"

As key sites of citizen–migrant interaction, marketplaces highlight how changing migratory patterns can engender new positions that are reserved for the migrant laborer and shift positions that were once reserved for citizens. For citizens, the changing demographics brought on by migration can mean that their race, location, or vocation suddenly place them in newly formed positions of "illegality." Scholars seeking to understand social change in the context of economic growth have historically studied the function that expanding migrant communities serve in national labor forces. However, far less attention has been paid to how particular public spaces or roles within the marketplace become imbued with racial, political, and gendered identities as migratory patterns change.

In Morocco, the association of "illegality" with hawking goods has had concrete impacts on the large number of citizens who make their livelihood through the *medina's* informal economy—citizens like Abdul-Aziz, who has worked at his father's fruit stand since he was old enough to count change. Now 16, he recounted the frequent torments of his peers, who often shout at him as they stroll down *Avenue Souika.* "He only speaks Wolof now" or "Where are your papers?" they say. Abdul-Aziz's work now places him in close proximity to the nation's growing population of migrants, illustrating how changes at the Spanish-Moroccan border have transformed what was once a space associated with lower-income Moroccan labor into one that is increasingly linked to political vulnerability.

In her seminal research on the role of gender in the marketplace, anthropologist Carla Freeman positions the Caribbean "higgler's" work (akin to the "hawker's" work in the African context) as a global process in and of itself, rather than the result of a global process (2001). She blurs the line between the local and the global, and she challenges the gendered identities that have commonly been linked to local or micro and global or macro processes of change. "In particular," she writes, "the higgler challenges any notion that global spaces are traversed by men and gendered masculine." If the feminine can be linked to the global, to formal economies, and to process of production, then the masculine, in some contexts, must be linked to the local, to informal economies, and to processes of consumption. Freeman disrupts familiar formulations in which the "Third World woman" is defined as either "outside globalization" or "the presumed back upon which its production depends" and instead posits women like Khadija as central players in forces of global and economic change (Freeman 2001: 1012).

Khadija's story gives lived experience this argument, as she routinely moves through spaces that are both symbolically and physically gendered masculine. Although she usually hawks on her own, I accompanied her one afternoon when she spread her cloth out on the corner of

Avenue Mohammed V in the city center with two other migrant women. They had just received several boxes packed with small jars of facial cream from Senegal, and Khadija expected high sales. Sitting together on the sidewalk, the four of us called out to the Moroccans who passed, "*Bon prix!*" "*Aji cheri!*" "*Zween bezeef!*" As the hours passed, the women spoke about the difficult spaces they are forced to occupy and how they feel doubly stigmatized by their "illegal" status in Morocco and their placement in Morocco's traditionally male sphere of public labor. Fatou explained, "In Morocco, the respectable woman stays in her home. Even to buy her groceries, the respectable woman brings someone—her daughter, her neighbor, her mother-in-law—with her. A woman walking through the *medina* alone is not respectable. A woman *working* in the *medina* alone, this is unthinkable!" Fatou and Khadija are forced to occupy a space that was first reserved for Moroccan men, but that, as Abdul-Aziz and others would contend, is quickly changing.

Conversations about shifting identities in the marketplace led me to think more deeply about my own position in Morocco—one that allowed me to sit at both men's and women's tables, to occupy both public and private spheres—and what it revealed about the experiences of women like Fatou and Khadija. My label as a foreign (*white, American*) woman affords me a more privileged position in Morocco. Their label as foreign (*black, African*) women pushes them to even more marginalized positions. In both cases, however, it is the combination of our status as "foreign" and "female" that opens up new spaces in the public sphere—spaces that are not offered to those who are local or male. It is this unique position of being both "othered" and gendered that allows us to transcend strict boundaries between male/female and public/private spaces. It is my whiteness, which is linked to a presumed status as educated, upper-class, and legal, and their blackness, which is linked to a presumed status as uneducated, working-class, and "illegal," that leads to the great disparity between the types of male public spaces that we occupy. If gender unites our experiences, then race certainly divides them.

Strangers Sleeping Side by Side

Khadija and her neighbors represent the new population of migrants from distinct ethnic, religious, and linguistic backgrounds who are being forced together in housing settlements around Morocco's urban centers. As these neighborhoods experience rapid demographic shifts, both migrants and the citizens who formerly inhabited them are formulating new and contested notions of belonging. In my early months of fieldwork, I remember being warned by one young man from Nigeria, "Be careful, because we are all desperate." As he explained, I heard the tensions that were rising between various ethnic groups in his neighborhood. "Some of us start out begging, but it doesn't take long to see that you won't get any kindness from Moroccans. So then you look for work, but you see that you won't get hired by Moroccans either. The Cameroonians are the only ones who figured out how to get by. If you want to live long enough to realize your dreams, then you have to '*trompe*' the Moroccans." Although he spoke to me in English, the young man used the French word "*trompe*," meaning "to trick or deceive." He told me how the Cameroonians created a scheme, relying on negative stereotypes about them. "They ask Moroccans for money to make counterfeit *dirhams*," relying here on the stereotype that Cameroonians traffic counterfeit money. "In order to provide the service, they need some money upfront to buy mercury because it's expensive. They take this money from Moroccans without ever returning the counterfeit *dirhams*, which they don't have the knowledge to make. They're playing on Moroccans' perceptions of them as thieving by actually thieving!"

Despite migrants from distinct backgrounds being forced into cooperative relationships in the forest camps and small apartments where they live, they are not a uniform or a unified population. Members of the community frequently warned me that "Cameroonians make fake money" and "Nigerians make fake papers," "Malians are kind, but simpleminded" and "Congolese are smart, but aggressive," "Ghanaians sell drugs," "Guineans sell women," and "Senegalese sell everything! They think they're better than us." There are divisions between francophone and anglophone, between Christian and Muslim, between lighter-skinned and darker-skinned, West African and Central African, those with status markers and those without. Within the camps and buildings that I came to know well, there are dozens of different groups struggling with the challenges of cooperation and cohabitation at any given moment. Yet, outside, they know migrants are seen as "*harragas*," and they are all seen as one.

In their studies of liminality, Victor and Edith Turner found that a unique form of community can emerge in the space between one known social structure and another. They apply the term "*communitas*," which refers to an unstructured community where all individuals are of equal status (1978). Their argument is easier to apply when imagining a sort of utopia that could emerge if all members of a community already occupied the same social status and shared a common culture. However, I contend that *communitas* can also be created when individuals are stripped of the social status markers that once differentiated them. It denotes the intense feeling of social togetherness and belonging that arises when individuals, standing between established social structures, are united through their common experience of liminality. In Khadija's apartment building, it matters little which school an individual attended or what kind of work they once did in their home country. What matters is where they are now.

According to the Turners' later work (1978), *communitas* can be found most notably in the act of pilgrimage, when members of both upper and lower classes are known to travel the same well-grooved paths toward a common goal (Turner & Turner 1978). As groups of pilgrims move together through space, they are physically distancing themselves from established social structures and symbolically distancing themselves from their social identities, leading to a homogenization of status within the group as they approach the liminal state. In fact, the concept of liminality has a long tradition in religious mythology. It accounts for such central ideologies as the Catholic Purgatory,[5] the Jewish *Da'at*,[6] and, arguably, the Muslim *Barzakh*,[7] each representing a temporary physical and spiritual space that lies in between one world, one identity, and the next. Although the Turners focus on the Christian tradition, the *Hajj*, or the annual Islamic pilgrimage to Mecca, represents another primary example from the Muslim faith. In the case of all ritual transitions and pilgrimages, the Turners argue that liminality induces positive community building. However, in the case of those who stand trapped between a past home and a future imaginary in Morocco, I find *communitas* to operate in a different way. Migrants share the feeling that in the public sphere, others impose an identity and a community affiliation on them. They are differentiated not by their ethnicity, religion, language, or even nationality, but by their race and presumed status of "illegality." Yet within the private spaces that hold their social lives, the "feelings of social togetherness and belonging," which define the Turners' understanding of *communitas*, are limited. Others may impose labels that forcibly group them together, but within the boundaries of their homes, migrants' social ties remain secured along lines of common culture, and their apartments and brotherhoods are established through shared nationality.

Mother, Sister, Daughter, Wife: The Vulnerability of the Female Migrant

As the oldest, Khadija plays a mothering role to many of the younger migrants in her building and to the other Malians—three women and two men—who share her small apartment with her. She left her own five children behind when she began her migration journey six years ago, and I could see her longing for them in the ways she cared for those around her. She was among the hardest working of all the men and women I knew, propelled by her dream of reaching Europe, where she hoped to reunite with her children through the family reunification programs that are available to refugees. When asked if she ever thought about bringing her children to be with her in Morocco, she told me that no one would want their children to live the way she does. "If God won't grant me a path to Europe, then I hope my children will stay." The lack of social services available to migrants in Morocco extends to the youngest generation, and even those who are born on Moroccan soil are routinely denied access to education in public classrooms or medical care in public hospitals. This, in addition to the public displays of racism and incidents of racially charged violence, makes it an undesirable alternative for most of the parents I spoke to. While there are relatively few women and even fewer mothers in Morocco's growing migrant community, the majority of them share Khadija's story of losing a husband before leaving home.

Khadija speaks to her children every week and sends what little she can home for their school fees every month. They now live in the home of Khadija's older sister and brother-in-law, where the family was forced to move after her husband left on his own migration journey many years ago. She explained that before leaving, he promised her they would be reunited after he reached Spain. At first, there were calls, messages, and the occasional money transfer. But then, there was nothing. The worst part, she said, was not knowing. "Did he grow tired of helping us? Did he die on the way? Did he find a new family in Europe?" To this day, her questions remain unanswered, and her loss remains unmourned. With no way to support her five children alone, she began saving money to pay the same smuggler who had hidden her husband in the back of his truck and dropped him at Mali's northern border with Algeria. Khadija's migration was spurred not only by her individual desire for her children to have a better life, but also by the lack of options available to her. Poverty and gendered inequality meant a complete lack of educational opportunities and limited work opportunities for her if she stayed home.

Just as Khadija described working toward the goal of reuniting with her children, many of the men I interviewed structured their narratives around the goal of reuniting with women on "the other side." Whether it was with partners they had left behind, women they imagined meeting in Europe, or wives they could afford back home only after a successful end to their journeys, they were motivated by the goal of marriage and, ultimately, the goal of having a family of their own. Despite this shared sentiment, I found it remarkable that none ever spoke about the possibility of finding a wife or even a temporary partner before reaching Spain. Seeing the centrality of marriage in their understandings of themselves as men and their complete inability to imagine becoming husbands while trapped on the migratory route or for many years in Morocco illuminates their relationship to the present. Although I was often shown photographs of the beautiful *cheris* that migrants left behind, the present represented a space in which all of their desires were suspended. In liminality, they are detached from their desired status as husbands and fathers and denied their physical desire for human connection.

Idrissa, a young man from Niger, lived in Khadija's building and occasionally accompanied us on our trips to hawk goods in the marketplace. On one trip, he explained that "The reason you only meet male migrants in Morocco is because of our culture. No one would ask a woman to walk across the city alone, so of course no one would ask her to walk across the country alone." His use of the verb *"demander,"* or "to ask," is important, as it portrays a scenario in which women are subjected to the demands of their families and are never the protagonists in their own stories. "You only meet women migrants if they accompanied their families here, and even then, I think they're a greater burden than they are a help." Perhaps conscious of Khadija's presence, he rationalized his opinion through the prevalence of violent (often sexual) crimes that are committed against migrants along the primary smuggling routes and the responsibility that all families feel to keep their mother, daughter, wife, or sister safe.

"In Muslim countries," one Moroccan respondent had explained to me earlier, "women are seen as vulnerable." The limitations placed on them and their movement stem from their families' desires to protect them. "A woman alone is seen as a woman without a family, and so she is free to be taken." I saw how this same line of thinking informed Idrissa's argument about the placement of migrant women. If a woman migrates to a new country without a companion, then she, too, must be seen as "free?" I asked. "Yes, she will be propositioned for sex. She will be seen as an object to be bought. This is not the case for male migrants traveling alone." Like the Moroccan man, he noted the responsibility of the family to protect female relatives, but he said little about how the same threats of violence loom for males on the migratory route. The difference between male and female migrants therefore may be less in the physical threats presented to them and more in the symbolic threats presented to the honor of the families left behind. The reputation of the family is uniquely threatened by violence against female migrants, and female migrants must carry with them the added responsibility of upholding the honor of their parents, siblings, husbands, and children on their long journeys north.

What Idrissa failed to examine was a situation like Khadija's in which the mother of a family is left alone and might view her own safety as secondary to the security of her children. Of course, there are female migrants who travel alone, and when presented with conflicting evidence, Idrissa agreed that, yes, he is beginning to see more women living in migrant communities in Morocco. "I've seen women from Togo, Ghana, and the Congo migrating alone because of the independence given to women in these cultures." His argument is a plausible one, but it could be based more on religious than cultural differences. He selected three countries with substantial Christian populations—Togo, Ghana, and the DRC—and the degree to which one can disentangle the influence of religion from the more broadly defined influence of "culture" is difficult. From my view, the restricted mobility imposed on women in Muslim-majority countries seemed to be the more likely reason behind their fewer numbers on the migratory route. Other migrants whom I interviewed highlighted the role of culture in shaping who migrates, but all of the arguments I heard ignored what I suspected was the most important part of the equation—labor. If labor is a primary pull factor in migration, then how is the demand for different types of work dictating who moves across which borders? Could the presence of a predominantly male migrant population in Morocco not be a reflection of the work that is available?

While the migrant laborer plays a visible role in Morocco's public sphere—through the selling of goods and, increasingly, through manual day labor—there is minimal demand for migrants to do domestic, traditionally female, work in the private sphere. I argue that this transition from the public to private sphere of labor indicates a larger shift in the nation's acceptance of a migrant population, and that in the case of the Maghreb, this shift has not yet occurred. With violent acts of racism on the rise and the tension between migrant and citizens groups high, migrant women are not considered by most to be viable options for domestic labor. Yet as second- and third-generation migrants are born in Morocco, I predict we will soon see more workers "invited" to transition into traditionally female spaces of work inside the home. With a new sector of the informal economy opened, the rate of female migration from across the continent is sure to increase. In addition, given the intimate nature of work in the domestic sphere and the desire that everything from food preparation to children's discipline be informed by Islamic teachings, those coming from Muslim-majority countries will likely be in even greater demand.

Neither Mother, Nor Sister, Nor Daughter, Nor Wife: The Role of the Female Researcher

When recounting stories from my research to friends and colleagues back home, I was occasionally met with concerned or incredulous looks, with comments like "*You* did this?" and with questions about how I navigated the "minefields" of working in male-dominated spaces. "What do you wear?" "Where do you sleep?" "But you bring someone with you?" Not only is my research population male, I was reminded, but they are *young* males, they are destitute, and they have long been relegated to spaces where they live in isolation from the opposite sex. It was true that respondents often brought forth acute feelings of loneliness and desperation in our time together. But the assumption that their isolation made me more vulnerable first assumes that it makes them more threatening. Comments and questions about my research, which accumulated over the years, left me feeling defensive. My responses grew terse and automatic. *I work alone. There is no place for any of us to sleep but the ground. I dress however I like.* I felt the need to defend my respondents and to honor the enormous kindness, openness, and generosity with which I had been greeted. My decision to finally reflect on the issue of vulnerability came out of a concern that by denying my sense of fear in the migrant-dominated spaces that housed my research, I am denying the fear that pulses through the veins of all of those who are there. It *is* a dangerous space, and once I was able to separate the danger that loomed for all us from any danger that loomed specifically for me as a female researcher, it was clear that our experiences were defined by our shared vulnerability.

Yes, there were rare moments in the camps and slums when I felt personally threatened. But more frequently, it was the uniformed officers raiding our spaces and aggressing us on the streets who were threatening to us all. There were moments when I was not certain who I should feel most threatened by. But are Idrissa and his brothers not also forced to constantly question who is a friend and who is a foe? In critical border regions like Morocco, identities and alignments can shift rapidly. When no person is clearly labeled and no group clearly defined, names and allegiances are for sale. An assaulting officer can become an ally with a bribe. A fake passport can turn a Senegalese man into a Congolese man, an adult into a minor, or a brother into a foreigner in a matter of seconds. In liminality, the established social structures have been broken, the self and the other are fluid, and a sense of trepidation permeates every encounter. *Who are you in this space? Who am I? On which side do we stand?* I now understand that for all who have ever occupied spaces like this and have experienced threats to our physical safety on a daily basis, the sense of fear can be dulled to the point of numbness.

I cannot even recount the number of times that one of the forest camps I was staying in was stirred to wake in the middle of the night by a police raid. Tents were left burning, as we ran blindly up the rocky mountain side, unsure at times who we were running from. In these moments, batons are swinging, and in the darkness, you can hear the dull thump of their blows and the pained screams that follow. It can take many hours and the light of a new day for the brotherhood to reassemble and for us to discover who is still alive and present, taking stock of the injuries of those left standing. As humans, we experience fear when we encounter danger—when something unexpected and unwelcome shakes us from our routine. But when danger is ever present, the mind reacts by elevating the threshold for fear. Equipped with a new survival mechanism, you start to feel nothing at all.

The truth is that throughout my research, I dressed in loose clothing, in old clothing, and in multiple layers of clothing to disguise any semblance of shape. Although I came to know the communities and brotherhoods that welcomed me as honest, respectful, and courageous,

I rarely had an interaction with someone of the opposite sex that was not marked by overt (and less overt) suggestions at my sexuality. The ambiguity of a woman who is neither mother nor daughter, neither sister nor wife, is difficult to place. My position as elite (a white American researcher), but unthreatening (a young female) fits none of the accepted models in a country where women are still tethered to the private sphere. I moved through public spaces of assertive masculinity and hidden spaces of vulnerable masculinity with physical tags that marked me as foreign in both—unwelcome at times and welcome at others. My presence not only threatened to expose a system of EU-sanctioned and North African-executed human rights abuse, but it challenged established social norms about gendered and racial segregation. In some cases, without directly removing me, authorities sought to make it increasingly difficult for me to be there, bearing witness at Europe's southernmost borders. In other cases, I was placed behind bars. My money and belongings were routinely stolen, and my equipment and research were forcibly "confiscated." Police officers searched me and border guards beat me. At times when I was not the target of their aggression, I sat powerless and watched as others were bruised, bloodied, and taken away. I lost some of those who I had come to call my brothers to the beating of border guards' batons—their nameless bodies tossed in mass graves. I listened to countless stories—raw and heart-wrenching—of rape and murder. High-ranking officials and street hawkers, Moroccans and migrants, boys the same age as my little brother and men much older than my father, in all of the many languages crowding Morocco's streets, shouted and whispered to me: "*Salope*," "Whore," "*Gazelle*," "Belle," "Sexy," "*Sopessa*," "Come here," "Go home!"

On a less than fully conscious level, I adopted new strategies for handling my encounters with foreign men in foreign spaces. Accessing the hidden forest camps where brotherhoods live, train, and wait for their next attempted crossing requires clearance at multiple levels. It requires months of paperwork and state-issued permits to do research in the region. It requires the hard-won trust of the smuggling rings and chief smugglers who control movement in and out of Morocco's informal camps. And it requires the generous acceptance of the brothers and occasional sister who live there. Before entering a new camp, I was generally met by one of the chief's most trusted brothers at the base of the mountain. Hiking several miles up the rocky mountainside, he would lead the way to his hidden home, our arms loaded down with the supplies I brought as a thanks for the brotherhoods' hospitality and an exchange for my "room and board." Sleeping far from the closest town below meant that I, too, must rely on what little food and water there was in the camp to sustain myself, and I was conscious of never being a greater strain on the group. In the bags, we carried the items most commonly requested by the brotherhoods: jugs of clean water, bags of rice, sugar, salt, blankets, nails, and duct tape. The nails are used to create climbing tools for the fences that separate Morocco from Spain, and the tape, when wrapped around the hands and feet, serves as a protective barrier against the razor wire. After many months in the camps, I compiled a list of other specialty items I thought the brothers would appreciate, and I brought them in smaller supply on my later trips: headlamps, gloves, shoes and socks, toothbrushes, cleansing clothes, pain medicine, bandages, matches, and an axe for chopping wood. Fires are not only the sole source of heat in the cold winter months but are necessary for boiling dirty drinking water year round.

Those who live in the mountains surrounding Ceuta and Melilla limit their movement to the hours of the day when visibility is lowest, so it was always past nightfall when I first entered a new camp. The shadows of those who would be sleeping beside me were visible only in the light of the fire, and the sense of trepidation on both sides was high. Although the state, the smuggler, the chief, and the brothers had approved me, questions lingered: who was I and what was I doing there? I would set the bags of supplies we had carried up the mountain at the feet of the chief, and after a brief greeting, I would wait for my space to be assigned. Sleeping in a makeshift tent or on a patch of forest floor with anywhere between 20 and 100 boys and young men, an occasional woman or child in the group among them, I slowly became known by my own name—"Isa." As soon as the group knew where to place me, our work began. With every passing day, I felt both less threatening and less threatened. My potential to bring awareness to the brotherhood's struggle in the long term became greater than what I or my belongings may have been worth to them in my first hours or days there. I grew into my role as researcher, as friend, and as comrade, and the brotherhood grew into accepting me. As soon as I was accepted as a member of the community, any crime against me became a crime against us. More times than I can recount, the brotherhoods protected and defended my honor when under attack. Not once was I ever aggressed by them. In fact, it was in their hidden homes that I grew to feel the safest.

In time, I observed how other migrants used similar strategies when they approached new camps, often offering their last remaining belongings—water, food, what little money they had—to those who were already settled in the space. It was not a payment for the right to sleep in a camp that no one owns. There is a shared knowledge that brotherhoods exist for the sole purpose of growing in numbers before their next attempted escape. Rather, it was a present payment for a future promise. I will feed you now, before I am starving, so that you will feed me later when I have nothing to eat. I will quench your thirst, so that you will tend my wounds. It is an example of the "intense feeling of social togetherness" that comes with *communitas* (Turner & Turner 1978). It is the bond that soldiers on battlefields and sailors on high seas throughout time have felt. In their shared experience of liminality, brotherhoods of African migrants create a unique form of antistructure that emerges only in the space between one home and the next. As the state abandons them, they must turn to one another for survival.

Because Melilla is less than 5 square miles—a small patch of Europe in the northwestern tip of Africa—and because foreign media is tightly controlled in the spaces surrounding the enclave, it is an ideal place for the state to test new strategies of border surveillance and control. There, migrant camps are regularly raided by officers, who leave nothing but the blue plastic of their makeshift tents melting. Yet I learned that a burned identity does not mean no identity at all. While Moroccans commonly use the term *"harraga"*—meaning literally those who burn—to discriminate against the growing migrant population, members of the migrant community have appropriated this term in recent years, and it has become a point of pride. A burner is one who has sacrificed himself or herself in the hopes that their family may someday know a better world. As Ibrahim, one of the members of Moneba's Guinean brotherhood, told me, "I am a *harraga*. I burn myself so my younger brothers won't ever have to." For Ibrahim, like so many others, his identity as an eldest son, as a brother, and as a man is tied to his sacrifice.

Migrants as the "New" Muslim Men

Gender, like other facets of identity from race to class, is a key point of analysis in anthropological research. However, a "gendered" study of a space has come to mean a study focused on the experiences that were historically overlooked by the discipline—namely, a study of women's experiences (e.g., Newcomb 2006). Anthropological research on masculinity, distinct from the larger body of work characterized by a biased focus on men's worlds, is still in its infancy when compared to the existing work on women (Peletz 1994). The growing body of research on masculinity in the Muslim world has drawn particular attention in recent years, as researchers struggle to confront and counter the gendered stereotypes of Muslim men that have been on the rise since 9/11 (Ouzgane 2006; Inhorn 2012). In *The New Arab Man* (2012), anthropologist Marcia Inhorn takes on the image of Muslim men as religious zealots and oppressors of women. Her research presents a "new" kind of man who is challenging the patriarchy of his forefathers through companionate marriage and gender equality in the home, often with the backdrop of war and poverty in their communities. Illustrations of how masculinity, and especially Muslim masculinity, is actively being constructed in the face of expanding migration from the Middle East and Africa toward Europe adds a new dimension to the research.

Moving away from the stereotypes of Muslims as zealots and oppressors, which the Western media has successfully, though problematically, linked to an Arab identity, there is a less visible Muslim man. Despite the invisibility of black Muslims in media, a recent demographic study found that 15 percent of the world's 1.6 billion Muslims live in sub-Saharan Africa, only slightly less than the 20 percent who live in the Middle East–North Africa region.[8] I argue that the migratory routes crisscrossing Africa present another "new" Muslim man—one whose decision to challenge the patriarchy of his forefathers may be more circumstantial, but who has nonetheless been forced to occupy a new role that upsets traditional divisions of labor. It may at first appear that male-dominated migrant communities in Morocco are spaces of hypermasculinity, but a closer look reveals that the men trapped there must take on a wider range of social roles than they would have played at home, including those reserved for women in their countries of origin. In the forest camps that many now call home, cooking, washing clothes, and caring for those who are injured are among the many tasks divided between the brotherhoods.

Moving from sub-Saharan Africa to North Africa, anthropologist Stefania Pandolfo studied young Muslim men living in the same Moroccan *banlieues* that many migrants now call home (2007). She takes on the same stereotypes that Inhorn writes about, focusing on Western media's representations of martyrdom and suicide in the Muslim faith and the influence these representations have had on the Muslim community. Pandolfo's study is set in the aftermath of Morocco's deadliest terrorist attack to date. In 2003, a total of 14 suicide bombers—all young Moroccan men between the ages of 20 and 23 from the slums of Sidi Moumen—attacked centers of foreign investment and leisure in Casablanca. Their targets included a five-star hotel, Spanish- and Jewish-owned restaurants, and the Belgium Consulate, killing 45 people and leaving more than 100 injured.[9] With global attention on this violent attack, questions about Morocco's future role as "the Western ally" loomed. Would the steady exchange of European tourists to Morocco and Moroccan immigrants to Europe continue? Pandolfo's subjects, all coming from slums like Sidi Moumen, struggled to conceive of any future for themselves in Morocco, given the limited (or complete lack) of economic opportunities available to them. They grew increasingly fixated on reaching Spain. In much the same language that African migrants used in interviews with me, they voiced an obsession with mobility and a sobering awareness of the risks they would have to take. "If 100 go, 90 will die; 10 will survive and fall into the hands of the Spanish police," one young man explained (Pandolfo 2007: 351). Still, they engaged in lively debate about the nature of such a gamble and how people choose to put their own life on the line or not.

"You go gambling with your life!" ("*Ghadi mghamar b rasek*"), says Jawad, one of the respondents in Pandolfo's study. He believes the decision to throw oneself into "a dream" is a form of suicide, and like any suicide, it is strictly forbidden in the Muslim faith. He argues that despite his poverty, there is value in living the life God has given him, "however unbearable its present condition" (2007: 339). Jawad's counterpart, Kamal, roots his argument in "an ethical struggle for a better life," rather than in religious doctrine (2007: 339). He sees no future for himself in Morocco outside of becoming "a common pickpocket" and believes migration is the only way for him to preserve his integrity. Yet, as their debate progresses, Kamal finds a link between his ethical beliefs and the religious accounts of migration that he has heard. Pandolfo explains that the Prophet's departure from Mecca to Medina in 622 CE, when the new faith was under attack, was a decision to migrate "from a land of injustice and oppression" (2007: 337). "A person oppressed," Kamal argues, "has an obligation to migrate rather than risk losing moral integrity" (2007: 340). Migration, seen from Kamal's perspective, is a struggle for a better life, a *jihad*,[10] and as such, death on the migratory route is no different than death in a religious war. In both scenarios, he believes that "the faithful find reward in the afterlife" (2007: 344).

Kamal tries to convince his friend that there is no other path open to young men like them, contending that he must leave "in order to support [my] family, feed them; they are poor, don't have anything, live packed in a single room, a prison" (2007: 345). His choice to put his life on the line is both a moral and a generous one. But Jawad counters that it is wrong to think of migration as war. The migrant, he argues, "seeks to resolve a personal problem, to improve his life, obtain a material gain" (2007: 345). In war, the soldier fights for the greater interest of the country. Most interesting to me in Pandolfo's sensitive ethnographic engagement with these young men was her attention to language and imagery. In the words of Kamal and Jawad, I heard my own respondents voicing their memories of a desperate past, their hopes for a better future, and the cyclical nature of their lives as they felt trapped in the present state. Pandolfo's scattered retelling illuminates how for migrants in North Africa, as for those in other corners of the continent, the pull to migrate has become as powerful a force as addiction or love:

> They describe the state of mind of the *harg* ["illegal" migration] in a language of addiction: *'l-harg keyjri f-l-'aruq bhal ddim, ana mbli* (burning flows in my veins like blood, I am addicted),' *mbli*, a term that is used for drugs, but also for being in love—I have lost all desire—*reghba* (desire, longing, for anything other than the burning itself). And in terms of rage, oppression: "*Ana hayr* (I am beside myself)," (*hayra* is confusion, helplessness, extreme anguish) and by the image of an elsewhere that becomes an obsession, and produces a cleavage, a rift, somewhat comparable to what happens in the phenomenology of dreams: "*Ddati hna, khat.ry lehe, bhal l-wsuas fiya* (my body is here, my Being is over there)" (with a gesture of the hand, far away, over there, in Europe), "as if with a constant whispering in my ear" (Pandolfo 2007: 353).

This particular feeling of "*hayr*" (confusion, helplessness, extreme anguish) is often voiced in narratives of struggle, and it raises the question of how migrants' desires for mobility challenge a feeling of helplessness and acceptance. While Jawad's decision to value his life, however unbearable, represents an acceptance of poverty, Kamal's decision to migrate—to fight, to sacrifice, to put his life on the line—represents the opposite. Both young men were raised in the same Islamic tradition, in the same situation of economic marginalization, and under the same flag. Yet, their reactions to the positions they were born into are diametrically opposed. One is driven by a religious doctrine that privileges God's will, while the other is driven by *jihad* in the original sense of the word—by man's continual war with himself—and by the belief that he alone can better his position in the world. Their debate highlights how, depending on the social conditions, the act of migration can turn a religious wrong into a right. Tunisian scholar Fethi Benslama proposed a similar phenomenon in the aftermath of Mohamed Bouazizi's now infamous self-immolation—an event that set off the Arab Spring movement across the region (2011).[11] Despite Bouazizi's suicide, the *mufti* of Tunis granted him an official pardon, claiming that Allah would forgive his act given the conditions that led to it. The socioeconomic state under which Bouazizi took his own life made it not a selfish act, but a sacrificial act for the greater good of his country—an act not of suicide but of martyrdom. When presented with the choice of death by poverty or death by migration, it is clear that only one provides the possibility for both physical and metaphysical transcendence.

In Morocco's hidden migrant camps, the brotherhoods speak of their struggle in a similar language—often referring to themselves as "*camarades*" (comrades), "*lions*" (lions), or "*soldats*" (soldiers), and speaking about their daily life as a "*guerre*" (war). In each brotherhood, there is a strong sense of community, and the eldest in the group, usually a young man in his early 20s, takes on the role of chief. He assigns his younger brothers, and occasional sister, their daily duties and remains focused on his primary task of preparing them for their next attempted crossing. Within the group, it is common for each individual to take on a new name—often including in their new name the names of actual people or places where they dream of going. A boy by the given name of Amadou Diallo, for instance, calls himself John Kennedy Jr. because he once saw a film about the American president and thinks he is a good man. Another calls himself Prince Souleman Money Pain because, as he explained to me, "Needing money is bringing me great pain, but once I have it, I'm going to live like a prince."

In the years since I started working in these camps, a new tradition has emerged among the brotherhoods. Each individual is now expected to tag a rock before making an attempted crossing—sometimes simply leaving their name behind, and other times leaving a more elaborate painting. A sampling of their art is pictured in Figure 4.1 below.

FIGURE **4.1   A sampling of images of rock art created by the brotherhoods in the hidden forest camps surrounding the Spanish enclaves of Ceuta and Melilla. Morocco, dates vary.** Source: *Photograph by the author.*

The term "Boza," which is often seen in their rock art, has been created between the multiple languages present in the camps to mean something akin to "Success!" It can be used to celebrate finding a new water source on the mountain, winning a game of stick ball, or evading a police officer who is chasing you up a rocky path at night. But most commonly, it is used to describe the ultimate win—reaching Europe. The news of every successful crossing is met with the brothers breaking out in chants of "Boza free! Boza free!" When I want to understand an individual's history of experience in Morocco, I walk around the mountainside with them. They show me their rocks, allowing me to note the number of attempted crossings they have already made, and by the level of decay on each, I can estimate how long ago they first arrived. Beyond just marking names, these tags have come to represent the passage of time in a space that often seems to exist outside of time and space and the cyclical nature of life for those who remain trapped there.

Learning from Comparative Studies of Migration

The movement of people, goods, and cultures across borders has long been at the heart of anthropological research. Yet Morocco presents a compelling case study for students and scholars of transnationalism,[12] a paradigm that has traditionally focused on "the process by which migrants build social fields that link together their country of origin and their country of settlement" (Glick Schiller, Basch, & Blanc 1992: 1). While the earliest approaches tended to depict migrants as embedded in fields of opportunity, more recent approaches place a greater emphasis on the "here" and "now" of individual migrants as they navigate a range of social institutions and relationships. The push and pull factors examined have therefore grown increasingly local and individualized. While this shift in the paradigm better accounts for the lived experiences of migration, it still lacks a means for accessing experiences of liminality—the very foundation of which challenges any fixed concept of a "here" or "now." This section provides a close lens on other recent ethnographic studies of transnational migration, interweaving central anthropological concepts with experiences from the field. Moving beyond the traditional focus on countries of origin and countries of settlement (Kearney 1986, 1995) and challenging later attempts to critique this binary by emphasizing points of interconnection between the two (Glick Schiller et al. 1992; Basch et al. 1994), I aim to better account for the complexities of movement that leave contemporary migrants feeling largely disconnected from both home and destination and push for a reconceptualization of the basic terms we apply in studies of the "migrant" and the "refugee."

The Transnational Paradigm

In the past decades, distinct approaches like the French "*circulation migratoire*" (De Tapia 1994) and the American "transnationalism" (Glick Schiller et al. 1992) emerged, cementing transnational migration in a list of subfields central to the social sciences. The transnational paradigm became known for its focus on three areas: (1) the influence of immigrants' remittances, absence, or overall migration on sending communities (e.g., Chu 2010), (2) the daily life of receiving communities within destination countries (e.g., Ong 1996, 1999, 2003), or (3) the socioeconomic networks that are created between sending and receiving communities (e.g., Basch et al. 1994; GlickSchiller et al. 1992). When coupled with the increasing interest in globalization, transnationalism highlighted the interdependence of "developed" and "undeveloped" societies in cultural and economic terms. The methodological frameworks that developed in Europe stemmed from research in postcolonial Africa, while those developed in the United States were rooted in research on the United States' own migrant populations. Despite geographic differences, both center on similar questions of how social and economic relationships are established across political and physical borders. The underlying implication is that with globalization should come new understandings of time, space, and mobility.

Viewing transnationalism as a process through which migrants create and maintain "multi-stranded social relations" between two communities challenges the association of geographic space with social identity (Gupta & Ferguson 1992). In *Nations Unbound* (Basch, Glick Schiller, & Blanc, 1994), for instance, the study of different migrant populations living and working in New York reveals how the groups are molded by sociopolitical processes in their old homes and their new. No longer is the Filipino linked exclusively to the space of the Philippines. No longer is Caribbean tradition linked exclusively to the islands that make up the region. With globalization, time and space have taken on new meanings, and a particular class of Filipino migrants is now linked to their mobility, just as particular neighborhoods in New York are now linked to Caribbean cultural practices of food, religious practice, and family structure. Through their mobility, Filipino migrants in New York adopt new understandings of the self that are not entirely Filipino or American, but a melding of the two. Those residing in highly mobile "sending" communities are similarly impacted—their identities shifting with the new cultural traditions and remittances that flow in. In contrast, those residing in "receiving" communities must adjust to the restructuring of socioeconomic systems that accompany an influx of migrant labor and changes to a cultural identity that is no longer rooted in nationality alone.

Transnational migration is a process that destabilizes the historically contingent relationship between the state, the government, and a clearly bounded community of citizens, and mass migrations can dramatically shift the location of the state's political membership. Transnational migrants, by nature of their physical location between two worlds, experience the power of the state as an "extraterritorial social formation" (Basch et al., 1994). To draw on another example provided in seminal research by Linda Basch, Nina Glick Schiller, and Cristina Szanton Blanc, El Salvadorian migrants in the United States are impacted by elections in their home community, just as those living in El Salvador are impacted by the American labor markets that determine the amount of remittances sent home. Sending countries like those across Central America have created policies to retain the involvement of migrant populations in their economic development by giving them a strong political voice (Glick-Schiller & Fouron 2001; Levitt & de la Dehesa 2003). In contrast to these policies, receiving countries have adopted policies that limit the political voice of migrant communities, including temporary visa programs that maintain migrants as laborers and economic subjects but not political subjects of the state.

In her research on refugee communities in the United States, anthropologist Aihwa Ong moves her level of analysis from the group to the individual level. Her work, *Buddha Is Hiding: Refugees, Citizenship, the New America* (2003), draws on Michel Foucault's argument that the modern state uses biopower to make populations and bodies "amenable to various technologies of control" with the goal of creating both citizen and migrant subjects that are "healthy and productive"—an argument that is seen later in the research of Dider Fassin (2005: 80; Fassin 2001; Foucault 2004). Yet Ong's research draws attention to one shortcoming in Foucault's original analysis by revealing how subjects often resist the technologies of control that are imposed on them. Cambodian refugees, she contends, have learned how to not only inhabit, but also manipulate the subject positions that were created for them in their home country and in their receiving communities throughout the United States. Just as elite Cambodians learned to disguise their education (a key marker of their social status) in hopes of being spared during Pol Pot times, Cambodian asylum seekers learned to craft specific narratives of vulnerability in hopes of being granted refugee status in the United States. Those who were granted refugee status were later instructed on how to inhabit their new "American-ness" through state-issued pamphlets and presentations on everything from proper dress to personal hygiene. Ong dissects a self-conscious form of presentation that I witnessed on a daily basis among migrants in Morocco, as they struggled to learn *when*, *where*, and *how* to be *who*. In the absence of official resettlement programs, those trapped in Morocco learn from the other migrants who live, work, and struggle alongside them.

The crux of Ong's argument is conveyed by the image of the hiding Buddha, or a refugee population that appears to accept new American values, while acting in accordance with their own cultural values behind closed doors. Being Cambodian American therefore involves a disjuncture from old home and new and demands the creation of something new and hidden. The natural comparison would be "Muhammad is hiding" among migrant communities in Morocco, where the promise of aid from European and Christian institutions and organizations pushes some to publicly present as non-Muslim while privately adhering to their own religious practices. In both cases, the migrant and the refugee similarly subvert the vulnerability imposed on them by the state through the act of crafting and inhabiting new forms of self and new narratives of vulnerability. At the Spanish-Moroccan border, where migrants are stripped of the rights that should be guaranteed to them, many rely on their ability to manipulate their histories in order to be seen as human. This in and of itself is a form of power.

Transnational Subjects at Home and Abroad

The complex relationship between fixed and mobile subjects is perhaps best exhibited through the study of their financial ties—through remittances, but also, through debt. In her study on fixed subjects in China, anthropologist Julie Chu examines the impact of migration on those who remain trapped in Longyan, a primary site for human smuggling to the United States, and the complicated systems of credit that have emerged. *Cosmologies of Credit: Transnational Mobility and the Politics of Destination in China* (Chu 2010) draws on Marcel Mauss's argument that the gift is the primary means of relationship building between humans and essential to all social structures (Mauss 1967). In communities around the world, credit, or the exchange of a gift in the present for the promise of a greater gift in the future, has become the primary means of financing migrants' mobility. Chu finds that the ubiquity of credit in lower-income Chinese communities has given rise to a "moral economy" in which a migrant's ability to acquire debt becomes a symbol of their trustworthiness and a marker for their future success abroad (Chu 2010: 239). This system binds migrants tightly to the families and communities that have supported their mobility and places even higher stakes on their journeys.

Among African migrants, the transfer of large amounts of debt to cover the high costs of smuggling has produced a distinct system of social relations. Migrants who are not successful in their final crossings to Europe know that their failure to repay their debts will damage the reputation of their families at home and, in some cases, lead to the confiscation of their family's property. As one young Congolese man explained, "This is not a situation in which my family is starting at zero, and I am risking my life to lift them up. I know that if I fail, I have lowered them down to $3,000 [USD] in debt. That is a debt that takes many lifetimes to repay." Failure to succeed damages a family's financial security in the present and leaves relatives to pass a high debt on to the coming generations. But if successful, the reward is equally high.

The notion of transnationalism has recently been expanded, with some researchers now defining "transnationals" as those who remain in a sending country but are dependent on a migrant family member who has moved beyond the country's borders (Levitt 2001, 2004).

The transnational exchanges they rely on come in the form of monetary remittances and social resources, both serving to place even non-migrants within a "transnationalized" space. Sociologist Peggy Levitt emphasizes the importance of moving beyond "methodological nationalism" to incorporate residents of home and "host" communities in analyses and reveals how migration transforms family, work, and social life for those who stay behind as much as for those who are mobile (Levitt & Jaworsky 2007: 132). Values related to gender, race, and religious practice are among the first to be impacted, giving way to new meanings of identity in both communities. Much like the conflicting value systems that Hicham's sisters struggle with as young Muslim women working and raising families in Europe, Levitt's subjects in the United States and their extended family members who remain fixed in the Caribbean are equally impacted by new ways of thinking about femininity.

For me, this raises the question of which of the fixed subjects in a given community should be seen as transnationals. Where, for instance, should we view those who are not receiving any financial or social resources, but are instead spending them? Whether through the impact that a mobile subject has on family reputation in their absence or the accumulation of family debt, the loss of a migrant family member can similarly situate fixed subjects in a transnationalized space, despite any ties to a community abroad. Khadija's narrative of a husband turned migrant turned mystery is not an anomaly. Every year, a similar chain of events leaves thousands like her with unanswered questions and no remaining connection to their family's transnationality beyond a missing person.

Questioning across Borders

Looking at what sociologist Douglas Massey terms "the world's principal international migration systems" (2005: 3)—North America, western Europe, the Gulf, the Southern Cone of South America, and Asia and the Pacific Islands—highlights the evolution of migration studies through the evolution of the places themselves. Massey supports the belief that as a twenty-first century paradigm, transnationalism must reach across geographical boundaries and explore how the increasing mobility of individuals is developing connections between sending and receiving countries at competing ends of the development spectrum. But there are challenges to this approach that others have failed to address. Different anthropological traditions have long been linked to distinct world regions, bringing one set of methodological tools and theoretical frameworks to, for example, Latin America (where inquiries tended to focus on economic relations between groups; e.g., Wolf 1972), another set to the Pacific Islands (where inquiries tended to focus on ritual practices within groups; e.g.,Oliver 1951), and yet another set to sub-Saharan African (where inquiries tended to focus on kinship and social organization in different groups; e.g., Evans-Pritchard 1940). The anthropological tradition in which studies have been conducted has therefore influenced the very questions that have been asked and, in turn, the answers that have been found. While gatekeeping concepts can be a good way to open the door to research, they can also limit one's findings once "inside" (Appadurai 1988), often requiring a form of translation between texts if one wants to compare ethnographic research conducted in different world regions. But what is the common language between studies of economic relations and studies of social organization?

These problems are not relegated to anthropology's foundational texts but continue to be present in contemporary studies of transnationalism, where the population under study often dictates the questions asked. The growing body of literature on North African migrants in western Europe, for example, commonly focuses on the role of religion in processes of assimilation. This makes it difficult to compare it to the literature on South and Central American migrants in the United States, which gives little attention to the role of religion in migrant experience.[13] Yet there may be far greater similarities between Moroccans in Paris and Mexicans in Chicago than the ethnographic data suggests. My research has been rooted not simply in an examination of how liminality is experienced by migrants trapped in North Africa, but how it forges new collective identities out of unexpected groupings. Past research has explored how the resettlement of distinct ethnic groups, like West Indians in New York, ultimately gave way to new meanings of blackness in the United States (Foner 2001). While markers of class or vocation may have been most salient to an individual's understanding of him- or herself at home, they often find that other markers are more salient to how they are read in their receiving communities. In the Caribbean, as in North Africa, conceptions of race differ from the historically dualistic (white/black) interpretations that are found in the United States and Europe. West Indians arriving in the United States therefore found that it was not their class but their race that suddenly determined how they were read. Attempts to distance themselves from the negative placement of blacks in the United States social order led them to align with other migrant groups, ultimately creating a distinctly black Caribbean identity that transcended cultural and linguistic barriers. Research on migrant communities that move between distinct systems of racialization draws on the knowledge established through Frantz Fanon's revolutionary writings, especially on the concept of realizing one's blackness only when entering nonblack spaces (1952, 1963).

Throughout history, migrants' desires to distinguish themselves from established minority populations, whether blacks in the United States or Muslims in Europe, have led them to actively use cultural markers to redraw what would otherwise have been understood as racial groupings. For most of the Moroccans I spoke to in Spain, it was their religion and not their race that they believed most differentiated them from the majority population. For most sub-Saharan migrants in Morocco, it is their race. I contend that in the face of demographic change, an overall narrowing of difference can emerge. The more nuanced categories of identification that fall outside of a strict Muslim/Christian or Arab/black dichotomy cease to be recognized. No longer Shia or Sunni,[14] Maliki or Hanafi,[15] devoutly or culturally religious, nuance is washed away with a sweeping generalization of all Muslims. No longer Malian or Nigerian, migrants like Khadija and Idrissa feel that their identities are being reduced to their race.

I approached my research with competing questions about how the experiences of migrants in Morocco are unique and how the Maghreb as a new "destination" reveals a global shift in transnational migrations from the global south to the global south more broadly. The transformation of the region reveals the concrete impacts of third-party political agreements on the ground, and Morocco continues to serve as a model for other nations seeking to trap migrants in prolonged states of transit. Egypt and South Africa are predicted to be among the next nations to transition into "destination" countries on the African continent (Fábos 2010; Crush & Frayne 2010). Mexico has already become another model, holding migrants from South and Central America in "temporary" states of detention just south of the US border.

When Is the Migrant a Refugee?

The migrants and the refugee have long been disassociated from one another by the terms of their movement—one chosen and the other forced, one searching for greater opportunities in a new home and the other searching for what was lost in an old home. Long before studies of migrants in liminal spaces, refugees were linked to extended states of temporality (Malkki 1995, 1994; Ramsay 2017). According to recent statistics from the UNHCR, protracted refugee situations now last an average of 26 years—more than two decades spent living with limited rights and opportunities (2015).[16] One Congolese asylum seeker whom I spoke with, for instance, spent one decade in a refugee camp in Gabon before reaching Morocco, where he spent another decade trying to reach Europe. Despite the actual permanency or temporariness of their stays in host countries, refugees are "in between" the homes they fled and the countries where they will be formally resettled. Tightened border controls, strengthened immigration policies, and increased externalization of borders from traditional immigration destination countries to other countries on their periphery have caused migrants' journeys, like those of refugees, to be interrupted by similar periods of "temporary" settlement lasting for years or, in some cases, even generations (Andersson 2014). This leads to the question of whether the two categories can still be so easily disassociated from one another by the terms of their movement.

The generalized category of refugees connotes images of suffering, displacement, and vulnerability (Malkki 1995). In order to be granted refugee status, one's narrative must first be accepted by the state, which requires both a demonstration of vulnerability on the part of the migrant seeking asylum and an acceptance of the demonstrated vulnerability on the part of the citizen evaluating the migrant's claim. The citizen relies on images and understandings they have of "the other" from the broader social imagination in order to evaluate the legitimacy of the migrant's performance. One example of this comes from anthropologist Miriam Ticktin's research in France—a country in which a policy known as "the illness clause" allows undocumented migrants with documentable illnesses to legally remain in the country for the duration of their treatment (2006). But as with all asylum claims, migrants' claims to illness must be throughly examined. They are inspected by a long line of immigration officials and medical professionals, placing their fates in the hands of these citizens. The potential danger of leaving such critical decisions to subjective interactions is highlighted by one immigration officer's sympathy for a Muslim woman's "familiar Orientalist narrative" of physical abuse and another officer's suspicion of an Algerian man's reported illness. Without an objective measure in place, the social imagination of what vulnerability looks like becomes the deciding factor. In the end, the officers' decisions lead to a woman with psychological trauma being welcomed under the illness clause and a man who later proved to be facing a terminal illness being turned away (Ticktin 2006). Ticktin's study further reveals how this policy has driven some who arrive on European shores, desperate for the chance to provide their families with a stable future, to take the only legal path that is open to them—contracting a serious illness. As awareness of the illness clause spread among migrant communities, fathers and husbands, brothers and sons, actively began seeking HIV, knowing the duration of their treatment would guarantee their families the right to remain in their new homes. Policymakers greatly underestimated how desperate migrants arriving in Europe are to keep their families from returning to the extreme poverty, conflict, or persecution they are fleeing.

In his research on the illness clause (2005), Didier Fassin explores how the body has historically been, and continues to be, a site in which states exert their power over subjects. But for migrants, in particular, the body has become a site in which they are compelled to display evidence of the horrors they have endured. With populist governments on the rise, migrants are being asked in new, multiplied, and increasingly convoluted ways to prove their eligibility for inalienable human rights. Across world regions, they are asked to reveal the scars of physical and psychological traumas, their bodies requiring evaluation by trained eyes and their stories by trained ears. Through their research, Ticktin and Fassin expose a new European political practice that has forced a population to exchange their health for their right to life. The transition from the category of migrant to the category of refugee is therefore a move from able-bodied (and economically threatening) to disabled body (and vulnerable). This raises important questions about the exclusivity of the two categories and the struggles of those who seek to develop lives beyond the confines of their state-assigned vulnerability. If one's right to life under the new state depends on a fluid transition into visible and verifiable vulnerability, do migrants seeking legal acceptance need first to dissolve all agency? Do refugees seeking to access their agency through work or education lose their vulnerability and therefore their claims to belong in the state? And perhaps most importantly, how has this system been constructed to privilege certain populations for whom a performance of vulnerability will come more easily? It is impossible to deny the fact that existing prejudices weigh in favor of women's claims to vulnerability over those of men and in favor of children's claims to vulnerability over those of adults. They also impact how state officials read the claims of migrants from varying racial, religious, and ethnic backgrounds.

In contrast to refugees, the generalized category of migrants has long been associated with the decision to "leave" rather than "flee" home. Yet the legal reality is that before being given the chance to apply for refugee status, the 68.8 million men, women, and children who are currently displaced around the world are categorized as migrants first. A rapidly expanding population of migrants is now setting out, or being forced out, on journeys that mirror the forms of punctuated movement examined in refugee studies (Collyer 2007). They spend years, even decades, trapped between their home countries and desired destinations, living in sprawling slums or makeshift camps that are akin to refugee camps in every way except for the social services provided. I contend that the persistent distinction between these two categories is less indicative of their patterns of movement or lived experiences of displacement, and more indicative of the political motivations to mold strict categories of inclusion and exclusion through the classification of "the other" as threatening or vulnerable to the state (Bosniak 2006). Distinctions between the migrant slum and the refugee camp should be studied not in terms of the different push and pull factors driving the movement of the individuals who inhabit them, but in terms of the different labels that are stamped on those individuals as they move and the legal pathways that are then opened or closed to them. As the UNHCR narrowly informs us, the migrant *chooses*, and the refugee lacks a choice.

> "A refugee is someone who, owing to a well-founded fear of being persecuted for reasons of race, religion, nationality, membership of a particular social group or political opinion, is outside the country of his nationality, and is unable to, or owing to such fear, is unwilling to avail himself of the protection of that country."
>
> "A migrant is someone who chooses to move in order to improve the future prospects of himself and his family."— UNHCR

Yet, as one caseworker exclaimed to me in an interview, "How often is one not the other?" The population of migrants trapped in Morocco is composed of both first-generation migrants and their children. The children commonly lack citizenship claims both to their parents' native countries and to their birthplace of Morocco until age 18 when it becomes, at best, incredibly difficult for them to receive citizenship.[17] In the language of refugee studies, the population of youth born in the Maghreb is a paperless or "invisible" population. Their liminal placement leaves them with the same limited work opportunities as their parents and without the necessary documentation to leave Morocco in search of greater social or economic mobility. Restricted access to public classrooms means that second-generation migrants lack any formal education or study of Arabic. Language, like labor, therefore becomes a marker of citizenship, perpetuating the social and economic marginalization of Morocco's migrant class into the coming generations.

Liminality has been applied to the refugee experience as both a legal and a lived state of being. While all of the migrants who I came to know well in Morocco view their homes as places of "temporary" settlement, regardless of how long they had been there, the second-generation youth born into these spaces challenge notions of temporality. How does their placement between "home" countries, which they have never known, and in a "temporary" home, which is all they have ever known, shape their expectations for belonging, return, or escape? For parents clinging to memories of a past and imaginaries of a future, it may be easier to live in a place that is neither here nor there. But how do they explain to their children that home is a point on the horizon?

Notes

1. In using the term "go-along" interview, I make reference to Margarethe Kusenbach's article "Street Phenomenology: The Go-Along as Ethnographic Research Tool," in which she argues that "by exposing the complex and subtle meanings of place in everyday experience and practices, the go-along method brings greater phenomenological sensibility to ethnographers" (2004: 455).
2. A *Derija* saying similar to "God blesses those who give alms to the poor."
3. During the holy month of *Ramadan*, Muslims deny themselves of worldly pleasures and end the ritual period of fasting and spiritual reconnection with a three-day celebration—*Eid al-Fitr*. Before the celebration begins, families undertake *Sadaqah al-Fitr* (charity of fast-breaking), donating food and money to the poor.

4. Depending on the conversion rate, 100 MAD (Moroccan *dirhams*) is equivalent to roughly 10 USD.

5. According to Roman Catholic doctrine, Purgatory is an intermediate state in which, after death, people who are destined for heaven "undergo purification, in order to achieve the holiness necessary to enter the joy of heaven" before being admitted. (Catechism of the Catholic Church 1030). Only those who die in the state of grace, but have not yet reached a sufficient level of holiness to enter heaven in life, will go to Purgatory, so it is assumed that none will remain forever in the liminal state.

6. *Da'at*, a Hebrew word meaning "Knowledge," is found in the branch of Jewish mysticism known as Kabbalah and is the physical location or mystical state where all 10 *sephirot* (or emanations) in the Tree of Life are united as one.

7. *Barzakh*, an Arabic word meaning "a barrier that stands between two things and does not allow the two to meet," is a physical location or spiritual state considered by some to be the Muslim equivalent to the Roman Catholic Purgatory. It is a period beginning with death and lasting until the Day of Judgment (*Bihar al-Anwar*).

8. A comprehensive demographic study of more than 200 countries found that there were 1.6 billion Muslims in the world, representing 23 percent of an estimated world population of 6.8 billion. The population is divided between 62 percent in the Asia-Pacific region, 20 percent in the Middle East–North Africa region, and 15 percent in the sub-Saharan Africa region, followed by less than 3% in Europe and the Americas. Of the countries represented in the sub-Saharan region, Nigeria has the largest population of Muslims and the sixth largest population of Muslims in the world (Pew Research Center 2010).

9. In addition to the hotel, restaurants, and Belgium Consulate bombed on May 16, 2003, there were attempted attacks on a Jewish cemetery and Jewish community center. In total, 33 civilians (8 Europeans and 25 Moroccan citizens) were killed and more than 100 were injured, along with 12 of the suicide bombers who died during the attacks. The remaining two were arrested.

10 Pandolfo distinguishes between two types of *jihad*: "On the one hand, *jihad* is a constant 'war' with oneself, against an internal enemy, impossible to eliminate, and in fact also necessary for life—a *jihad* that only ends at death. On the other, it is a war against an external enemy who represents a threat for the community of Muslims" (2007: 344).

11. Tarek el-Tayeb Mohamed Bouazizi was a Tunisian street vendor who set himself on fire in 2010, in protest of repeated harassment by officials and confiscation of his wares. The population's outrage intensified after Bouazizi's death, leading then-President Zine El Abidine Ben Ali to step down in January 2011, after 23 years in power. Bouazizi's act is now remembered as a catalyst for the Tunisian Revolution and the larger Arab Spring, inciting riots in Tunisia that would later spread throughout the region. In 2011, he was posthumously awarded the Sakharov Prize for his "historic changes in the Arab world," the Tunisian government honored him with a postage stamp, and *The Times* named him "Person of the Year."

12. Throughout my analysis, I use the term "transnationalism" in its broadest sense to indicate a social phenomenon that grows out of the heightened interconnectivity of individuals and the receding economic significance of boundaries between nation-states. However, what I challenge in the popular understanding of transnationalism is that the interconnectivity of *all* individuals is heightened, rather than being heightened according to hierarchical structures of privilege, often along the lines of gender, race, and class (Freeman 2001: 1017).

13. Research conducted by Geschiere 2009; Geschiere and Ceuppens 2005; Cherribi 2010; Brubaker 1996, 1998, 2009; and Balibar 2003 in comparison to research conducted by De Genova 2005; De Genova and Peutz 2010; De Genova and Ramos-Zayas 2003; Chavez 2007, 2008; and Bosniak 2006.

14. Sunni and Shia are the two major denominations of Islam. Following the death of the prophet Muhammad in 632 CE, the group now known as the Sunni chose Abu Bakr, the prophet's adviser, to become the first successor, or caliph, to lead the Muslim state. The Shiites chose Ali, the prophet's cousin and son-in-law. Ali and his successors are now called imams. They not only lead the Shiites, but are considered to be direct descendants of Muhammad.

15. Maliki and Hanafi are two of the four major schools of jurisprudence within Sunni Islam. Maliki doctrine is predominantly traced to North and West Africa. The Mosque of Uqba in Tunisia was a major historical center of Maliki teaching from the 9th to 11th centuries, and it continues to be the primary school for Muslims in both regions today.

16. According to the 2015 UNHCR report titled *Global Trends: Forced Displacement,* the number of people displaced from their homes around the

world reached a record high of 65.3 million, a dramatic rise from the 37.5 million people displaced only 10 years earlier.

17. Moroccan nationality law is the subject of the Moroccan *Dahir* (Decree) of 1958. According to Article 11, a foreigner applying for Moroccan citizenship must fulfill the following conditions: (1) reside continuously in Morocco during the 5 years preceding the application; (2) be of legal age at the time of the application; (3) be mentally and physically fit; (4) have a record of good conduct and reputation in addition to not being convicted of any crime or offense punishable by Moroccan law [*including "illegal" migration*]; and (5) have sufficient knowledge of the Arabic language and (6) be able to fully provide for himself.

CHAPTER 5

Burning Yesterday for Tomorrow: Images from the In Between

Introductory Case Study: A Journey to the Space In Between

I saw Phino many times before I first spoke with him. He was doing construction work on the building next to my rooftop room in Rabat, and he was often standing on makeshift scaffolding—sanding, caulking, or painting the crumbling walls—as I passed beneath the wooden beams that suspended him in the air. The building had been purchased by a French couple planning to open a new bed and breakfast in the *medina*, where throngs of European and American tourists were increasingly seeking "authentic" Moroccan experiences. Phino was happy for the chance at consistant work. He always wears the same boots with holes where steel toes may have once been, the same pair of tattered blue jeans, and one of two stained T-shirts with foreign phrases printed across the back. He keeps his hair closely cropped, his face cleanly shaven, and he looks a decade younger than his nearly 50 years. But his hands show every day of his hard labor. The gloves that he and the other five workers shared were made of camel skin, and I guessed they belonged to the foreman in charge.

A small but growing population of migrants was working in the construction industry during the time that I lived in Rabat, and I was interested in learning more about what they were doing, how much money they were making, and the opportunities that this kind of work might be opening up for others in the public sphere. Would more desirable work opportunities postpone migrants' plans for escape? Would it ever suspend their plans entirely? I lingered long enough to catch a hint of an accent that would trace Phino and the other workers back to their countries of origin. He was on a team with one other migrant and four *Soussis*, or Moroccans who had moved from the rural South in search of work. Their foreman, a middle-aged *Soussi* with a full beard, strong build, and small, watchful eyes, was often on site—drinking mint tea, eating *hersha*,[1] and discussing the intricacies of the project in a series of outbursts over his cell phone.

This particular pattern of speech, which is not only loud, but seemingly aggressive and adversarial, shaped my assumptions about the men I encountered in my first weeks in Morocco. Men standing on the street corner by my bus stop, men seated at the table next to me in the café, men queuing in long lines to buy fried potato sandwiches in the marketplace every afternoon—they all seemed to be deeply immersed in arguments with one another. Yet with time, I came to understand it as just another way in which Moroccan men perform their masculinity in the public sphere. It is not a sign of anger, but rather of interaction between men of equal social status in a space outside of the home. It is, in fact, friendly. As is true with many things in fieldwork, the meaning of their speech became clear to me not through its presence, but in its absence. I began to notice the times when this pattern of speech was missing. When I sat awaiting interviews with governmental officials, I heard it behind closed doors, but listened as the men working in the main offices adopted hushed, even demure, tones with those who ranked above them. In all conversations across divisions of social status—conversations between husbands and wives, fathers and sons, Moroccan nationals and those born beyond the country's borders—the patterns of speech shifted. I even began to hear a distinction between how *Rabatis*[2] spoke to other *Rabatis* or to *Soussis*, a population that was sometimes stereotyped as being poor or uneducated, having left their rural communities for Morocco's urban centers (McMurray 2001).

With dress, bodily comportment, and speech all being important tools used by individuals in the process of identity making (hooks 1999), the accent of migrant workers not only helped me detect their countries of origin, the volume, pitch, and deference or aggression of it also helped me guess their placement in Morocco's emerging hierarchy of political inclusion. In contrast to the outbursts of the *Souissi* foreman over his cell phone, I heard the hushed conversations between Phino and his friend, Stephan, who shared the same Congolese accent. As Phino's foreman explained to me, "We [*Souissis*] took the work no Moroccans wanted. We worked for wages no Moroccans wanted." But now, many like him have moved up the ladder to oversee teams of migrants, who travel from even farther south and are willing to work for even less. "*Harragas*," he continued, referencing Morocco's new migrant class, "are trapped here until they can save enough money to leave. They're desperate to leave, so they don't turn down any work or complain about any pay." I learned that if race alone does not serve to mark day laborers as "*harragas*," then their work under the direction of a *Souissi* certainly does. They lack the tools needed to feign any form of political inclusion in the public sphere.

Phino took the most common route for Congolese migrants to Morocco. "Camels," as they are called, charge upfront for their services, and for those making the long journey from Central African countries, the payment due is around $5,000 USD. Once smugglers have accumulated a group of at least one dozen migrants, they produce the fake papers that are needed and arrange the guides. The group is handed off from one guide to another as they cross international borders—some transporting them through cities hidden in the backs of their trucks and others walking with them across stretches of desert. Once in Morocco, the migrants are responsible for arranging a guide who will take them across the Mediterranean. Those who lack the funds for this final leg of the journey search for odd jobs in the city, where they will work and save, or join a brotherhood in the forests of northern Morocco, where they will attempt to cross the fences surrounding Morocco's Spanish enclaves. While each country in the sub-Saharan region has its own smuggling network, many work in conjunction with one another, and it is not uncommon for a migrant to pay a "camel" in his country who will quickly pass him off to a local guide from another country. Morocco's own smuggling network is also quickly expanding to serve the needs of an expanding migrant population. For Moroccans like Kareem, a middle-aged man who returned from his low-paying job as a farmhand in Italy to work for his uncle's business in human smuggling, the choice was a simple one. "I can make much more money helping Africans go to Europe than I can make going to Europe myself!" he exclaimed. But as a clandestine business, there is no protection for the buyers. I have heard countless stories of migrants whose journeys never materialized—their guides disappearing shortly after being paid. Even more common are stories like the one Phino shared with me in which migrants pay to be delivered to European shores and are instead extorted for more money at every leg of their journeys until their pockets run dry, leaving them stranded somewhere between point A and point B. After finally reaching Bamako, Phino and his group traversed northern Mali and then Algeria by foot. They spent weeks crossing the vast, trying expanses of desert. When their guide abandoned them, they spent months in a makeshift camp at the Algerian-Moroccan border, before finally scaling the fences that divide the two countries on their own and reaching the town of Oujda.[3] Yet Phino never made it beyond Morocco. His story is full of theft and exploitation, imprisonment and deportation, abuse and brutal gang rape by a group of teenaged Moroccan boys armed with glass bottles. It is a series of events so brutal and commonplace that it seems difficult to imagine how any man, woman, or child in his shoes ever makes it to the other side.

After more than a decade spent living in Morocco's forest camps, Phino is grateful for the odd jobs that make it possible for him to sleep indoors in a small room that he rents with seven others and, on most weeks, to afford his daily bread. He explained how working in construction gave him enough money to survive, but rarely enough to send anything home to his family at the end of the month. Every morning, he stands on a particular street corner outside of Rabat's *medina,* where Moroccans know that migrants will be waiting in search of day labor. He is happy when a job promises work for more than a day and always eager that the steady pay might allow him to save some money for the final leg of his journey that he is still desperately awaiting. However, he has been in Morocco long enough to know that a week rarely passes without any money he has managed to save being stolen from him by police officers in a routine pat-down on the street, or if not by them, then by his landlord in a routine apartment search. This has become his way of life.

Although stories of migration float heavily in the air throughout Morocco, it is not as simple as one might imagine to find a migrant willing to recount his or her journey from start to finish. Trust is needed first, and in a community so accustomed to deceit, nothing is harder earned. My relationship with Phino and his friend Stephan started with casual greetings as I passed beneath them. Gradually, it progressed to offerings of "extra" couscous from my *riad's* kitchen on Fridays and eventually to shared meals on the small table I set up on the roof. Multiple models of acceptable behavior had to be broken in our interactions with one another—a woman speaking to a man, an "elite" to a laborer, a white to a black—but it was the last of them, a foreigner speaking to a foreigner, that made our relationship possible. Phino later laughed with me, explaining, "You Americans, you talk to everyone!" Our friendship was built largely on our common experiences as foreigners in the Maghreb, and it was relegated to spaces of secrecy—the only spaces where we felt free to speak. I remember the moment he first agreed to share his story with me. It was a sweltering summer day, and we sat together on the roof, sweat beading down our faces. He had just finished work, and I set a plate of traditional almond paste cookies and a kettle of hot mint tea out on the table between us. I had learned in our previous interactions that Phino adopted the Moroccan belief that drinking hot beverages is one way to cool the body down—a belief that still eluded me. I clicked my voice recorder on. "Tell me about the day you first imagined a new life beyond your home country."

In many ways, Phino's narrative is a familiar one, although he is older than the average migrant who travels his route. He grew up in a small town, where families survived on subsistence farming—cassava, plantains, mangoes, and guavas. As this way of life became increasingly difficult, women began taking their staple crops to the local markets to sell or trade, and men began venturing beyond the boundaries of their rural communities to seek labor in small neighboring cities like Bongandanga. "When I was young, mine was a small town full of families. Today, I hear it is a strange town full of women and children. The men have all left to find work." Through hundreds of interviews with Morocco's diverse migrant population, I learned that the majority of men who make migrations from small towns like the one where Phino was born have been chosen by their families or communities for a reason. I heard common refrains of past successes and a sending community's high hopes. Whether deemed "the smartest" or "the most talented" student in the schoolhouse, "the hardest working" or "the most successful" worker in the family business, there is always a reason why others band together to support the dreams of one migrant over the hundreds of others who are seeking to escape. It takes many people pooling their resources to afford the high fees demanded by smugglers, and communities are thoughtful about this investment. The young men who are chosen have been deemed the most likely to succeed abroad, and there is an expectation that the sacrifices of the community will be richly repaid in the future. As I learned from Phino, it is both a privilege and an honor, an expectation and an obligation. It is the impetus for freedom and mobility, but it is also a heavy burden to carry, binding one tightly to a place as it disappears into the distance behind them.

Memory Making: How One Man Builds a Narrative (and One Researcher Rebuilds it)

Memory is wildly inaccurate. Despite the detail with which I poured the day's events into my field journal every evening, despite the quality of my recording equipment or the resolution of my photographs, despite all of these pieces of "data" that comprised my postfield analysis, I am aware of the limitations of my own memory. My Nikon captured the collection of belongings that were neatly arranged on the floor beside Phino's mattress and the squalor of the hidden camps surrounding Morocco's Spanish enclaves, but where did he say he found that silver coin with the horse's head on it? And what did it smell like, that mixture of fresh mint and trash piled high, stagnant in the summer heat?

As ethnographers, we are trained to be aware of how our relationships in the field shape our research. But rarely are we pushed to question how our memories of these relationships continue to influence our analysis. Most prized to me now, in the final phases of writing, are my memories of the individuals who brought my fieldwork to life. It was not the objects they carried with them that proved meaningful to my analysis, but the time we spent together, cultivating the trust that allowed them to share their own memories of those objects with me. As Ruth Behar noted about her fieldwork experiences, "an anthropologist's conversations and interactions in the field can never again be exactly reproduced… gone before they happen, always in the past, even when written up in the present" (1996: 7). So what does it mean to base one's analysis on memory? It means first to think of memory not as fact but as fiction. It means to think of memory as storytelling and to think of stories as holding truth. I have come to understand that it is the way Phino remembers his wife's voice or remembers the color of the mud underfoot in his native village, the way in which he has constructed and reconstructed a thousand times the story of his "sending ceremony," which holds truth for his lived experience of migration. His experience is, in fact, what he remembers of it. My challenge was being invited into those memories.

After 15 years spent trapped in a place where he never intended to be, Phino explained that the power he has to manipulate parts of his story depending on his audience—emphasizing the war-torn land-scapes of the Congo for the immigration officers who were reviewing his claim to asylum or the beauty of the village that he still calls home for me—is the only power that he has left. The power of ethnography is in hearing not only the story that is constructed for you, but all of the stories that are constructed over the time you spend with a subject. Competing memories of one place or one event combine to ultimately give more layers of truth, not less. If analyzed thoughtfully, each layer reveals the subject position of the storyteller in relation to the listener. In Phino's depiction of a war-torn home, I heard the most torturous moments of his youth *and* I heard his imagined future on safer soil—a future that he would find only after gaining refugee status. I heard him building the narrative that was most likely to grant him an escape beyond Morocco's borders. As ethnographer, I was uniquely positioned to hear multiple stories and, through them, to create a full, complicated, and layered picture of his experience. Phino is a migrant, but that is only one of the myriad ways in which he understands himself. He is also a father, a husband, a son, a brother, a friend, a worker, a student, and an adventurer. Although an outsider may never guess it based on how he dresses and the work he performs, the easiest way to get him talking is to start with one of his two favorite subjects—American fashion or Afri-can history. He is excited by the contemporary designers who are incor-porating what he calls "traditional African style" into their fashion lines, and his tone shifts when he speaks with pride about his "heroes," who include African leaders Patrice Lumumba and Nelson Mandela. Phino defines himself to me as a Christian, an African, and a migrant—though he does not ever describe himself as a migrant in Morocco. Rather, his narratives assert his identity as a migrant en route to his desired destina-tion within the EU.

The traditional focus on sending and receiving communities has tied researchers to narratives of the past and future. As an increasing number of migrants end up trapped in transit countries, it is impor-tant to add a third dimension to our analysis. Studying the collected narratives of men like Phino and their common oscillation between a remembered past and an imagined future, it is difficult to overlook their denial of the present state. My research in Morocco spurred my interest in how we can study the space that lies in between and better under-stand the present-tense stories that are told (and un-told) there. In the following section, I propose a new research method that I term "visual life history collection," and I argue for the need to adapt the traditional methodologies that have long been applied in studies of transnational communities.

Traditional Life History Collection and a Call for Visual Data

I was best able to observe migrants' present-tense space through their interactions with family members and close friends, although neither group occupied the same physical space as them. Their family members were usually located in their home communities, and their close friends were scattered at different points on their own journeys—some still at home, some in transit like them, and some successfully on the other side of the Mediterranean Sea. When I observed how Phino used messages and photographs, narratives and images, to actively construct his life in Morocco for his family at home, I realized that I was standing in the middle of his process of memory making. Much like he had built a narrative of his "sending ceremony," recounting it so many times before he first told it to me that it had already become one of the better worn grooves in his brain, he was now building narratives of his present. These narratives would be told again and again by his family members in the DRC, ultimately shaping how they view migration and how some of them would come to imagine their own futures. In the process of memory making, that which is remembered or revealed can be just as important as that which is forgotten or concealed. My unique position as ethnographer allowed me to explore the different pushes and pulls that determine how migrants weave their narratives in the present tense. When speaking to his daughter or writing to his wife, what did Phino choose to reveal and conceal and why? In our visual life history sessions together, I questioned how the time, the place, and, most importantly, the audience, shaped the words and images that he chose to share and what they ultimately revealed about his understanding of himself.

Sociologist and photographer Douglas Harper (2002) claimed that including images in research, through a process termed photo elicitation, not only produces more information, but new kinds of information. Photo elicitation is based on a simple concept: one inserts images, usually photographs, into a research interview. In some cases, interviewees are asked to bring their own photographs, but more commonly, the interviewer provides them. Photographs can be selected around broad themes of the interview, such as news clippings from a recent article on migration in the Mediterranean, or they can be selected to elicit specific memories, such as images from an interviewee's home country. The primary difference between a standard interview and a photo elicitation interview lies not in the interviewer's questions but in the interviewee's responses, and the difference has biological roots (Harper 2002; Clark-Ibañez 2004). As humans, we respond differently to these two types of information—images and words. The brain's visual cortex is evolutionarily older than the parts that process verbal information. As Harper explains, "Images evoke deeper elements of human consciousness than words. ... Exchanges based on words alone utilize less of the brain's capacity than exchanges in which the brain is processing images as well as words" (Harper 2002: 13). Interviews that incorporate visual data are therefore likely to produce more numerous *and* more complex responses from interviewees.

One year into my fieldwork in Morocco, I felt there were still aspects of individuals' migration narratives that I was having trouble accessing—parts of their journeys I was unable to map. At this point, it no longer seemed due to a lack of trust. With time and deepening friendships, respondents were increasingly comfortable narrating even the most intimate details of their physical journeys to me. I worried that I was not asking the right questions to access the emotional journeys they had taken along with their physical steps. I wanted to know more about the individual pushes and pulls, the past realities and the future imaginaries that fueled their movement to the present state. I wanted them to dig a little deeper in their retellings and find threads of their narratives that had not been shared yet.

It was at this time that I decided to start augmenting my collected data with what I called "visual life histories." Traditional oral history collection is used to establish a complete history of life experience (Yow 2005), and in more recent adaptations, it has been used to condense an interviewee's complete experience in relation to a specific, often traumatic, event—a veteran's experience in Operation Iraqi Freedom, for instance, or a Syrian refugee's journey to the EU. I realized that an adaptation of this method, combining it with photo elicitation techniques, could encourage narratives, whether complete life histories or complete event histories, to be built around visual material culture instead. I relied on the interviewee's *own* photographs to open up new pathways in the brain, allowing me to explore what stories they carried with them and what stories they sent back home.

In my experience collecting traditional oral histories with migrants, I had observed how the process opens up a unique space for incorporating material culture into narratives. Because oral history interviews must be conducted over many long sessions together and because these sessions often necessitate meeting in respondents' homes, greater rapport builds with each meeting. Just as tea is offered and dinner is shared, family photographs and other mementos are often passed back and forth across the table. Intentionally centering my visual life history sessions on the incorporation of material items—specifically photographs, but also maps, books, journals, clothing, and found objects—I discovered that I was eliciting from respondents both more narratives *and* different kinds of narratives about their experiences of mobility, belonging, liminality, and identity in transitory spaces. With an assortment of images and objects spread out before us, questions that I had not known to ask naturally arose. These questions opened deeper levels of communication and more emotional connections to past experiences and future aspirations. I asked: what had "home" come to mean in light of their journeys? How had their imaginaries of Europe changed? How was their current "temporary" situation explained to those left behind? And most importantly to me, in what ways had their own conceptions of identity been transformed? Who were they now, in this space where they never intended to be?

In all of my time spent working with migrants in Morocco, I have never met a single one whose material possessions have not at least once, and usually multiple times, been stolen from them. If they left home in their best clothes, they are gone. If their parents bought them a new pair of shoes for the journey, it is gone. If they set out with a cell phone or a watch, a pocket knife or a wallet, a flashlight or a hat, they are all gone. Whatever money they had in their pockets, it is certainly gone. I am always curious about what migrants pack on their day of departure, leaving home with the knowledge that they may never return and able to bring no more than what they can carry on their backs. The answers I have received are surprisingly similar, even across socioeconomic divides. What migrants deem "the necessities" usually include a spare pair of clothes, a cell phone and phone charger, a jug of water, a box of crackers and possibly a can of sardines, and whatever money they have to their names. Many also carry a copy of the Bible or the Qur'an, which I find notable given the weight of both and the high rates of illiteracy in the population, and nearly all carry a small and cherished collection of old photographs. By the time I am sitting across from these men, women, and children, they have already been hustled and abused by a long line of smugglers, bandits, border agents, police officers, and detention center guards, and they have lost nearly everything they started out with, backpacks included. Photographs are the one possession that hold no value for others, and I have found that, as such, they are often the one possession that migrants are able to keep. They become increasingly valuable to them as the other parts of their material pasts disappear. The images respondents shared with me, faded and wrinkled when I saw them, had become their only physical connections to home. Their photographs had become their memories. Looking at them, I remembered what John Berger famously wrote on the connection between photographs and memory:

> The thrill found in a photograph comes from the onrush of memory. This is obvious when it's a picture of something we once knew. That house we lived in. Mother when young.
>
> But in another sense, we once knew everything we recognize in any photo. That's grass growing. Tiles on a roof get wet like that, don't they. Here is one of the seven ways in which bosses smile. This is a woman's shoulder, not a man's. Just the way snow melts.
>
> Memory is a strange faculty. The sharper and more isolated the stimulus memory receives, *the more it remembers*; the more comprehensive the stimulus, *the less it remembers*. This is perhaps why black-and-white photography is paradoxically more evocative than colour photography. It stimulates a faster onrush of memories because less has been given, more has been left out. (1992:192–193, emphasis added).

Because the migrants who shared their images with me had so few material possessions, the photographs they had hidden in their pockets or folded in their sweaty palms as they were smuggled across borders served as both sharp *and* isolated stimuli. The less they have, the more they remember. I draw on Douglas's argument that photo elicitation produces new kinds of information, and I take it further by considering how photographs that connect subjects to particular places (but are *not* reflective of their lived experiences) conjure a different kind of response than those that connect subjects to their pasts. In each of my visual life history sessions, I provided some general images of people or places that respondents would likely recognize—past leaders of their countries or geographic landmarks close to their homes. Next, they provided their own images of their pasts. While the former served to highlight migrants' feelings of connection to a people or a place, the latter more commonly highlighted migrants' feelings of disconnection.

Placement within larger and more anonymous social structures therefore brings a sense of belonging, while placement within familial and more intimate social groups illuminates migrants' feelings of isolation. A *National Geographic* image of the Congo River, for instance, pushed Phino to voice the connection he felt to his home country (*"I am from a beautiful country." "I am Congolese." "In the Congo, we have all the natural resources man needs to survive."*) An image of his actual home pushed him instead to voice his distance across time and space and the disconnection he felt to the place he once knew as home. (*"I've never seen this home before." "My family has grown since I left." "That big man is my little brother."*) Because the first image exists outside of his personal experience, he can assume that it remains unchanged in his absence. It was his home country, and it remains his home country. In many ways, the image serves to collapse the time and space between Phino and the place he left. The second image, a photograph included in one of his wife's letters mailed to him in Morocco, shows a home that has evolved since his departure (in large part thanks to the meager remittances that he sends). It is a home that he has never and likely will never see. It is a home that instead marks his many years of absence. Phino's reactions to these images spoke to his competing understandings of home and belonging from his place in between—the nostalgic connection he has to an imagined place that has come to represent home and the real connection he has to a previously known place that still holds his family within its four walls. His wife's photograph which he brought into our interview illustrated how both homes, real and imagined, are now foreign to him. I contend that by amending traditional photo elicitation and oral history interview techniques, they can be used in combination to assess how individuals creatively reconstruct a past and reimagine a future in new spaces of liminality. This methodology is especially useful when working with transnational populations whose material histories may be largely destroyed. The following examples walk through two visual life history sessions with Phino and a young migrant named Santigie. I explore in detail what was selectively revealed and concealed to me through narrative and image, as they constructed their stories in active rejection of their present states of suffering. What was created, I find, is both an oral history and an oral future.

Phino: A Visual Life History

Home Country: The Democratic Republic of the Congo
Destination Country: France
Current (Dis)Location: Morocco

Phino is originally from the DRC and left his home in 2004 with the goal of migrating to France by way of Morocco. He and two friends, who paid the same "camel" and started out in the same group, posed for formal portraits on the day of their departure. These photographs, pictured in Figure 5.1 below, were the first ones he showed me when we met for our visual life history session in the small apartment he now shares with seven others in a migrant-populated slum outside of Rabat. The three friends had taken turns posing in the corner of Phino's uncle's kitchen, dressed in their finest clothes—Phino in a tan jacket given to him by his uncle, matching pants he purchased at a store in Kinshasa, brown leather shoes brought home to him by a cousin working in Europe, and a striped tie that he described as "My wife's favorite. She thinks I'm a big man when I wear this tie!" The styles worn by his friends range from what I would call "business casual" to what Phino called "street glam," but the positions they chose to take for their portraits were remarkably similar: gaze confidently placed on the camera's lens, arms resting easily at their sides, left foot placed forward, as if each man's journey had already begun. The fact that, like the majority of migrants I interviewed, they chose to wear jackets and sweaters, dress shoes and ties, despite

FIGURE **5.1   A collection of "departure day" portraits of Phino and his two friends.
DRC, 2000.**
Source: *Photographs courtesy of Phino Ngiaba and copied with his permission.*

knowing that their journeys would require days spent hidden in the backs of trucks and weeks spent walking across deserts is also notable. They were dressed for the lives they hoped were awaiting them on the other side of the European border, and not for the sweltering heat, exhaustion, and brutality that their journeys north would certainly bring. The objects they chose to wear—the pen in Phino's pocket and the digital camera looped around the wrist of his friend—similarly marked the status they hoped to attain as migrants in Europe and the status they already carried with them as mobile subjects. They were dressed the part of the businessman and the tourist, the objects that completed their ensembles underscoring the important roles that words and images would continue to play in their constructions of self.

In our first session together, Phino showed me a second collection of photographs, pictured in Figure 5.2 below, that were taken at a "sending ceremony," held in honor of the departing migrants. As he remembered, "This day was important because it marked the beginning of our journeys. Our families had worked so hard to send us, and they wanted to pray for our success. It makes me sad to see their faces—to see the faces of the people who sacrificed so much so I could go to France. It makes me sad to think about how I haven't made it yet." His initial reaction pushed me to consider how it would feel to have your entire social network band together to send you on a journey that, despite your best efforts, you repeatedly failed to complete. Phino explained, "Communities spend months, sometimes years, working to finance one journey. You cannot return without at least the money to repay them." For this reason, reverse migrations—returning empty-handed to those

FIGURE 5.2 A collection of "sending ceremony" photographs from Phino's departure day. DRC, 2000.

Source: *Photographs courtesy of Phino Ngiaba and copied with his permission.*

who supported you—is rarely seen as an option for migrants, regardless of how difficult their current situation is or how unlikely their final crossing may be. When I returned to questions about Phino's second collection of photographs at a later session, he replied, "They remind me that my journey was blessed. I haven't made it to France yet, but when I look at these photographs, I know that someday I will." His later reflection reveals how the same images can be used to narrate two competing stories of migration—one of failure and one of success. They also highlight what I found to be a theme among migrants trapped in spaces of liminal settlement—the feeling of being neither here nor there, neither successful nor failed. It is a conflicted and unresolved personal narrative that they often tell.

In addition to the prized photographs from his sending ceremony, Phino has a third collection of newer photographs displayed around his one-room apartment. Some are taped over peeling paint in the "kitchen"—a hot plate and large metal pot on the floor in the corner of the room. Others are taped up in the "bedroom"—two old mattresses on the floor in the opposite corner. Phino and his roommates share the mattresses in rotating shifts and cook quietly to avoid disturbing those who are sleeping. Beside the pot there is always a large bag of rice, which is the sole ingredient in most of their daily meals. Beside the mattresses there is a small pile of clothing which includes all of the possessions shared among the eight men. Without even a hole in the wall for a window, a thick heat blankets the room night and day. Flies start buzzing at the crack of dawn, and rodents and insects scurry throughout the night. Each floor of the building has one "bathroom" shared between the multiple apartments. It is a small closet-sized room with a hole in the floor and a spigot on the wall at knee height for washing. Some days, there is a slow trickle of water; other days, there is none. When I asked Phino about the images he chose to display around his apartment, he explained that he often included a photograph in letters home to his family, so they could "imagine" his life in Morocco. Occasionally, he kept a copy of the ones he liked best for himself.

The third collection of photographs, pictured in Figure 5.3 below, are the only ones that travel south to the home he left behind, and while they allow his family to imagine what lies beyond their borders, they reveal nothing of the life that Phino is actually living. Instead, they feed into an imaginary of the other as being more desirable than the known—a notion that Phino himself described having before leaving

FIGURE 5.3 A collection of photographs Phino sent home to his family in the DRC. Morocco, dates vary.
Source: *Photographs by Phino Ngiaba and copied with his permission.*

the DRC, and a notion that he continues to hold for France, despite Morocco's failure to meet any of his expectations. Included in this collection are photographs of him standing beside a car, which is not his, and in front of some of Rabat's most popular tourist destinations, which he has never entered. When we reached the photograph of him standing outside of Mohammed V Mausoleum, he commented, "I've never visited the monument, but I had a friend take a photograph of me here." The entrance fee of 100 dirhams (approximately $10 USD) would be a significant sacrifice for Phino, who makes an average of 200 dirhams a month and goes some weeks with less than 10. "I try to spend as little as I can," he told me in an earlier interview, "so I can send some money home to my family every month. They think that if you're living abroad, you should be making lots of money. They don't understand how hard it is here. Even when I do work, there is no guarantee that I'll be paid for it." He was both embarrassed by his present living conditions and resentful of his family's inability to understand what they could not see.

Many of the photographs use one of the city's many bed and breakfasts as a backdrop, and he explained how he took them while visiting a friend who was briefly employed there. He showed me photographs of himself posing beside a portrait of a Victorian-era European woman, paging through a coffee table book on Morocco, standing beside flowering plants in the open courtyard, and leaning against weight machines in the small fitness center. When asked about the photographs taken in the kitchen of the bed and breakfast, Phino explained that he wanted his wife to see that "I am eating well. And I even have a sink to clean my dishes!" Ironically, this particular pair of images hangs above the hotplate in his own gritty apartment—a space that his family will never see. The only photographs that do not picture Phino were ones taken inside of one of the guest rooms—starched white sheets and pillowcases beneath a framed collection of African art. Did Phino's family really believe that he slept in this room, his roommates and rotating sleep schedule hidden from them? Did they really believe that his days ended with exercise on these modern machines and not with muscles aching from hard labor in the hot sun? I asked him, "Do these photographs not make your family question why you don't send more money home to them?" I had found that the issue of remittances is a sensitive one for migrants, and Phino acknowledged that yes, his family was unsatisfied with the money that he sent home to them. But he was resigned to the fact that however much or little he sent home, it would never be enough. He also knew that his family had little way to assess how much one earns from working abroad or how much daily life (especially a life as luxurious as his photographs suggest) in Morocco would cost. Before he left home, he too was operating under the assumption that "everyone abroad lives well." Interview after interview had revealed that regardless of migrants' country of origin or socioeconomic status, the life they found beyond their borders was far from their expectations. Looking through Phino's third collection of images, I found it easy to see why.

The final photograph Phino showed me was of him and a female tourist who had been staying in the bed and breakfast where his friend was employed. I asked him why this image was important to him, and he explained that she had been kind to him. Her kindness, it seemed, was illustrated through her acknowledgment of him—not as a migrant but as a human. Her willingness to engage him in conversation, to share a pot of mint tea with him, and to take a photograph with him transgressed social norms in much the same way that my own interactions with him did. The woman greeted him and his friend, asking Phino his name, where he was from, and simple questions about his life back home. "She was from London. She told me to contact her if I ever come to London. She was kind to me. She even bought a doll for my daughter in the marketplace before she left." Phino fell silent, and for the first time, I saw him cry. I had known him for more than one year, and I wondered if, in that moment, recounting this story to me, he suddenly felt how impossibly far London was for a man like him—born in the DRC and now trapped in a cycle of routine exploitation at the borders to the EU. His voice cracked, "I haven't seen my family since I left home.

My daughter is 15 years old now." This poignant moment brought about by the images that Phino shared with me in our life visual history sessions revealed the very paradox that he was living. As he clung to memories of a past and hopes for a future, the world around him had kept moving forward, leaving him trapped in between with little to his name but a doll for a daughter who had long since outgrown the world of make-believe. His wife's pregnancy had been his impetus to leave home in search of a better future for his family. "I have never known peace in my life, but I hoped that someday my child would," he said. He and his daughter's relationship exists solely through phone calls and messages exchanged via Skype, WhatsApp, and Facebook Messenger—through the letters and images he sends home to her.

The collection of photographs that Phino took in Morocco highlight what I found to be a second theme among migrants trapped in spaces of liminal settlement—the desire to continue the imaginary of what life abroad will be, even as lived experience proves otherwise. The majority of those with whom I sat down for visual life history sessions perpetuated this vision by sending home photographs of places where they did not live, cars they did not drive, and friends they did not have, often accompanied by remittances that stretched them far beyond their means. In Phino's case, the images he sends home paint a very different picture of his present state for his family, while the images he receives from those one step ahead of him on their migration journeys sustain his own belief that a different future is still awaiting him. Of the three men pictured on their day of departure and celebrated in the community's sending ceremony, Phino is the only one who remains trapped in Morocco. One is back where their journeys started, now a receiver of the images that Phino sends, and the other is in Phino's desired destination country, now sending him images of an idealized migrant experience in France. Although the bed pictured may not be the bed his friend actually sleeps in, it reveals deeper truths about expectation, aspiration, and the universally human feelings of pride and shame.

In interviews with migrants at various points on their journeys, I heard shared sentiments of sadness, loneliness, and loss. I heard a desire to return home and a recognition of the intangible social ties that are lost in migration and no longer seemed worth sacrificing. At the end of each interview, I always asked the same series of questions, one of them being, "If you knew that you would never make it to France [or insert here the migrant's desired destination country], then would you choose to return home tomorrow?" To which every interviewee re-sponded, "Yes." The present conditions offered little in exchange for all that had been lost. It was not what they had expected life abroad to be. My follow-up question was, "If you knew there were still a small chance that you would eventually make it to France, then would you choose to never again return home?" To which the answer was also consistently, "Yes." Despite the failure of Morocco to live up to expectations, there remained a strong conviction that other countries would. With only a sliver of hope that there might be a better life on the other side of the next border, they asserted again and again that they could imagine no path but the one forward (Zuluaga 2015).

Included in Phino's collections of photographs were three distinct depictions of home: the home built by remittances in the DRC, which he had never seen; the home awaiting him in Europe, which he had never seen; and the "home" in Morocco, which was never his. They illustrate that for him, home, traditionally defined as "the place where one lives," is understood only through the past and the future—through memory and imagination. The place where Phino lives in Morocco is the one home that is never pictured, the one that he refuses to claim as his own, as he works to obscure and forget his present state. His desire to continually remember a past and reimagine a future speaks to the contemporary state of transnational migration, which leaves those who have fled their countries of origin perpetually seeking the destination that was promised to them. Unable to return home and unable to find a destination better than the last, the physical and emotional dislocation of this seeking leaves individuals like Phino—even those who eventually reach European soil—forever in the unresolved status of the migrant.

Santigie: The Digitization of Visual Life History

Sending Country: Sierra Leone
Destination Country: England
Current (Dis)Location: Morocco

My second example of visual life history collection comes from a very different case study. Santigie, who left his home in Sierra Leone two years before I met him, has been alive for the same number of years that Phino has been trapped in Morocco. He had just turned 16 and had one photograph to his name. The photograph, pictured in Figure 5.4 below, was one of his few material possessions. "They took this photo of me

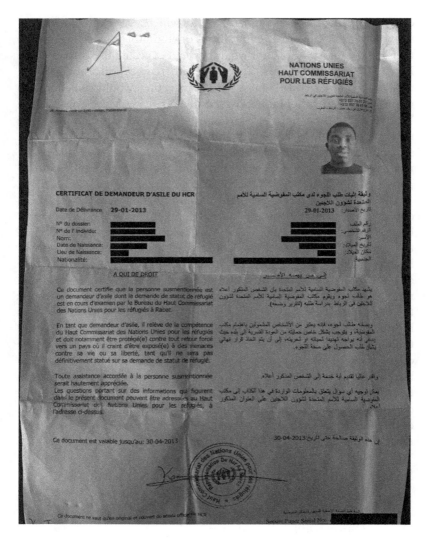

FIGURE 5.4 Santigie's UNHCR asylum application and attached photograph. Note: sensitive information has been removed.

Source: *Image copied with Santigie Achuo's permission.*

when I went to the UNHCR to ask for asylum papers," he explained in our first session as we sat together at a café in central Rabat. "I asked them if I could take it with me, because I'd never had a photo of myself before. I don't think they're supposed to give you the photos they take, but this woman was kind, so she let me take a copy of it. It'll always be special to me because it's my first one. Someday, when I'm a big man, I'll probably laugh at this old photo."

I met Santigie through my work with the *Centre des Droits de Migrants* (CDM), one of Morocco's largest migrant-aid organizations. He came in seeking advice on how to apply for asylum, and I explained to him that given the lack of social services available to even those with refugee status in Morocco and the pervasive abuse by local authorities, many choose not to apply for asylum until they reach a country where they will be able to rebuild their lives. After this standard warning, I directed him to the UN Refugee Agency (UNHCR), where he would be able to pick up an asylum application and asked him to bring it back to CDM, where I would help him fill it out. From there, it would be his decision whether to file it or carry the completed application in his pocket in hopes that he would someday be able to file it on foreign soil.

Most respondents preferred to schedule our visual life history sessions in the privacy of their own apartments, but when I offered Santigie the options available to us (including my home, his home, the desolate university library, or a local café), he picked the café. He explained that his roommates, who took shifts sleeping in their crowded one-room apartment much like at Phino's, might be disturbed by our conversation. He also enjoyed the chance to eat a real meal. Taking me up on my "order anything you like" offer, Santigie devoured an astonishing amount of food in each of our many sessions together—ordering Coca-Cola, beef brochettes, and French fries, and happily eating the second plates I requested when he was done with his first ones. I tried my best to shield him from the rude remarks from waiters and the stares we always received from surrounding tables. It embarrassed me when we often had to walk to three or four cafés before finding one that would agree to seat us. But none of this came as a surprise to him. Santigie reassured me that this was "normal," as I apologized for the management's behavior, and I realized that he felt just as embarrassed for me, knowing the assumptions others made about what kind of a woman would be eating with a "*harraga.*"

In our first session together, I asked Santigie what he brought with him when he left home, knowing that he did not have any photographs to his name but might have other objects to propel his emotional reflection on the steps of his journey. I soon discovered that, like many other teenaged boys, Santigie considers his phone to be his single most prized possession, and his phone is full of images. He was happy to show me his collection of digital photographs—images of his favorite soccer team and favorite female celebrities, familiar images of Messi and Ronaldo, Beyoncé and Rihanna—which told a story not about where he came from, but where he was hoping to go. For the youngest generation of migrants, digital culture often takes the place of material culture, and Santigie's phone and Facebook profile are rich archives of data to be mined. His profile, a still frame of which is pictured in Figure 5.5 below, is not only a compilation of his "favorites," but a collection of images he is actively curating to illustrate his imagined future for the world. Walking through the collection with him one photograph at a time filled in holes in his narrative that traditional interview techniques alone had failed to access.

The first theme to emerge was Santigie's desire for triumph. Scanning through his images, I saw material goods that he did not own but desired, and I saw images not of him but of others whom he aspired to be like, in large part because of the buying power they had attained. His Facebook profile is filled with images of sports heroes, entertainment stars, African Americans who have long been idealized by popular media for the stories of triumph they represent—a rise from the underbelly of social and economic marginalization to the courts and stages where they perform their success for others to see. This narrative of "zero to hero" is not unlike the narrative that many migrants ascribe to themselves, and like them, Santigie is driven by his desire to consume the goods that represent "the West"—both materially and ideologically. He explained that reaching London would be his own performance of success. "Everyone's got a good job there, a nice place to live, a nice car to drive, everything you could ever want. They're living big." His narrative perpetuates the ideal of Europe as a land of endless opportunity. But unlike Phino, whose narrative is fueled by the images of those further along the path to "success" than he was and whose own images fuel the desires of those left behind, Santigie's narrative exists in an undefined virtual space. It is driven more by the promises of popular media than by the journeys of other migrants who have traveled before him.

The second theme to emerge from Santigie's digital archives was a history of tribulation. There are a select number of photographs on his profile that tell stories of discrimination and abuse—a narrative true to his lived experience at home, on the migratory route, and in his present state in Morocco. Included are an image of a black man in shackles, reminiscent of the long tradition of slavery across the region, and a cartoon animal proclaiming, "*Je n'ai pas le temps de détester les gens qui*

FIGURE 5.5 Santigie's Facebook profile page. Note: sensitive information has been removed.
Source: *Image copied with Santigie Achuo's permission.*

me détestent, car je suis trop occupé à aimer ceux qui m'aiment," which
Santigie translated as meaning, "Don't worry about your haters, worry
about your lovers." His reflections highlighted a fundamental connection between his own feelings of tribulation and his awaited triumph.
He explained, "No one wants to be here [in Morocco], where they treat
us like dogs, but you've got to lose before you win."

Phino's visual life history revealed how his present is intrinsically
tied to his past—he is committed to repaying the community that had
made his journey possible, to lifting his family from poverty, and to reuniting with his wife and daughter. Santigie's visual life history revealed

how his present is instead tied to his aspirations for the future. He lost both of his parents at a young age and claimed, "There was no one at home to notice when I left." His narrative is the one that first led me to question if, among some migrant groups, researchers should begin thinking about the collection of "oral futures," or imaginaries of what lies ahead, as equally important as "oral histories," or memories of what was left behind. In the case of Santigie and others who make up the youngest generation of migrants trapped in Morocco, it is these visualizations of the lives yet to be lived, the places yet to be seen, and the people they are yet to become that are most defining of their journeys. "Money," Santigie said to me in one of our final sessions, "I think it's like wings. Someday when I have enough, I'm going to fly." While the eight miles that separate Morocco from Spain cannot be flown by those who lack the papers to travel, for Phino and Santigie alike, it remains a journey full of promise and expectation.

Mapping Migrants' (Dis)Location

Along with applying new methods to access the lived experience of displacement by incorporating visual culture into narrative-driven analysis, I encourage researchers to question how extended periods of displacement are pushing migrants to continually reconceptualize what space, mobility, and detention mean to them. Reaching across disciplinary boundaries in search of better ways to visually represent migrants' experiences of liminality at Europe's borders, I discovered the work of Moroccan-born artist and migrant Bouchra Khalili. Born in Casablanca, Khalili now calls Paris home and works in the Mediterranean, where she collects the narratives of migrants and transforms their journeys into visual representations of transnationalism. In interviews, she explains how she travels to places with concentrated migrant populations (Marseilles, Istanbul, Malaga) and awaits a natural interaction with one of the many migrants settled there—a moment when an outstretched hand begs for change on the corner or a stranger asks her for directions. Her *Mapping Journey* film series and accompanying screenprints map the migratory trajectories of these men and women whom she happens to meet. After each "chance encounter," Khalili asks the migrants if they can trace the route by which they arrived at their current location. She pulls out a paper map and pen, steadying her camera's eye on their hands as they begin. Their journeys never follow a straight line from point A to point B. Rather, they underscore the increasingly convoluted routes that contemporary migrations are taking.

The contorted lines take center stage in each of Khalili's short films, as the audience never sees more than the hands of the men and women. Yet, the lack of visual stimulation allows the dialectical qualities of each voice to rise, hinting at who the narrator may be. Khalili does not ask about the push or pull factors driving their migrations, but they find it difficult to trace their journeys without noting how the various legs involved years spent working under exploitative conditions to save money, years spent waiting on legal (or forged) paperwork to pass the next checkpoint, and repeated experiences of deportation, imprisonment, and failed attempts at movement—each one accompanied by extortion, abuse, and humiliation.

One such journey is described by a middle-aged man named Younes, who began with a move from his small town in rural Morocco to the bustling city of Tangier. Jagged lines then connect his next move from Tangier to the southern coast of Spain—Algeciras, Marbella, Malaga, Nerja, Almunecar, Almeria. This series of dots indicates stops of varying lengths in Younes's journey—some being no more than a few days, others being many months spent washing dishes in the back of the house at touristy restaurants in order to support his next move. Many of the towns along Spain's southern coast rely on the exploitable labor of passing migrants, and the migrants, knowing their own dispensability, have come to expect that hours will routinely be rounded down, tips will be pocketed by management, and questions will cost them their jobs. In Madrid, networks of friends or family make it slightly easier for Moroccan migrants like Younes to find work, but he found that the exploitative working conditions (especially in the service industry, where the majority of migrants are employed) are not much improved. After a few years in Madrid, Younes continued his journey northward, more jagged lines connecting a series of dots through France to Paris. "From Barcelona," he explains, "we took a small road to avoid the police at the border." In addition to being drawn by the promise of greater economic opportunities in new cities, the men and women in Khalili's short films recount the measures taken to hide their movement from place to place. Primary border crossings are always avoided in favor of less traveled and further-flung points on the map. From Paris, Younes was eventually pulled farther north to Belgium and then the Netherlands, before traveling south again toward the promise of work in Italy's construction industry. Rome is now the place that he calls "home," although at the beginning of his journey, he never could have imagined the route his migration would take or the country where it would end.

While geography itself can make it nearly impossible to travel directly from point A to point B (air travel being an excluded option for the majority of migrants), political borders have further complicated human travel for millennia, molding how and when humans can experience physical spaces. The accompanying screen-printed series, *Constellations,* may at first seem secondary to Khalili's short films, but it represents the sense of emotional and geographical detachment that accompany migrants' journeys. A sampling of this series is pictured in Figure 5.6 below. By removing the political boundaries of nations, each screen-print presents viewers with curious lines indicating a geography distorted by long histories of territorial disputes, colonial legacies, and contested political agreements.

Khalili's work succeeds in creating visually stunning, yet simple, depictions of an increasingly complex global phenomenon without losing the nuance of migration as a diverse human experience. But even in her innovative visual scholarship, she perpetuates a myth of migration as a finite journey from point A to point B—albeit along convoluted lines and punctuated with many unanticipated stops along the way. She collected the narratives of the privileged few who survived their final crossings, feet planted within the boundaries of the EU. Working instead with migrants in Morocco, I collected the narratives of those

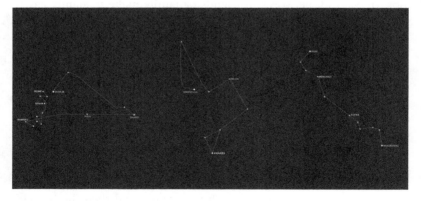

FIGURE **5.6** *Constellations* **by Bouchra Khalili.**
Source: *Image courtesy of the artist.*

whose homes were still disappearing points on the map, far south and far north of where they stood. My research with those who consider their current points to be places of "temporary" settlement, despite the duration of their time in Morocco, suggests that migration is, much like De Genova states, a never-ending process (2005). Even in the fortunate (and rare) cases in which one reaches the desired destination and begins the process of rebuilding one's life, the constant threat of deportation looms for undocumented migrants. In many cases, there also arises a desire to continue moving in hopes of finding greater opportunity— the elusive new home that was promised to them when their journeys began. The idealized images of home that are perpetuated through the narratives and images of migrants like Phino are rarely met in reality, and so the idealization continues. *Paris is not what I hoped it would be. But Lyon—Lyon will be a land of opportunity*!

A sense of dislocation arises with the first step in a migrant's journey and that, as many explained to me, remains a constant state of being from the first step onwards. Just as the migrant never feels entirely a part of the destination country or the spaces of temporary settlement that are found along the way, they will never again feel "at home" in their countries of origin. The financial and social challenges of return migrations aside, the home they left is no longer there to greet them. In Phino's case, a new home had been built and new social ties established. His role of father had been subsumed by his brother, with whom his daughter shares her daily worries and joys. Over the course of his long absence, his wife, his siblings, and his closest friends have all found ways to replace his physical and emotional presence in their lives. "Home," he said simply, "it has changed." In Santigie's case, the loss of home was his impetus for movement. His physical home and the relationships that brought meaning to it were destroyed with the loss of his parents. "My home was already gone when I crossed the border," he explained. "I left to find a new one." Memories of homes lost and imagined remain a driving force for both, propelling Santigie's dream to rebuild his sense of belonging in a new place and Phino's dream to return a "big man" to the place that was built in his absence.

Notes

1. *Hersha* is a Moroccan bread made with cornmeal, eggs, sugar, salt, and animal fat. It is dense, filling, and often described to me as "the worker's bread" because it provides enough sustenance to complete long hours of physically demanding work.

2. *Rabati* is a colloquial term used to demarcate those born in Rabat from those who move to the city. It can be used to elevate *Rabatis* from other Moroccans in conversation, as Rabat is considered by many who were born there to be the epicenter of intellectual life, and to produce the most educated and elite population of Moroccans. However, any *Fèsi* or *Marrakechi* would contend otherwise.

3. The border controls between Morocco and Algeria have increased significantly since the time that Phino crossed. Migrants traversing this route in more recent years claim that the difficulty of crossing the Moroccan-Algerian border is comparable only to the difficulty of crossing the borders surrounding Morocco's Spanish enclaves. Both are surrounded by trenches and multiple rings of razor-wire fences, and they are under constant surveillance by armed military forces.

CHAPTER 6

"Le Peril Noir": The Racialization of Political Status

> *Is Morocco not a part of Africa? But here, I am the African, and here, being the African is a bad thing. In Morocco, Africa is associated with sex, with AIDS, with alcohol, with drugs, with a loosening of traditional values and a twisting of Islamic traditions. Here, I am associated with all of these negative things. I have never heard anyone ask, what can a migrant contribute to my country? No one imagines that I might have anything positive to add.*
>
> —OUSMANE, M, 22, Senegalese, exchange student
>
> ....

Introductory Case Study: The Senegalese Exchange

As the population of migrants in North Africa continues to grow, Moroccan media has been addressing the new challenges this population brings, linking it the "mounting racism of Moroccan nationals" (*L'Economiste*), the "spread of disease, drugs, and prostitution" (*Telquel*), and a "growing humanitarian crisis concurrently produced and ignored by the EU" (*Al Massae*). But as early as 2012, the popular Moroccan news magazine, *Maroc Hebdo*, drew international criticism when it ran a cover story titled *"Le Peril Noir,"* along with the face of a young black man and assumed migrant, pictured below in Figure 6.1.

Ousmane had been living in Rabat for four years when I met him, but he still called Dakar home and returned there to visit his friends and family when his classes were on break. Of course, not all migrants travel the same route to Morocco, and not all imagine boarding rubber boats or scaling razor-wire fences when they arrive. Morocco is also home to a small but significant population of students who migrate from

FIGURE **6.1** *"Le Peril Noir"* **magazine cover.**
Source: *MarocHebdo archives.*

Senegal and other African countries under a university exchange program every year. Like Ousmane, they tend to come from upper-class families and communities in their home countries. Rabat's "University Village" was developed in the 1980s when the United Nations Educational, Scientific, and Cultural Organization (UNESCO) created the first university exchange program for African students in Africa. The program's current director explained to me how they choose Morocco because it was seen as both politically stable and in need of financial aid (lacking in oil reserves) at the time. Moroccan universities, still in a state of disrepair following the colonial period, were reconstructed with

UNESCO funds over the following decade. Although UNESCO failed to create similar programs in other African nations, as was originally promised, and eventually cut all funds to Morocco's African Exchange Program, King Mohammed VI has maintained it. Morocco continues to offer scholarships to a large number of Senegalese students in exchange for generous taxation and importation policies, and has even expanded the program to include students from other African nations and former French colonies in the Caribbean in recent years. This makes "The Village," as the students call it, a unique space, home to a diverse population marked by their racial minority and upper-class status. My engagement with this population helped me to disentangle how factors of race and class distinctly and simultaneously impact the experiences of all foreigners—exchange students and migrant laborers, documented and undocumented—in Morocco.

In theory, the open borders between Senegal and Morocco[1] should make travel between the two countries easy for all Senegalese with the funds to purchase airfare. However, Ousmane's experience illustrates that it is his student ID and what I came to identify as a particular set of "class markers," not his Senegalese passport, that facilitate the ease of his travel back and forth. It did not take him long to realize that in Morocco, his race is linked to presumed economic marginalization and political vulnerability in the public sphere, and as is true for other documented foreign nationals, it is critical that Ousmane's public image be carefully constructed. Foreigners who are marked by their racial minority status, whether they are African, European, or American, can work to disassociate themselves from Morocco's emergent class of migrant laborers through a performance of their status as educated. However, Ousmane found that his performance was not successful in distancing him from migrants unless he could use speech, dress, and bodily comportment to be read as a European or American foreigner. As he explained to me, it is only within the walls of The Village that he feels comfortable "being African" in Morocco.

The Village is located just outside of *centre ville*, along the rail line of Rabat's newly completely tram. I was introduced to it by a Moroccan friend who had taken classes with Senegalese exchange students during his undergraduate years and arranged an interview for me with a current student who was studying for his baccalaureate in Engineering. I knew nothing about the man I was going to meet except that his name was Ousmane, he was Senegalese, and he had family members living in the United States. The Village reminds me more of military barracks than a safe haven, surrounded on all sides by high concrete walls once painted white, but now cracking and covered with graffiti. At the entrance is a small house with uniformed officers inside. On my first visit, I found two officers, who were absorbed in the match playing out on the small television screen in front of them. In order to understand the interrogation that ensued, it is important first to understand the kind of privilege that is more commonly granted to white foreigners in Morocco. There were multiple times when protocol was waived in place of courtesy for me—times when I was waived through security checks at airports or welcomed into the offices of governmental officials with little questioning. This is not to discount the constant barrage of street harassment and police aggressions that also structured my experiences in Morocco. It is simply to acknowledge that in North Africa, as in the rest of the world, whiteness equals privilege. The list of privileges afforded is long, and in some cases, the lines between privileging a particular racial identity and pursuing a particular gendered identity become blurred. Suffice it to say that while I may have anticipated a denigrating sexual comment when approaching the two officers that afternoon, I did not anticipate their level of hostility.

Again and again, I was asked about the purpose of my visit. The two men were clearly dissatisfied with my explanation that I had an interview scheduled with a student who was living in The Village. They made copies of the identification card I provided, wrote my name in their book, and took my photograph for their records. They needed to search me before I could enter. They laughed as they touched me, pushed me against the wall, and pulled my clothes aside. "Salope,"[2] they called me in neither their native language nor mine. I was told that Ousmane would be called down, not to meet me, but for "further questioning." I sat for hours on the sidewalk outside of the University Village gates, sweat pooling in the sweltering sun, as I waited for the officers to finish their interrogation. I was never granted access to the grounds that day, but six hours after our scheduled interview time, Ousmane was finally released to speak to me on the street outside. I was notified that my name and photograph had been added to the University's file of "restricted visitors" (which Ousmane later translated to mean "suspects"). The other officers needed to know who was and was not allowed inside of the gates.

"No one visits us here," he began in his native language of French. "None of us have family in Morocco. We don't have any friends who don't live here [in The Village] with us. They think it's only drug dealers and prostitutes who would visit us. I guess you don't look like a drug dealer." While Ousmane was only trying to lighten the tension that the officers on duty had created, his comment echoed what I heard frequently in my interviews with Moroccans—the familiar cry against *"drugs and prostitution!"* Which rose up whenever the subject of migration was broached. As I came to know Ousmane and his fellow exchange students better, it was clear to me that the concern of university officials is a reflection of societal-level xenophobia and is not motivated by any past incidents with Rabat's Senegalese student population. They are a studious, highly motivated, and socially isolated group.

> *I want to go to Europe to finish my studies. With a degree from Europe, you have the chance to find a good job—in Europe or even in America. And if you don't succeed at finding a good job abroad, then at least you can return home and find something good. You can't find a good job abroad with a degree from Morocco, and even in my country, it's not worth too much. But I'm not crazy. I know it will be hard, and if I can't find a job in Europe, then eventually I'll return home.*
>
> *—Ousmane*

Ousmane acknowledged how the simple fact of having been in Europe, even if he is unable to earn a degree or find a job there, will grant him a higher status on the job market in his home country. His narrative highlights the primary distinction between foreigners living in Morocco for the duration of their student exchange programs and those trapped in Morocco for undefined periods of time. The difference is in the imagined futures they hold for themselves. Like the tens of thousands of others who cross through Morocco en route to Europe every year, all of the exchange students I spoke with dreamed of someday finding work on European soil. "We all dream of finding a good job in France or England or Germany," Ousmane's roommate, also from Senegal, explained. "No one wants to stay here. In Morocco, you'll always be black. You'll always be stuck at the bottom of the ladder. In my country, at least I have the chance to move up through hard work." While Ousmane and his roommate's desires to leave Morocco in search of social and economic mobility echo those of Morocco's migrant laborers, Ousmane's eventual return to Senegal is not contingent on his success. He is aware of the expectations his family holds for him, but upper-class migrants like him do not carry the memory of their families, or entire communities, sacrificing to make their journeys possible. "My parents want to tell their neighbors that I live in Europe, that I have a good job, that I drive a nice car. They want this because it gives them pride. They don't need this because it puts food on their table," Ousmane explains. His future success (or failure) will be weighed for the social value it holds—for its ability to uplift his family's standing in the community—but he knows he will never carry the weight of physically lifting his family from poverty like so many others do. He will try to reach Europe, and if he fails, he will return home empty-handed. This is a luxury not afforded to all. The experience of Morocco as an island or a holding cell is most salient for those whose footsteps cannot be retraced until they have the debts that they owe in hand.

In Ousame's case, an expansion in the realm of possible futures is linked not to his status as documented—and therefore legally free to move—but rather to his class, and his narrative reveals how, in most cases, the two are intertwined. Ousmane grew up in a "nice home," he and his brothers attended "good private schools," and his family "never worried over change." In fact, he said it was not until he moved to Morocco and saw the communities of West African migrants settled throughout the country that he truly appreciated the depth of poverty that exists in Senegal. That part of Senegal had been hidden from him. His mother and father spent the majority of his childhood years living in New York, where his uncle ran a small car rental company. His father worked for the family business, and his mother held a number of odd jobs, including working as an administrative assistant in the local elementary school. Ousmane and his brother stayed in Senegal with his grandparents. After retirement, his parents were eager to return home to them. They used most of the money they had saved working in the United States to buy an apartment in Dakar, where they now live with Ousmane's brothers and grandparents. The remainder of the money they had saved was used to send Ousmane, their eldest son, north. Although the Moroccan university exchange program does not hold the same prestige of studying in Europe, it is considered one step closer. Much like the communities that band together to send migrants like Phino through Morocco en route to Europe, Senegalese families participate in this program with the hopes that it will provide a launching pad into European universities.

Ousmane acknowledged that if he failed to reach Europe, his Moroccan degree would hold little social value in Dakar. Yet his attempt to migrate would reaffirm his upper-class standing. "The fact that I came to Morocco, that I tried my best, whether I end up finding work in Europe or not, this is an expected step." Across West Africa, attempted migration to Europe had become an expected rite of passage for all young men, especially first-born sons who have the means to search for greater social and economic mobility abroad. While I often sensed that Ousmane was underplaying the shame that would accompany his return migration, the fact that he even spoke of this kind of "failure" as a possibility set him apart from the other young men I interviewed. He saw Europe not as a land of boundless opportunity, but as a place where earning a degree and finding work would be challenging, and his imagined future did not begin and end on European soil. There remained in his imaginary the space for an alternative trajectory that led home, and the very imagining of this alternative future distinguished him from Morocco's larger class of migrants. It is only among those whose chances of "making it" abroad are slimmest that there is no other future envisioned.

University Village: A Space for Here and Now

I returned to University Village several times in the months following my first meeting with Ousmane to continue my conversations with him and other students. On later visits, I was finally granted access by a guard who was on duty alone. He asked me a few questions, I showed him my passport, and he wrote my name in his book without looking over the list of "restricted" visitors. Inside The Village is a large, open courtyard surrounded by dormitory buildings four stories high. There are six dormitories in total, each marked with a letter above the entry door. Ousmane explained that Buildings A and B are female dormitories, C and D are male, and E is reserved for students from the Caribbean. The courtyard that links them is a dusty patch of land with concrete benches and a cracked concrete slab. A basketball goal with the netting torn off sits at one end of the slab, and at the other is a narrow one-story building that serves as the cafeteria and recreational room. I arrived early one evening, and the "house," as the students call it, was bustling with life. In one corner of the room is the "cafeteria," which is no more than a miniature refrigerator, an old microwave, and a pair of vending machines selling Coca-Cola brand drinks and prepackaged snack foods.

Sandwiches are for sale at lunchtime, but most of the students choose to eat in their rooms, where many have their own mini refrigerators and hot-plates. In the opposite corner of the room, there was a group of students seated around the television screen—piled onto two sofas and overflowing onto the floor below. They were laughing and cheering as a match played out on the screen.

It was not until this moment that I recognized the complete lack of leisure in my other spaces of observation throughout Morocco—in the apartments and marketplaces, the detention centers and forest camps where most migrants' lives were playing out. In many ways, this group was not unlike the other population with whom I spent the majority of my days. Both were young, male-dominated groups of mostly West and Central Africans who viewed Morocco as no more than a temporary home. But here, within the walls of University Village, I recognized the sunken cheeks and deflated voices that had become so familiar to me. I recognized them in their absence. Here, young men shouted at the television screen, many of them wearing the jerseys of the players they admired most. They showed off their skills on the basketball court outside, smiling at the young women who watched. They ate the *akara* and banana fritters the women prepared in their rooms. They all sang along to the music playing through their cell phone speakers and danced. The striking difference between this space and the spaces that confine the lives of Morocco's undocumented migrants is how it allows for shouting and playing, for flirting and dancing, for eating and enjoying. It is a space that permits them to be seen and heard. It is a present-tense space, concerned with neither the past nor the future. They were young college students, and for a moment, they appeared to be just that.

Students like Ousmane argued that their embodied experiences of marginalization in Morocco are even more difficult than those of undocumented migrants because they are moving from elite positions in their home countries. "We're not accustomed to this kind of abuse," he said, as a group of younger Moroccan boys held their noses and shouted racial slurs in his wake. Phino would later counter Ousmane's assertion, as he talked about the experiences of lower-income migrant laborers like himself. He argued that while they may be more accustomed to social marginalization, they are weighed down by a constant fear of returning home empty-handed to the communities that supported them—or never returning home at all. "My brothers with deep pockets don't know how this feels," he said. Yet my engagement with both communities revealed that students like Ousmane and migrants like Phino, who come from drastically different class backgrounds, have more in common than they may imagine. Their experience of marginalization runs parallel in Morocco, where they are grouped together under the common category of "African." Moreover, although one may have deeper pockets than the other, they tend to come from similarly privileged social positions. Migrants like Phino have been chosen by their communities as the most likely to succeed abroad, and despite being from lower-income families, they are held in high social regard. Contrary to what antimigrant sentiment in the media would have you believe, Europe is not being flooded with all of Africa's "fighting-age men." Instead, Europe has Africa's best and brightest at its doorstep—and all too often, Africa is losing their best and brightest on their journeys toward uncertain futures there. Ousmane's friend, Moussa, explained that Morocco is best seen as a bridge. It is not a home, temporary or permanent, but a bridge to where they want to be.

> *Those people who tell you that they don't want to go home because life is better in Morocco, they're only telling you part of the story. It's not that life is better. It's that they're closer to their dream. I know how it is to work hard in your country and think you have it good—you eat, you sleep, you enjoy your family. But as you grow, you start to see those who left for Europe coming home with cars, coming home to build big houses, and you start to realize that no matter how hard you work in your country, you will never have a car, you will never buy a house. This dream of leaving for Europe starts to burn in your heart, and once it does, it will never burn out. So you leave your good life behind for a dream. You say you will make it to Europe, even if it means dying. This dream becomes worth dying for. You will spend your whole life in Morocco if you have to, because it is one step closer to your dream. No one chooses Morocco. It is only a bridge to where we want to be.*
>
> —Moussa, M, 22, Côte D'Ivorian, exchange student

New Racisms on the Rise

One of Morocco's leading experts on migration, sociologist Mohammed Boudoudou, has written extensively on how new migration patterns can impact a county's existing structures of social stratification (2004, 2012).

In one of our many conversations, he took my questions about how the class markers carried by students like Ousmane or laborers like Phino might impact the frequency and intensity of discrimination against them in a new direction. "We could ask the same thing about the Moroccans who are doing the discriminating because their education [and class] also play a role!" Boudoudou's research has revealed that the more educated or the higher class a Moroccan individual is (the two being related for the purposes of his argument), the higher their degree of acceptance to change will be. In our conversations, we expanded this notion of change to include the new patterns of migration and a growing migrant population in cities like Rabat. "Certainly, there's a class effect in Morocco, where we see that lower and middle class Moroccans are the most prejudiced against Africans, and this prejudice exists regardless of the Africans' socio-economic status. If you're black, it doesn't matter if you're educated or uneducated, rich or poor" (M. Boudoudou, personal communication, 2018). Bringing my ethnographic lens into focus, I agreed that I had observed how the population he deemed both "highly educated" and "high class" was the most open to legal reformations that would grant migrants (especially minors) trapped in Morocco greater access to basic social services. Within this population, there is a larger awareness of international human rights law. And among the university students, professors, and other academic "elites" I knew, there was a desire to elevate Morocco's standing by supporting the mandates of this international law. "This is our chance to show the world that Muslims aren't all bad. We can lead the way in addressing the migrant and refugee crisis humanely," suggested one of Boudoudou's students in a class discussion. However, I did not find the same level of support for the principles of international, or arguably "Western," law among less progressive circles of educated and socioeconomically elite Moroccans. While there is a clear correlation between education and class, the correlation cannot always be extended to political persuasion. In my observations, a low degree of racism toward migrants was better predicted by the combination of class standing (and presumed level of education) and progressive politics than by class and education alone.

Boudoudou made a second point that I later challenged, urging him to draw a distinction between racist ideologies and "everyday" acts of racism. Over my years of research, he and I had become friends, and I started helping his twin sons prepare for their college entrance exams on the weekends when I was in Rabat. Both were 18 years old, bright, and dreamed of attending university in the United States. In our time together, I was welcomed into a Morocco that even after eight years was still foreign to me. Their Morocco was manicured, air-conditioned, and isolated. I could not believe they had spent their entire lives in Rabat and never once set foot in the main marketplace, where the majority of the migrants I knew hawked goods and the majority of the Moroccans I knew bought their daily food. They could not believe I had. I remembered Boudoudou once telling me a story about how the boys had been "punished" by having to take a public bus to school in the morning when they were younger and how they had come home that afternoon to recount the horrors of it. "We were packed in so tightly we could hardly breathe!" they had told their father. I remember their faces when they discovered that I took that same bus to our study sessions together every week and that I traveled to Morocco's eastern border with Algeria and back by bus many times. Each *banlieue,* including the upper-class neighborhood of Hay Riad where Boudoudou and his family live, gives access to distinct experiences of work, school, and leisure. The experiences of his sons illustrated how class molds Moroccans' interactions with public space. I argued to Boudoudou that simply because those in higher-class positions are significantly less likely to have daily interactions with racial minorities of migrant or even citizen status, we cannot assume that their "everyday" acts of racism would be any different if they did.

Working-class Moroccans like my friend Hicham frequently made comments that revealed their proximity to and different history of experience with Morocco's growing migrant class. Hicham is significantly more likely to have daily interactions with migrants—on the buses he rides to work, on the streets when he walks back to his home, and in the marketplace where they sell the goods he buys. For him, this population represents a different kind of threat. While upper-class Moroccans buy private cars and gated homes to protect themselves against the physical dangers they fear, Hicham argues that migrants pose a greater threat to working-class men like him. Similar anxieties were expressed to me in interviews with Moroccans in the marketplace: "Africans will work for nothing." "Africans are stronger than Moroccans." "Africans will take pennies for the work I do." With the national unemployment rate hovering around 25 percent in Morocco, the fear is two-fold—one, migrants will drive down the wages of hourly labor, making already undesirable jobs even more undesirable, and two, migrants will soon monopolize the day labor market altogether. Counter to Boudoudou's hypothesis, a low degree of racism toward migrants was best predicted by the combination of class standing and the daily interactions presumed by one's standing in the social hierarchy.

The Language of Difference

Anthropological studies of social inclusion and exclusion have long centered on racial and ethnic identities. Although the two are commonly conflated in practice and analysis, it has been argued that racial constructs alone are "based on biological features that are facts of birth," and, unlike ethnicities, they are mutually exclusive (Williams 1989: 425). "Race-making" is a process of social stratification, and like others, it is founded on the ascription of "moral, social, symbolic, and intellectual characteristics to real or manufactured phenotypical features" (Stanfield 2011: 161). This ascription justifies the institutional and societal dominance of one group over another. Racism, as the generator of race-making from one generation to the next, transmits the ideologies and practices that lead to stratification along otherwise arbitrary lines of physical difference. Race, though constructed, becomes real in its tangible effects across individual lives. Racist ideologies transmitted through everyday processes of socialization across generations impact major life decisions about everything from education, housing, and healthcare to work opportunities, partner selection, and family planning, shaping the structures of power, authority, and prestige in a society. Because border regions bring together diverse groups of individuals, they serve as a primary site for observing the creation and proliferation of new racisms.

Only recently has political identity become another key dimension in understanding social stratification, leading me to question how studies of race and ethnicity inform what we are beginning to understand about citizenship and "illegality." My interest was not only in the legal and social construction of new categories of differentiation—citizen and migrant, legal and "illegal"—but in their embodiment. I know the construction of new legal categories allows society to legitimize new forms of difference. What I sought to examine was how subjects are embodying, evading, and manipulating these categories on an individual level. Yet before political marginalization is experienced in the everyday, there must first be language to describe it.

Representation is an essential part of the process through which race is socially constructed and communicated between members of a social group. In his seminal research on the subject, sociologist Stuart Hall stresses the importance of language—or representative signs and images—in understanding the construction of racial identities (1997, 2000). Like related semiotic and discursive approaches (de Saussure 1916; Foucault 1980), Hall's constructionist approach relies on viewing representation—or the way humans use language to give meaning to the concepts in our minds—as a two-part process (1997). First, there is the internal system through which all objects, individuals, and events are correlated with a set of images we carry around in our minds, such as the image of "a chair," the image of "my friend's wedding ceremony," or the image of "my father." Second, there is the external system of language through which all of our internal images are correlated with a set of words that give similar meaning to similar images within a cultural group.

You and I might picture a different "chair" when we read the word, but we are both likely to imagine an object with four legs and a seat, regardless of its exact color, size, or style. Although the images brought to the forefront of your mind when reading the words "wedding" or "father" are specific to your own experience, you are familiar enough with my experience to generate images in response to my words. You could not picture *my* friend's wedding ceremony, but the words likely conjured similar, even clichéd, images of women in white dresses and colorful floral bouquets. You could not picture *my* father, but you likely pictured an older male. Depending on your degree of familiarity with my family history, you may have even pictured an older male with olive skin, black hair, and Mediterranean features. Those who know me more intimately may have an image of my father that comes to mind. This is the internal system at work. The external system provides the words that give meaning to these images. The ability to share common under-standings of the connections between images and words—internal and external systems—reveals the degree of connection between speakers. Are the speakers friends, acquaintances, members of the same cultural group, or citizens of the same country from different cultural groups? For some cultural groups, picturing a "father" may generate words like "family" and "love," while for others this picture may generate words like "discipline" and "fear" or "absence" and "anger." These words place individuals on multiple scales of belonging, revealing where they stand in relation to one another and to the dominant system of language. The two-part process of representation serves as the critical link between objects, concepts, and signs, which leads to the production of meaning in language. It also explains why researchers have found that migrants moving between linguistic systems feel the most significant "cultural impact," regardless of the actual distance traveled (Manning 2005).

In the same way that the word "father" carries multiple meanings across linguistic systems, words marking racial, ethnic, and gendered identities are distinct to the cultural contexts in which they are created and used. The words "black" and "Muslim," for example, connote a different set of meanings in rural America than they do in urban Morocco. This presents a unique set of challenges to transnational subjects, as they are forced to negotiate the different meanings of the identity markers they carry as they move across borders and between different cultural groups and linguistic traditions. One young migrant from Nigeria explained that he moved from a place where "everyone was like me," or where being black and Christian made him part of the majority, to a place where "everyone assumes I'm a Muslim migrant." In the context of Morocco, his race marked him as being outside of the majority cultural group. It made his political state of vulnerability visible and marked him as part of a religious group that he did not identify with internally. While it may be assumed that assimilation into the majority religious group would better insulate some racial minorities from racism, there exists a strict delineation between Moroccan-born and foreign-born Muslims in the neighborhoods that I called home.

Some Muslim migrants explained how they chose to assimilate into Morocco's minority Christian population after feeling unwelcome in their neighborhood mosques, although it is unclear what role the aid provided to migrants through European, often Christian, organizations, might play in this decision. In other cases, migrant women who identified as Christian explained their decision to adopt traditional Muslim forms of dress in public. They all agreed that wearing headscarves had diminished some of the verbal street harassment they were subjected to on a daily basis in Morocco, but they also pointed out how the strategy was more effective for those with lighter skin. One young woman from Nigeria elaborated on the distinction she made between performing and accepting a religion. "Wearing a *hijab* doesn't make me a Muslim," she said. "It makes me a woman who wants to walk down the street in peace. When I'm in the privacy of my apartment, I practice what I am."

Some Moroccans suggested to me that this tactic could be motivated by a desire to receive aid from Muslim organizations, but I have not observed anything that would support this. Instead, I found that the motivation behind migrants' decisions to publicly perform a religion other than the one they privately practice is connected to their agency.

Much like anthropologist Saba Mahmood whose work pushed scholars of Islam to consider the act of veiling as an act of liberation—an act that gives women the power to assert their piety—I began to view migrants' acts as expressions of agency dislodged from resistance (2004).[3] The decision of Muslim migrants to worship privately, given the lack of acceptance in community mosques, can be seen as an assertion of their piety rather than a lessening of it. The decision that some non-Muslim women make to publicly perform piety through the act of veiling can similarly be seen as a form of resistance to the social structures that bind them. Donning the dress of the dominant power structure is an overt ascription to dominant social norms, but it is also a subversion of traditional Islamic values—one carrying no less agency than the other. Overt displays of religiosity from dress to practice should be examined as tools that allow individuals to create and curate their self-image and larger societal images of their religion (D'Alisera 2001).

Through religious, vocational, and educational separation, Moroccan citizens are able to establish and maintain socioeconomic division from the country's growing migrant class. It was especially interesting to observe how the physical division of Morocco's mosques, marketplaces, and classrooms could be used to affirm distinctions between two populations ascribed to one race—Moroccans who identify as black and migrants living in Morocco. In the capital city, this is illustrated by the relegation of migrants to distinct and impoverished neighborhoods outside of the city center and the isolation of upper-class African exchange students to the well-defined space of University Village. Within migrant-dominated neighborhoods, the separation of migrant and citizen groups is further enforced by minimizing the number of Muslim migrants worshipping in community mosques and the number of migrant youth studying in public classrooms.

While there is no policy that officially bans migrants from enrolling in public school, the enrollment process presents significant barriers to those with limited resources or linguistic skills. Assuming a migrant family has the resources and necessary level Arabic language, as a limited number of the families I interviewed did, teachers and fellow students present a new set of challenges for migrant youth. Among the small number of parents whose child had at some point attended a public school, I could not find a single one who did not report abuse. They reported abuse from fellow students, and in a shocking number of the cases, they also reported abuse from the teacher. "Go on, tell her what happened," I remember one mother coaxing her 12-year-old boy as we sat side by side in the small apartment they shared with another family. "I . . . I . . . I begged my mom not to send me back to school." The boy covered his face with his hands as tears streaked down his cheeks. "It had been going on for months," his mother continued his story where he stopped. "He kept telling me the other students would tear up his assignments and then laugh at him when he had nothing to show the teacher. They would call him names, throw rocks at him, and drive him under the steps at the entrance to the schoolhouse where I would find him hiding many afternoons." She was conflicted. Her primary goal in fleeing her home had been to provide her children with opportunities that were out of reach for her, and though she did not want her son to be tormented, she also did not want him to grow up without an education as she had. "The last time I sent him to school, he came home with his two front teeth missing. He was beaten so badly I couldn't see his eyes. His little body just collapsed into mine, purple and bloodied. I thought, what have I done?"

In the weeks that followed, I continued to collect stories from other parents who knew all too well the pain she felt. Kia, a young mother from Mali, stopped sending her daughter to school when the teacher beat her daughter so badly that she had to be carried home. "She beat her with a stick in front of the whole class. Her legs were bleeding and her foot was swollen for weeks. Mari [her daughter] kept asking me why the other kids didn't stand up for her. I told her they were just scared." Sofia, a young mother from Guinea, sent her three sons to public school until her family received repeated death threats from their neighbors. "They were going to kill us before they would accept their children sharing a classroom with my children." She now passes on what little arithmetic and literacy skills she has to them at home. "I want them to know more than me, but how will they ever learn if I'm the only one who teaches them?" Like the first mother I interviewed, Kia and Sofia felt they had failed to reach their primary goal of providing their children with greater opportunities. Even beyond the borders of their countries, they saw the futures of social and economic marginalization that awaited their children in Morocco.

Race as Nationality: Placing Black Moroccans

Drawing on Hall's main argument about representation, we can understand social inclusion or belonging to mean interpreting the world—or literally, the words that are used to describe the world—in a similar way as those around you (1997). Border regions are a fascinating place to apply this argument because along the imaginary line where one country meets another, an individual's sense of belonging, or ability to interpret the world around them, can shift rapidly. Over the past decade, as rates of African migration to and through Morocco have increased, the local interpretation of racial, ethnic, and political categories of identity have been shifting rapidly as well. The history of collision between distinct groups of Africans, Arabs, and Europeans has long informed Moroccan conceptions of race, but only in recent years has blackness emerged as *"le peril,"* or the region's most pressing "danger." The primary difference in contemporary interpretations of race is the introduction of political status as an added marker of difference. In Morocco today, the line between foreignness and belonging is often drawn along lines of racial (and assumed political) minority status. This shift means that as the boundaries of *Jazirat al-Maghrib* are being challenged, contested notions of belonging are beginning to impact the identities of black Moroccans who "look like," "work like," or "live where" migrants are expected to, in what I term new "zones of illegality."

I developed many close friendships over my years in Morocco, but one family in particular grew to feel more like an extension of my own than any other. Adil, a middle-aged Moroccan man born in one of the most impoverished corners of Salé, Rabat's neighboring city, is like a brother to me. Even now, I speak to his family regularly—his sisters filling me in on the neighborhood gossip, his younger brother recounting his weekly soccer games for me in great detail. Adil's brother, Simohammed, was eight years old and attending the local public school like all of the neighborhood boys when I first met him. Now, he has left school in favor of playing for a local soccer team, following in his older brother's footsteps. Adil was recruited by a soccer team at a young age and relocated to "the barracks" with other promising young athletes from across the country. A grueling training regimen quickly replaced his schooling, and at the age of 18, he went on to play for Rabat's team. It had been decades since Adil last wore his uniform, but he was still recognized by former fans, who would often stop him on the street to ask,

"Barihsina?" He would reply, "*Na'am. 'Ana* Adil Barihsina," telling them, "Yes. I am Adil Barihsina." Adil maintains the physique of an athlete and looks younger than his years, but he now sports dreadlocks down to his waist and is hardly recognizable from the old photographs I have seen of him with his teammates. He might argue that these fan sightings are rooted in his memorable scoring record alone, but I would contend that his race—as one of the few black Moroccans to play for a recognized team—also contributes to the city's lasting memory of him.

Despite Adil's years of employment on the field, he is no better off than his family and often laments how he missed the opportunity to complete his education. He and his family live in an old *riad*, which like most of the other buildings in Sidi Moussa, looks eternally under construction. The walls are all cinder block, covered in graffiti, and the floors are roughly poured concrete. Many of the doors and windows are missing, rebar decorates the rooftops, and electricity is spotty at best. Adil shares the one small kitchen, living room, and bathroom with his parents, two brothers, four sisters, two brothers-in-law, two cousins, four nieces and nephews, and his maternal grandmother. But unless it is raining, he prefers to sleep on the roof. It was on the roof, with clothes-lines and clucking chickens around us, that I had some of my deepest conversations with him and his extended family about Morocco's grow-ing migrant community and the increasing discrimination that families like his are experiencing.

Adil's mother, Rafika, is a "*mqaddima*," or "welcomer' of the spirits" in the Gnawa tradition—a spiritual group that has long been prevalent in Rabat's poorer *banlieues* and is starting to gain traction with young, urban, and upper-class members.[4] While there are more black Moroc-cans who identify as Gnawa, it is not an exclusively racial subgroup, and those I spoke to were quicker to link Gnawa to particular styles of dress, music, or spiritual beliefs than to skin color. In Moroccan popular culture, the Gnawa are considered experts in the treatment of scorpion stings and psychic disorders, but among their followers, priestesses like Rafika consult on a wide range of issues ranging from financial troubles and infertility to broken bones and colicky babies. They fill a void in neighborhoods where "Western" medical care is often cost prohibi-tive. I had the honor of watching Rafika treat many patients over the years—converting their one bathroom into a sacred space for trance and using her knowledge to apply music,[5] dance, and special offerings to evoke the ancestral spirits thought to drive out evil—the root cause of all maladies. She showered her patients with the same enormous kindness and generosity that she always showed me, taking her payment in small change, food, or appreciation.

Lacking official data, Adil and I estimated that his surrounding blocks included approximately 75 percent whom he identified as "Moroccan," 25 percent whom he identified as "black Moroccan," and none whom he identified as African or migrant. Adil and his extended family members all consider themselves to be part of the subset that is politically identified as Moroccan citizens and racially identified as black, but when I asked them about their experiences of racism in the community, they could cite none. I was also at a loss to recall any experiences, although I knew the subject of race was ever present within their home. I often spoke with his younger sisters, who are a few years younger than I am, about their friends' love lives and their own prospects for marriage, and I cannot remember a single time when race was not central to the conversation. "He's too dark for you!" Hanan would say to Najia. "She's so beautiful—she has such straight hair!" "She's the lightest one in her family, so she'll marry first." I remember them writing to me years later to tell me that their younger cousin had in fact married a "very handsome" and "very light" man from one of the newer, middle-class housing developments outside of Rabat just before her 18th birthday.

Race was most central though in conversations with their youngest sibling, Simohammed, who is notably darker skinned than the rest of the family. Many of our dinners together ended in eruptions of laughter as the children taunted their mother, Rafika. "Where did Simo come from, Mama?" one would say. "Simo is from the Sudan!" another would joke. "Was there a *special* cousin we don't know about, Mama?" Adil would ask, shaking his finger in Rafika's direction as she rolled over in a fit of laughter. Their father, a man of few words, always smiled as the scene unfolded. "We don't know why Simo is so dark," he would sometimes say to me in his quiet tone, as if to offer finality to the conversation. But this conversation unfolded again and again, almost word for word, as Simo grew older. It was never mean spirited, yet Simo was certainly becoming aware of how his sisters linked race to beauty. I wondered when he would become aware of how it is also linked to marginalized political status outside the walls of his home.

The family's jokes about Simo being "from the Sudan" reminded me of the insults shouted at Abdul-Aziz, the Moroccan boy who works at his father's fruit stand in the *medina*. "*He only speaks Wolof now!*" the other boys would shout at him as they passed. Abdul-Aziz is what Adil's family would classify as "Moroccan," not "black Moroccan," and even so, his work in Morocco's informal economy had pushed him into a new zone of "illegality." How, then, are contested notions of belonging affecting black Moroccans who occupy similar spaces of "illegality" at work or at home? Just as the racial prejudices of Professor Boudoudou and his sons are shaped by their limited orbit beyond the boundaries of their home in Rabat, Adil and his family's experiences of racism could be linked more to the orbit of their lives in Sidi Moussa than to the changing sociopolitical climate. They live in a home built by their paternal grandfather, and their daily routines rarely take them more than a few blocks away from it. They are poor, but they are well respected within the confines of their community. Adil alone demonstrated greater awareness of the changing perception of blackness in Morocco, and this was in large part because of his role in the same informal economy where Abdul-Aziz is employed. When I first met Adil, he had been selling used shoes in Rabat's main marketplace for more than a decade.

Once a week, he takes the bus north to Nador, where the global second-hand trade brings thousands of tons of used clothing into Africa annually.[6] In Nador, he buys clothing by the "bale"—mechanically compressed and tied together—and waits until he is back on his rooftop in Sidi Moussa to sort through the goods he has to sell for the week. Crouching over the piles of clothing, Adil works through the night, marking the items that will sell best. He is keenly aware of which foreign labels he should look for as he sorts the clothing into "high," "middle," and "low" price items, and occasionally, he saves the best finds for himself. Spreading his goods out on a blue plastic tarp in the middle of the main thoroughfare every weekday, he sells socks for as little as 1 *dirham* and shoes for as much as 20 (approximately 2 USD). If he makes enough to cover the cost of his trip to Nador and back, he considers it a success. Adil has seen the dramatic transformation of this space since the months when migrants first began selling their goods alongside him in the early 2000s. "Every day," he explained, "it seems like there's one more migrant hawking here. One less Moroccan."

Lacking any formal schooling beyond the third grade, Adil taught himself the basic arithmetic necessary to run his business. He learned to speak Arabic, French, Spanish, and English, although his literacy level stops short of being able to read a newspaper in any language. He has devoted much of his adult life to learning, and speaking English has always been his primary focus. He explained how English is one of the tools he uses to present himself as someone who belongs—as distinct from the migrant men working in the marketplace with him. Yet, I realized that he also uses English as a tool to present himself as distinct from other Moroccans. Much like Ousmane, he believes his belonging is rooted in his performance of foreignness. Adil credits his love of foreign (mostly American) films for his American accent and his frequent use of American colloquialisms. On any given night, he can be heard calling out in English, "Twenty bucks!" "Hot deal!" "Cool styles!" He wears his hair in a nontraditional style that, for an outsider, links him more to Rastafarian than Muslim culture, and he carefully chooses every article of clothing to fit his performance. He speaks freely about these being his "tactics." His mission? "I try to look cool, American, you know, like Michael Jackson or Bob Marley," he told me one night, standing beside his tarp in his signature second-hand Nikes, tight black jeans, foreign-logo T-shirt, and black fedora. "I'm not an African, like 'I walked here from the Congo' African, but if I don't dress like I'm foreign, then everyone will think I'm Congolese!" Unable to draw on the upper-class markers that Ousmane can as a Senegalese exchange student, Adil finds other ways to self-consciously present himself as distinct from the country's new migrant class.

I could tell Adil was growing concerned about the impact that new migration patterns would have on his younger brother when he started coaching him on how he, too, could "act cool." "When I was a soccer player," he recounted to me in a Skype conversation in 2016, "I wasn't the black one. I was Adil. I was the one with the fast feet. None of us worried about race. But I hear the things they shout at Simo on the field now." Unlike Adil, who played in the late 1990s, Simo is constantly singled out for his race. Coaches, fellow players, fans, and opponents alike define him by his status as a racial minority. "Last week, they were all shouting at him, 'The African!' 'Pass it to the African!' No one would have called me the African when I played." For someone born on the African continent, why was this an insult that Adil do deeply feared? I wondered if he thought about the brutal treatment of some young migrant men in Morocco, and worried that his brother was coming of age in a distinctly different country than the one he had grown up in less than two decades before.

Racial minority Moroccan citizens and African migrants alike are grasping for markers of foreign identity to assert their belonging in the public sphere. It is outside of the University Village gates, as is true for Adil outside the orbit of Sidi Moussa, that race marks Ousmane and his peers as not belonging. "Can you imagine the fear that we walk down the street with everyday?" he asked me in one of our last conversations. He told me that his friends in The Village, like him, were concerned about the escalating violence against blacks in Morocco, but that when he tried to explain his fear to his parents, they brushed it off. "I think it's hard for them to imagine that something like this would ever happen to me because I'm from a good family. I'm a good kid. They don't understand that here, everyone who's black is seen as a criminal." When speaking to Adil and his family about the recent murders of black migrants, including Faye, Ndour, Seck, and Bété, which dominated the news during my early months of research, they expressed a similar fear. "It's getting harder and harder for us to fit in," said Adil. He argued that as a lower-income family, they have even fewer tools to draw on when trying to manipulate their identity in the public sphere than upper-class students like Ousamne have. "We can't always afford the right clothes. My siblings can't afford to study English. My parents work all the time." In his research on identity making, Hall noted the significance of the "material and symbolic resources" required by individuals who aim to maintain control over their identification (Hall 1997: 17; Bourdieu 1999). The experiences of Adil's family underscore how those individuals already inhabiting positions of privilege are the ones most likely to possess the resources needed to remain in control of their identification in changing times.

How We "Other": From Racialization to Legalization

Examining political categories of "citizen" and "migrant" alongside racial categories of "white," "black," and "Arab" allows researchers to integrate studies of racial inequality with those of global inequality. This new form of racialization, I contend, is structured by the state's production of "illegality." It has been argued that Foucauldian techniques of governmentality are used to stamp labels of inclusion and exclusion on the bodies of migrants as they move, producing a condition of "illegality" (Foucault 1980; Chavez 2008). This condition of "illegality" is then embodied through lived experience (Willen 2007b). While migrants remain physically unchanged by the process of labeling, the ways in which they are read by receiving communities, and therefore their daily experiences and opportunities in those communities, are determined by the label. Anthropologist Leo Chavez's argument highlights the government's central role in producing social and economic exclusion through various labels that mark one's status as "illegal," "undocumented," "paperless," "clandestine," or "alien." In the case of North Africa, however, the European states exercise even greater control over the labeling of migrants than Moroccan officials do. This shift in power indicates how traditional immigrant-receiving countries like the United States and those across the EU are increasingly exporting their immigration and asylum controls and reaching into neighboring countries to shape new forms of global inequality beyond their own borders.

To draw on Chavez's example, a Mexican who is stamped as "legal" at the border enters a distinctly different United States than a Mexican who is stamped as "illegal" in the same space. Yet, it is important to consider the agency that migrants have in this process. Many of them choose to be rendered "illegal" by crossing in places that fall beyond official border check points and bypassing the legalizing process of being stamped altogether. It is also important to remember that labels of inclusion and exclusion are more fluid than this example may suggest. Theories that assume the labels assigned to migrants at the border alone will shape their daily experiences in receiving communities do not account for the impact of competing factors of race, class, and gender. As is evidenced by exchange students like Ousmane, race can label one as "illegal" in the public sphere, despite documented legal status and attempted performances of belonging to a foreign, educated, and upper-class subject-position. In this case, stereotyping by the general public proves more powerful than government-sanctioned processes of legalization. Class, gender, and other factors from ability to sexual orientation can similarly shape access and opportunities in new communities.

Past research on racialization has illustrated how race can be "written" on subjects in much the same way that legality is "stamped" on migrants in border regions (Fikes 2009). Like political labeling, race is not contingent on physical characteristics alone. Across North Africa, an individual may be alternately labeled as "Arab" *and* "black," "Moroccan" *and* "African," "citizen" *and* "migrant" in the course of one day, depending on their dress, speech, and the particular physical spaces that are occupied by or denied to them. Since a range of skin colors exists among Moroccan nationals, and some like Adil and his family are read as *"noir"* or *"khal"* (darker skinned), the emergent migrant class is not always physically identifiable. The mutable nature of racial and political identities is driving an ongoing negotiation of assigned labels by both migrants and citizens, and new understandings of what it means to be black, African, or "illegal" are emerging daily.

Using the example of borders and those who regularly cross them, anthropologists Akhil Gupta and James Ferguson (1992) examined the connection between culture and space, highlighting how subjects marked with one identity (e.g., "Moroccan" or "Senegalese") can inhabit spaces that are marked with another (e.g. "Spain" or "Algeria"). I take this argument one step further by examining how a single subject can embody competing identities ("illegal" and "legal") in the course of one day depending on the spaces they occupy. Those who carry visible markers of "illegality," such as the color of their skin or the type of work they perform, are marked even beyond the physical border. As Adil's experience illustrates, the subjects carrying these markers can be migrants or citizens whose race or work has positioned them in zones of "illegality." On many occasions, I observed how Adil was comfortably read as a black Moroccan within the confines of his neighborhood where his family was well known and respected, and how he fought the stereotypes associated with being a black migrant when working in the marketplace. Gupta and Ferguson's work suggests that physical location is no longer the only grid on which cultural difference can be mapped. It is increasingly necessary to privilege multiple grids of power, including race, nationality, and as I contend, political status.

The limited ethnographic data available on Morocco as a critical border region pushed me to seek out comparative research from other borders. I was especially influenced by Kesha Fikes's work among African migrants in the EU (2009) and Nicholas de Genova's work on interactions between migrants, citizens, and state structures in the United States (2005, 2002). Both anthropologists focus their ethnographic attention on migrants who are assumed to have traveled north in search of greater economic opportunities. De Genova examines the border between the United States and Mexico as a site where "illegality" is performed by the state and observed by the public, suggesting the need for a visible space of confrontation in order for abstracted legal binaries to be seen and heard. The border holds the power to shape a nation's understandings (and misunderstandings) about legality, as is evidenced by the common misconception that Mexicans account for the majority of all "illegal" migrants residing within the United States or that the majority of migrants arrive in the United States by crossing a land border. According to the Pew Research Center, more than 60 percent of the United States' estimated 11 million undocumented migrants first enter the country with legal visas. De Genova's research shows how the conflation of "Mexican" and "illegal" makes it difficult for Latinos in the United States (documented and undocumented) to escape the stigmatization of migrant–laborer. It could also be argued that this conflation molds larger understandings of migrants (Latinos and others) as all being unskilled laborers of undocumented status. By way of the border spectacle, Latino becomes synonymous with "migrant," regardless of immigration status, just as Asian or African migrant workers become synonymous with "Mexicans," regardless of nationality. Like Moroccan citizens whose race or work in the black-market economy places them in zones of "illegality," Latino citizens, who make up the largest ethnic minority group in the United States, are impacted by the United States' social and economic marginalization of migrants.

While de Genova's work reveals the American fear that migrants are depressing wages within the national workforce, Fikes reveals the Portuguese fear that migrants are making it harder for their nation to fit the EU's standards for continued inclusion. The majority of Fikes's research centers on the outdoor markets where Cape Verdean migrants are informally employed and the ways in which the majority female migrant population is read through their work. She shows how the spatial contexts that migrants move through and the citizen–migrant interactions that take place in those spaces can mark them as either vulnerable or threatening to the future of the state. In Lisbon, the spatial boundaries of "illegality" are not policed by the state's border guards but by the citizens themselves. Fikes's description of the daily lives of four migrant women captures how each subject can move back and forth along a scale of social stigmatization, depending on the spaces they occupy and the roles they play in each space. As one woman transitions from the fish market to the home of a middle-class woman, she moves from being vocally excluded as a fish hawker (and assumed "illegal" migrant) to silently included as a domestic servant (and assumed "legal" migrant). She shoulders the racial slurs hurled at her in public as she performs one job and is welcomed into a family in the private sphere as she performs another. In the EU, as in Morocco, clothing is commonly read as a marker in contexts where political identity cannot be determined through physical difference alone. Much like Adil's second-hand designer clothes offer him protective armor in the marketplace, the fish scales covering the arms of the four migrant women whom Fikes followed made their migrant status inescapable. Whether seen on a city sidewalk or a public bus, the scales connote a particular spatial orientation in the social hierarchy.

By examining the critical roles citizens play in policing "illegality," it becomes clear how the socialization of groups to recognize new forms of difference serves to reproduce border sites and continually reinscribe labels of inclusion or exclusion in public spaces. The work of de Genova and Fikes reaffirms the notion that political categories of identification, like racial ones, are fluid and that what is understood to be a concrete category of citizenship exists only in relation to the exclusions surrounding it. Identity is not a naturally constituted unity lacking in internal variations. Like Hall, de Genova and Fikes find that identification is the "the marking of difference and exclusion" (2000: 17). The creation of new categories of political exclusion for African migrants in the Maghreb therefore necessitates a restructuring of the inclusive categories of Arab, Moroccan, and citizen.

If we take for granted that no society is bounded in space or fixed in time, as Gupta and Ferguson argue, and if the lines between different racial and ethnic groups are always overlapping, then a key question becomes, how are distinct categories of identification maintained as subjects move across space and time? In other words, how does an individual's identity remain bounded and fixed, even as that individual traverses physical borders and inhabits new subject positions over the course of the day and ultimately over the course of their life? Anthropologist Fredrik Barth's work grapples with what exactly qualifies as an ethnic or racial distinction, and how these distinctions are affected by the increasing migration flows of globalization (1969).[7] Noted for establishing the fact that "boundaries persist despite a flow of personnel across them," Barth suggests that even with an increased mobility of goods, capital, and labor in the contemporary age, racial and ethnic distinctions that delineate groups will persist (1969: 10), or as others have argued, they may even be on the rise. Although the lines may be redrawn to include or exclude new populations, the lines of inclusion and exclusion themselves never cease to exist. Rejection is a key component in the making of any group, and so the boundaries between groups are dependent not on an absence of mobility and contact, but rather on the presence of some form of exclusion. "Woman" and "black" are marked identities in contrast to the unmarked identities of "man" and "white."

It is only in relation to what one is not that the positive meaning of any identity can be constructed, solidifying the link between white and black, man and woman, and, I would contend, legality and "illegality."

By highlighting how boundaries are not actually maintained through racial difference, physical separation, or language barriers alone, Barth's later work suggests that more institutionalized forms of political and economic segregation are increasingly determining the discrimination of ethnic minorities (1987). Applied to the context of Morocco, this would suggest that it is the state's policies and practices, such as the routine abuse of migrants by military police forces, and not the routine "micro-aggressions" or everyday acts of racism perpetuated by citizens, that position migrants in spaces of marginalization. If, like me, you view the state's polices and citizens' behaviors as deeply intertwined, this distinction is not as easy to make. The macro approach requires overlooking how even state policy is eventually embodied by the individuals who execute it. When watching brutal beatings unfold over the course of my research, I often questioned how officers justified their behavior. Did they not have sons and daughters the same age as those I saw them brutalize? Were they unable to see the bodies of migrants as human? Like migrants, guards working at detention centers and border checkpoints have agency in their decisions to enact or subvert the state.

Inside and Outside of the Lines

In his most recent work (2000), Hall makes an important distinction between studies of racial identity—or "the relationship between subjects and discursive practices"—and studies of identification—or "the process of subjectification to discursive practices" (16). He argues that identification, as a process, is never complete. It can be "won or lost," "sustained or abandoned" by an individual at any given moment (16). While the notion of winning or losing one's identity evokes a sense of powerlessness, Hall acknowledges the possibility that some subjects play active roles in maintaining or abandoning their identities. Yet, his work does little to examine the important distinction between empowered and disempowered subject positions, leaving the questions: Under what circumstances do subjects wield control over their own processes of identification? Is this control limited to particular facets of identity (i.e. gendered and racial identities, which are widely seen as immutable—or religious and political identities, which are seen as more malleable)?

And, as my research suggests, does the control that subjects have over their identity vary depending on the social spaces that they inhabit and those that are denied to them?

The study of borders no longer means simply the study of political boundaries that physically delineate states. It has expanded to encompass the multiple ways that borders operate symbolically and conceptually in everyday life. It can mean the externalization of borders by those in power, the experience of borders by those crossing them, or the manipulation of what have been termed "bordered" identities. Borders can politically label migrants as legal or "illegal"; symbolically label migrants and citizens as included in or excluded; and geographically distinguish between the socioeconomic interests of competing regions. Morocco's land borders with Spain, encircling the two enclaves of Ceuta and Melilla, are the region's most obvious example of a political border and serve to physically push back the bodies of those seeking to enter the Spanish state. They are also unique in their status as contested borders, indicating an unequal relationship between the nations on either side. They create and sustain the social hierarchy, and in their production of identity—both national and individual—these borders create binaries, the two sides of any binary opposition rarely being given equal status.

In attempting to make sense of the self in a transnational space like the Maghreb, a third element beyond the previously known or imagined self is born. It is born from neither the old home nor the new. It is born from neither the past nor the future. It embodies and denies the present time and space. The third element is a new self, a new consciousness—a "mestiza" consciousness, as Gloria Anzaldúa termed it—and although it is a source of pain and longing, loss and loneliness embodied, its energy comes from the continual creative motion of breaking down and rebuilding the self anew (1987: 102). In this understanding of transnationalism, migrants are quintessential postmodern subjects. They belong to and yet do not belong to two distinct nation-states, they live in a period of time suspended, and their movement across the border challenges our very understandings of self, culture, and nation.

Through Anzaldúa's "borderlands" (1987), I was first introduced to colonial borders as spaces defined by the domination of "other" over "other" and by the conflict of distinct cultural traditions. Postcolonial studies taught me that borders can instead be defined by the mixing of "other" with "other," by the "mestizaje," the creolization (Glissant 2008), the hybridity (Bhabha 1994) that comes from distinct racial and cultural traditions. In later theorizations of cultural hybridity, the border has been presented as a more harmonious version of cultural contact and collision, a modern multiculturalism devoid of any analysis of power (Canclini 1995). Regardless of the approach, the border as a site of contact has always been essential to identity studies, challenging fixed categories of identity, the tendency to tie identity to place, and the hesitancy to rethink cultural difference through connectivity. The border itself remains an affront to our "self-here/other-there" structuring of the world.

We tend to think of borders as spaces where inequalities come head to head. We are presented with images and imaginings of great political borders where Morocco meets Spain or Mexico meets the United States, where suffering meets hope or poverty meets opportunity. Iconic borders are never found where like meets like, where the United States bleeds into Canada or where Spain and Italy lay side by side. To delocalize the border is to see it, instead, in all of the lines that unite and divide beyond the physical border. Bordering, after all, is the practice of defining the self in relation to the other, and research has shown us that just as borders divide, they unite. They bring together "other" and "other," creating contact and collision, community and combat.

The border is a curious object of study, shifting its mechanisms of power for the same subjects at various times and places. Whether through the enforcement of a physical border or the social stigmatization of those who carry its scars, "illegality" is best understood as a form of identification, and, like other forms, it will always be in a process of transformation. Constructions of race and legality are never singular. They are constructed across different, "often intersecting and antagonistic," discourses (Hall 2000). To access the migrant experience, it is critical to understand the physical, sociopolitical, and discursive spaces in which the narrative of the migrant is imagined and the ways in which it is concretized through language and practice. All processes of identification require the marking of symbolic boundaries, and that which is left outside of the boundary constitutes the identity of what is permitted inside. Even as "the most inclusive category," the citizen exists only in relation to the migrant (Gledhill 2003: 209). The border, as the line that divides, unites the two.

Notes

1. Morocco and Senegal have a long-standing relationship "founded on values rooted in the soil of faith and culture" (Sall 2018) and strengthened through trade agreements and multilateral regional investments by Senegalese president Macky Sall and King Mohammed VI in recent years. As of 2014, Senegal was Morocco's leading African trade partner with a volume estimated at 122 million USD.

2. A derogatory French term from the French word *sale* (n. "dirty"), meaning "whore."

3. In *The Politics of Piety*, Mahmood claims that existing scholarship has long hindered conceptualizations of Islamic revival movements, and, in particular, the women's piety movement. Mahmood challenges assumptions about the relationships between "action and embodiment," "resistance and agency," and "self and authority" that inform most studies of nonliberal movements (2004: 38).

4. There are two types of spiritual or devotional groups in Morocco—Sufi and popular—with the division between the two based primarily on social class. Sufi devotional groups have a book, a lodge (*zawiyya*), and a leader (*sheikh*). Popular groups such as the Gnawa, in contrast, have historically been nonliterate and do not have a book that holds their prayers, songs, or histories. In some cases, they use a pilgrimage site that belongs to a local Gnawa group or a shrine connected to one of the saints claimed by the Gnawa. The most striking difference is that they are not hierarchically organized under a *sheikh*.

5. The traditional instruments of the Gnawa include the stringed *gimbre*, the rhythmic *krakebs*, and the drum, which are used together to create hypnotic trance music, marked by low-toned, rhythmic melodies, call-and-response singing, hand clapping, and head spinning.

6. A massive 387,000 tons of clothing (equivalent to 2.9 billion T-shirts) are traded annually from the United Kingdom alone (*The Guardian* 2015).

7. Anthropologists traditionally understood ethnic groups to (1) be "largely biologically self-perpetuating," (2) share "fundamental cultural values," (3) represent "a field of communication and interaction," and (4) have "a membership which identifies itself and is identified by others as constituting a category distinguishable from other categories of the same order" (Barth 1969: 11). This definition is linked to an outdated assumption that race equals culture, culture equals language, and society equals a group that maintains its cohesion through the rejection of others.

CHAPTER 7

....

Where The Story Ends

Until the lions have their own historians,
the history of the hunt will always glorify the hunter.

—CHINUA ACHEBE

....

*I*was born by the water. I met Alphonse in my first weeks of fieldwork in Morocco. *It was almost 35 years ago.* His voice is soft, rising and falling as he speaks. Sometimes, it sounds like the voice of a child. *I stayed home when the Civil War began, but when it grew stronger, I had to leave.* He comes from a small village called Wamba in a war-torn region of the Congo. *For two years, I lived as a refugee in the neighboring countries. I was alone. I lived like a scavenger bird, only there was little to scavenge.* At the height of the first Civil War, Gabon was bursting with Congolese refugees. Lacking official camps, they were left to sleep in the streets. *Day to day, I was just trying to survive.* A tall, thin stalk of a man, he walks a head above the others. *My parents, all of my family, they stayed behind. My father owned a small store. My mother worked there every day from sun up till sun down. They couldn't afford to leave it behind.* He is always the last one to speak, a listener. His face gives way easily to a smile. *I was young, and I wasn't afraid to lose everything in my search for something better. My mother was happy when I left, because the boys who stayed behind had no choice but to fight in the war. I was her oldest child, and she wanted more for me.* Away from the crowds, across the table from me, his stories flow quietly and steadily. His words are deliberate, poetic at times. His hope is persistent in the face of pain. *I don't have any family left in the Congo. My mother, my father, most of my family has been killed. Those who haven't been killed have gone off to fight in the war.*

Still, I am alone. He was one of the few men I met who had successfully made the crossing. *I was born by the water 35 years ago. I have never shared my story with anyone before. No one has ever asked.*

Those who arrive on southern European shores seeking asylum are immediately faced with difficult questions—questions that will determine their futures. Many ask themselves: "Has my suffering been enough? Will my story be enough?"

I met Alphonse Ngiaba in the summer of 2013 at a Moroccan prison being used to detain migrants from across the continent—many coming from Central African countries like he did. His journey had taken him all the way from his home in the DRC to Europe, although it was punctuated with many stops along the way—two years spent crowded with thousands of other refugees in Gabon, one year spent traveling the treacherous route north to the Maghreb, and many more years spent working in informal economies to save money for his final crossing. For caseworkers who would later review his asylum claim, his narrative hit all the right keys: his village ravaged by war, his family members killed by rebel forces, many of his friends forced into the uniform of the rebel soldier. His only possible future was one of military conscription. Yet despite his narrative, he was seated across from me. His journey had not ended in Europe but had returned him, like so many others, to Morocco, where he sat awaiting his chance to escape once again.

Africans make up the largest percentage of asylum seekers arriving on European shores. But for the fortunate few who survive their final crossings by boat across the Mediterranean Sea or by foot over the rings of razor wire separating Morocco from the Spanish enclaves of Ceuta and Melilla, their journey to a better life has only just begun. They must next prove that their cases are strong enough to allow them to stay. Those entering Europe from Syria and other countries across the Middle East have more encouraging odds. Last year, the acceptance rate of their asylum applications was 72 percent, leaving only 28 percent without a safe path forward. Alphonse knew that his odds were not as good. The acceptance rate of asylum applications coming from the region defined as sub-Saharan Africa last year was less than 8 percent, leaving more than 92 percent of them rejected. This rejection rate far exceeds that of any other world region. Through my work, I argue that the criminalization of blackness—and especially young black males, who make up the majority of sub-Saharan African asylum seekers—on a global scale has made it virtually impossible for them to plead their cases of vulnerability. Skin color is determining the application of international law. But the first step to positive change is a recognition that this inequality exists in the first place. As someone who regularly has a seat at the table when international bodies come together to debate human rights and the growing refugee "crisis," I can tell you that at this moment, race is rarely a part of the conversation. The experiences of men like Alphonse reveal how certain populations of asylum seekers continue to be stigmatized in their interactions with citizens, state agencies, and even international aid organizations. Too often, they are seen in terms of the presumed threats they pose, raising the critical question: Is Alphonse not among those whom our international human rights laws were written to protect?

The Legality of Undocumented Movement

Throughout my fieldwork, I spent many months conducting interviews in Morocco's detention centers and living in the country's hidden forest camps, spending time with detainees and members of the camp brotherhoods, with those awaiting their first chance at crossing and those who had made it to the other side, only to be "repatriated" back to Morocco. I wanted to understand how all of their journeys, regardless of their home country or the reasons why they first left home, kept returning them here. As the trust between Alphonse and me grew and he shared more details of his own journey with me, I realized that he had an unusual story to tell.

We sat in a small courtyard with the prison's high concrete walls rising around us, but Alphonse's mind was in a different time and place. He was a boy in the small village of Wamba. There, he had attended a one-room schoolhouse, although he remembered more about the soccer games that unfolded on the dusty streets after school every day than about what he had studied in school. In the late 1990s, the fighting between rebels on the side of the Congolese Liberation Movement (MLC) and those on the side of the Rally for Congolese Democracy Movement (RCD) finally reached his home. According to a statement released by the UN Refugee Agency (UNHCR) in 2001, the DRC's civil wars killed 2.5 million people in their first decade alone. Alphonse's father made just enough money to keep food on the table, but nothing more. Higher education was the only way out of military conscription, and Alphonse knew that for those born in his village, there was no hope of earning a college degree. Most children would never make it past elementary school. He told me about the first time he saw the huts around him burning and about losing his youngest brother not long after that day. He remembered having the realization, sometime in his early teens, that he would soon have no choice but to flee. He worried about what would become of his family in his absence, but he held the dream of helping them escape once he reached the other side. "I thought once I was safe, I would be able to reach down and pull them up with me," he said. "I was naive. I didn't know how hard it would be for me to find a safer place to be."

Traveling on foot and hidden in the backs of smugglers' trucks, Alphonse covered nearly 5,000 miles from the DRC to North Africa. It took him six years in all—many of those years spent hawking goods and saving money on the streets of Libya and Morocco—before he had enough to afford his place on a boat. "I remember the day I left for Europe. I will always remember it. It was in January of 2005. It was a long ride to the water, and I was packed into a truck with many others. The air was hot. I was worried there wasn't enough for all of us. When we made it to the boat, we spent many days on the water before we saw land again." As is common in Mediterranean crossings, Alphonse was on an inflatable raft that went adrift when the outboard motor they had purchased from a smuggler stopped working only hours into their attempted crossing. They were eventually pulled to safety by a rescue ship that was operated by one of the many NGOs patrolling the Mediterranean before search and rescue actives like this were criminalized.

Those who live to see European shores know that difficult questions await them there. If they arrive without detection by the coast guard, they must decide if they will present themselves to authorities as formal asylum seekers before being found by local police, or if they will attempt to escape the systems of legalization that are in place and begin their new lives as undocumented migrants. In that moment, Alphonse remembers carefully weighing his odds. Official refugees (those who have been granted asylum) have the benefit of better work and educational opportunities; the possibility of bringing spouses, parents, and children to apply for legal status in Europe through family reunification programs; and the chance to walk down the street without the constant fear of deportation. They can send their children to school, go to the hospital when they are sick, and report a crime if they are victimized.

But if their application for asylum is denied, as most applications from sub-Saharan Africa will be, then deportation is the next step. Deportation rarely returns rejected asylum seekers to their proper country of origin. Alphonse knew that instead, deportation meant the likelihood of being returned to his last point of departure—the Maghreb. There, hundreds of thousands like him remain trapped until their next attempted escape.

Those who have less faith that their asylum claims will be accepted by the assigned caseworker—that their stories will be chosen above all of the others—can take advantage of Europe's overcrowded detention centers and "disappear." In some ways, this form of escape symbolizes the completion of the migrant's long journey and the attainment of a dream, but it comes with a sense of defeat. For migrants, accepting the status of "undocumented" means accepting that they will never have the chance to reunite with their families. As one Spanish caseworker explained, it means accepting that they will likely end up "in condemned houses, in trains they find in abandoned rail yards, or outside in the elements, sleeping on mattresses covered in plastic sheets." For the few who are able to find paying work, he explained, "Work will be temporary, under the table, and for low pay—no more than a couple of euros an hour. This is what they risk their lives for." But in reality, most risk their lives not knowing that they will continue to be trapped in zones of "illegality," facing economic exploitation and social ostracization even in Europe, and will remain at risk for the multiple forms of institutionalized abuse that structured their daily lives in the Maghreb.

When the small rubber boat that carried Alphonse across the rough waters of the Mediterranean washed ashore in Spain, he decided to take the risk. He would apply for official refugee status. He had been instructed on exactly how he should tell his story to those who greeted him on the other side, and he was prepared. "I memorized every word of it," he said, "and I practiced it again and again in my head: I was born in the Congo. I fled my home when the war reached my village. I am a political refugee."

Policy and Practice on the other Side of the Border

Although the international laws protecting basic human rights trace their origins to the refugee crisis that followed World War II, European nations are still struggling to protect the rights of refugees, and the issue is growing increasingly politicized with every new election cycle. Most central for Alphonse in the Universal Declaration of Human Rights is Article 14, which guarantees all citizens of the world the same basic right to seek asylum in other countries, regardless of their place of birth. Yet today, the future of asylum seekers is left to a series of short and subjective interactions with local caseworkers or, in rare cases, to local judges ruling on asylum seekers' appeals. Formal interviews often take less than 30 minutes—a brevity that Alphonse said was difficult to understand given the many years, thousands of miles, and thousands of dollars it had taken him to finally reach Spain. For asylum seekers, the future rides on first impressions. Like Alphonse, they routinely trade advice on how best to tell their stories: How does one dress to look both vulnerable and responsible? Which details are best revealed or concealed? One woman I interviewed, whose application had recently been denied, regretted not having cried in her interview. "Sometimes, speaking your pain isn't enough," she said. For interviewers, the prejudices they hold, which no adult is without, can easily seep in to the decision-making process. Interviewees who have been numbed by their past traumas may have trouble convincing an interviewer how dire their circumstances really are. The interviewers, neither highly paid nor highly trained for dealing with psychological trauma, may not realize all of the ways in which trauma can manifest itself or how their own emotional reactions to an interview can shape their final judgments.

It now takes upward of 24 months for cases to be heard, and during this period, asylum seekers are limited in their ability to work, leaving many in abject poverty. Having arrived before the current migrant and refugee "crisis" began, Alphonse had to wait only 12 months for his case to be heard, and he was able to find temporary work in Madrid while awaiting his hearing. Over the phone, the man who owned the small shop where Alphonse once worked told me, "I was moved by his story—by how much he endured to get to where he was—and I was impressed by how hard he worked. He was the hardest working employee I ever had. He was quiet, but he always asked me what else he could do. Sometimes, I would catch him sweeping the floor or organizing our titles in alphabetical order when there was nothing left to do and the others had already gone home. Never once did I catch him sitting idle. He always had a smile on his face, like he was happy to be useful." Alphonse, too, had fond memories of the time he spent working in what I learned was a bootleg DVD shop. "Those were my happiest days," he said, reflecting on a period of his life when the dream of rebuilding his life in Europe still seemed possible.

At Alphonse's first hearing in 2006, his asylum application was denied. With a language barrier between him and the ruling judge and a lack of legal support, it was not immediately clear to him what had happened. "I later learned that I hadn't been granted asylum because I spent too long in another country before arriving to Europe," he explained. Under the guidance of his employer, he began saving all of his money to hire an immigration attorney who could help him file an appeal. "We were sent to another court to have my case heard by another immigration judge, and that judge asked me if the government of Gabon had given me a home. I said no. He asked me if the government of Gabon had given me three meals a day. I said no. He asked me if the government of Gabon had given me a doctor or an education. I said no. When you are a refugee in Africa, there is little given to you. Some days you have food and some days not. Only those who are dying ever have any medicine. I never saw any books." In the end, the judge ruled that Alphonse was provided no means to survive in Gabon, opening up, once again, his path to asylum in Europe.

Alphonse had been living in Madrid for two years, finally settling into the feeling that he could walk down the street without fear, when his journey back to the other side began. "The officers came for us in the early morning. I had just returned home from work," he explained. "I was sharing a small apartment with five other Africans, and they came for all of us. I will never know why. Had one of them done something wrong? Had one of us been reported by our neighbors? We couldn't ask any questions. They threw us on the ground and handcuffed us. I was hit by one of the officers when I asked if they would remove my handcuffs so I could show them my papers. I was hit even harder when I told them that I was a refugee, that I had a job, that I had an attorney. I thought, how can I get this far only to be sent home? I have papers now! I am safe!" His deportation back to Morocco was likely a mistake. He was swept up along with a group of undocumented migrants he was living with, but there is little hope that the mistake will be rectified. Our international laws were written to protect vulnerable subjects like Alphonse, and yet like the others, he was returned to his last point of departure to begin the cycle of attempted escapes once again. Alphonse's story contrasts the utopian view of Europe held by those who have yet to make their first crossing, but his hope of returning to Europe and eventually finding a better life for himself there is unwavering to this day. From the Moroccan prison where he was detained, he shared parts of his story with me in his own words, and that is how I will share it with you.

The civil war broke out after the Congo's first democratic election. The former president took his position back from the leader who won, and the people split, some supporting the old leader and some the new. When there is civil war in a country, the citizens take advantage of one another. There was looting everywhere. There were soldiers everywhere. The good people were terrorized by them. The government's military was voluntary, because the economy was so poor that the government couldn't pay the soldiers, and the country couldn't survive without the workers. For this reason, the soldiers were young. Education was the only way out. If you had a good job, then you were left free, and if you had a high school diploma, then you were made an officer. I would have been a simple foot soldier.

In the Congo, children start school at age six. After six years in the schoolhouse, you have a graduation. It is a challenge to make it through. Once you finish, you are proud. Your family is proud. Your community is proud. There weren't many students who finished school in Wamba. The students who did finish had the chance to move on to high school. The public schools require a small fee. All of the children whose families can pay the fees are allowed to start, but those who aren't good are sent away. There were more than 60 children in my school. There was one teacher. Some children came in early, some late, and the one room held all of the different levels of learners. If a child required any attention from the teacher, he was sent home to his parents. It is sad, because I now see that it was these children who needed school the most, but the system has no place for them. If a child is weak, there is no place for him in the schoolhouse. I now say, there are no weak children, only weak educations. Many teachers in the Congo have other jobs, because the economy is so poor that the government can't pay the teachers well either. There were days we didn't have a teacher at all. The private schools, they are stronger. I always said, when I have children, they will go to private school. But I never really believed it would be possible. I never knew anyone who had the money for school. I am from a poor family.

The official reason I was in Spain is because my country is no longer a safe place to live, but the truth is that all of my life, I dreamed of going to Europe. Going to Europe means having opportunity. When I was a child, I heard wonderful things about it. I thought, someday I will go, and I will give my family the things they never dreamed were possible. When I finally made it, I thought, all of my dreams have come true! I wanted to work hard. I wanted to study. I wanted to do something good with my life. I had dreams of returning to my country with an education and fighting the political corruption that drove me and so many others away. In my first months, I worked with an old man who burned movies and music onto small discs in the basement of a building. I worked with computers, with all kinds of new machines. I loved it. I worked in the night, and he paid me with cash. I started saving all of my money to afford classes. That was before all of my money went to an attorney. I learned that maybe Europe isn't so different from Africa after all.

In the Congo, the government wants the power, they want the money. They use the power to build their own fortunes and help their own children, but they care nothing about the children of their country. This is the big problem in Africa. Countries like the Congo are rich in oil, but the people never see these riches. For decades now, bad things have been done, and bad things have been ignored. We had our first democratic election in the nineties, but it meant nothing. To this day, the leader who loses the election takes his position back by force if he wants it. I don't have any answers for you now. I don't know what will happen in the future of my country. I am tired. We look to the youth to make a change, but the schools teach you about European history and not about your own. What can you do in a country that you don't understand? I learned nothing about the history of the Congo until I left.

When you lead a country, you don't lead the trees, you don't lead the rivers, you lead the people. A country is its people, not its oil. A country is a living thing. What are you going to lead now, big man? What are you going to lead now that all of your people have left? Thomas Sankara was a great African leader. He would travel to the villages and eat what the people were eating. He would sleep where the people were sleeping. He never wore the nice clothes of the politicians, always the uniform of the soldier. He preached to his army, "A soldier without education is a murderer!" He educated his army. He was young and handsome. Sankara was a true revolutionary. A lot of people think that he was the first person to see what the people really need, to listen to what the people really want. He was a hero for saying to the Europeans, "You aren't treating us like humans!" And for saying to the other African leaders, "Our land is for our people, nothing is for us!" He changed the name of his country—"No longer will you carry a French name!"—he called it "Burkina Faso," the land of the honest people. He was murdered by one of his closest friends in 1987. The man who killed him took his place as the ruler of the honest people. But it was Sankara who gave hope to his country, and that couldn't be taken away. I borrowed a book about Sankara from the library in Madrid, and when I was sent back to Morocco, I still had it with me. I had that book for many years. It was like a friend to me. I read it once, twice, so many times. It was like a very good friend to me.

When I think about my small days in the village, I think about playing soccer in the streets. The streets were dusty, and the sand would burn your feet. The old ball we played with was held together with string. I never knew there was anything wrong with that ball until I saw something better. We played every day until sun down. Before dinner, the other boys and I would run to the river. We washed in the water, and our mothers would call to us, warning us not to wade out too far. "The water is dangerous!" they would say. None of us knew how to swim. Sometimes, the older boys organized fights between dogs after school. They each had strays they named, and they would walk their dogs to other villages to fight the strays those boys had named. I followed the boys from my village, cheering them on in the fight. But at night, I would think about the dogs, and I would cry. As I grew older, I stopped going. Even now, I feel badly when I remember how we treated those dogs. I can still see them, ears torn and bleeding, like it was yesterday. It makes me wonder if we're born with more than goodness in our hearts. We were children, and we each wanted to believe that we had the strongest dog.

—Alphonse M, 34, Congolese migrant [DRC]

Border Externalization: A Modern Spanish Ruling of The Moroccan Border

There are so many perilous points on the primary smuggling routes crisscrossing the African continent that migrants' final crossings over razor wire or across rough waters are only the most recent memories that they hold—not always the most traumatic. For those who have reached safety within the borders of the EU, images of fatal fence and boat crossings, of skin shredded by razor wire and bodies washed ashore, continue to serve as powerful visualizations of how European policy is acting on individual bodies. "It's hard to ever feel safe," one Guinean migrant settled in Spain explained to me, "when every day you see that your brothers and sisters are not." The Lampedusa disaster brought international attention to the dangers of migration from Africa to the EU in 2013 when news broke that more than 350 migrants had drowned just 75 miles from Italian shores. For the 518 men, women, and children on board, the lights in the distance signaled that the end of their long journey was near. According to one report, "They had made a difficult journey across the Sahara and through Libya, packed into trucks and walking long stretches over sand on foot, only to pay several times the price of one plane ticket to be packed in again—shoulder to shoulder—on a boat much too small and much too old for their numbers" (Schwartz 2014).[1] They saw lights on the Italian island of Lampedusa in the distance, but that was before the water started pouring in. That was before the fire erupted—their captain's failed attempt to signal to those ashore that they were in crisis. That was before the boat capsized—the passengers' failed attempts to escape the flames. That was before everyone on board had to choose, in the final moments of their lives, to go by water or by fire.

Body bags lined the beach—shoulder to shoulder once again. "Pray [to] God for the victims of the shipwreck off Lampedusa!" called Pope Francis. "An immense tragedy!" called then Italian Prime Minister Enrico Letta. "A European tragedy, not just an Italian one!" then Deputy Prime Minister Angelino Alfano followed. Rescue workers added powerful images to the story with their words—a mother clutching her child to her chest, a teenage boy in a T-shirt that read "Italia," and a young woman who had given birth on the boat, her infant still attached to her by umbilical cord. In the weeks after the incident, survivors came forward revealing that the casualty reports had been grossly underestimated. In fact, hundreds of others had been locked in the hold of the vessel by their smugglers. The few who survived the tragedy were taken into custody by Italian officials, where they awaited trial to determine their alleged status as "illegal." A "guilty" verdict would result in fines of up to €5,000 and immediate deportation.

Six years later, in 2019, the remnants of yet another tragedy are on display at the Venice Biennale (*La Biennale di Venezia*)—a prestigious visual art exhibition in Italy. Visitors are faced with the monstrous remains of a 90-foot fishing boat, pictured in Figure 7.1 below, that capsized on the route between Libya and Lampedusa in 2015. It is the remains of the Mediterranean's largest tragedy to date—a tragedy in which between 700 and 1,100 men, women, and children lost their lives in the sea. There were only 28 survivors. The boat was brought to Venice by artist Christoph Büchel, who calls the project "*Barca Nostra*" ("Our Ship") and hopes it will provide a somber reminder of recent Mediterranean tragedies. The project name represents the collective politics that allow for daily tragedies in the Mediterranean to continue and our shared responsibility for the lives lost. It is not "their" ship—it is "ours." But Büchel's work also raises important questions about the ethics of making art from tragedy. Europe did not want the bodies. Do they deserve the boat?

Figure 7.1 Tourists enjoy a break in front of the "*Barca Nostra*" exhibit by artist Christoph Büchel. Venice Biennale, Spring 2019.
Source: *Photograph courtesy of Martin Herbert.*

According to the UNHCR, an average of 14 migrants drowned in the Mediterranean every day in 2016—the year following the capsizing of "Our Ship." The International Organization for Migration's Missing Migrants Project reported that a record 629 died in one month of 2018 alone. These numbers are good estimates at best. As my research has shown, Mediterranean crossings are poorly reported, and authorities on both sides of the sea have incentives to underreport the deaths that occur there. But there is no denying that the three paths commonly referred to as the Western Mediterranean (Algeria and Morocco to Spain), Central Mediterranean (Tunisia and Libya to Italy), and Eastern Mediterranean (Turkey to Greece) routes are active and increasingly deadly, raising alarm in destination countries in Europe. Italy, Spain, and Greece each receive tens of thousands of individuals fleeing their homes across the African continent every year. Yet their individual responses to migration are beginning to diverge.

Italy's newly elected populist government signals a major shift in the country's response to Europe's ongoing migrant and refugee "crisis." No longer are migrants simply being pushed back at border fences. Now, their boats are being turned around in international waters, and the critical work of search and rescue missions attempting to prevent more tragedies in the Mediterranean is being criminalized by the states that should be protecting migrants' basic human rights to asylum. "If more people leave, more people die," Italy's new deputy prime minister, Matteo Salvini, stated in a recent press conference. His party line focuses attention on the threats that are present along migratory routes, but it fails to recognize the even greater threats that migrants face in their home countries, from Sudan to Syria. Italy has drawn criticism from human rights groups for its new "zero tolerance" approach, which includes closing all of the country's ports to humanitarian rescue ships and a plan to institutionalize deportation before migrants have time for their asylum claims to be reviewed. In 2018, the humanitarian ship *Aquarius*—operated by Doctors Without Borders and the French organization *SOS Mediterranée*—saved 629 lives in a three-day search and rescue mission, only to spend the following 12 days stranded in the Mediterranean as they were turned away from one port after another. Italy was the first to close its ports, followed shortly after by Malta. Doctors, aid workers, and the rescued migrants aboard all struggled with dwindling supplies and the threat of a forced return to North Africa until Spain finally agreed to open its ports to the *Aquarius*.

Spain, under a new and comparatively progressive administration, took its moment on the global stage to tell the world it saved one ship, but it cannot possibly save them all. Days later, 70 men, 30 women, and 6 children drowned off the coast of Libya in the same waters where the *Aquarius* had been patrolling. Every time a ship is turned away from European ports, those aboard—if they do not become another Mediterranean statistic—are forced to return to the countries they are fleeing. For many migrants, the choice between a forced return to North Africa or death is an easy choice to make. As so many have said to me over the years, "I will make it to Europe, or I will die trying."

The Weight of their Journeys

According to Spain's Law on the Right to Asylum and Refugee Status,[2] every man, woman, and child arriving on Spanish shores has the right to apply for asylum. Once their application is filed, they have the right to interpreters, legal counsel, and emergency medical assistance. They have the right to state-sponsored accommodation in one of Spain's four detention centers for 60 days, or until their case has been reviewed. Approval of their application guarantees the right to a work permit and social welfare, which includes subsidized health care and education.[3] Those whose applications are denied are required to leave Spain within 60 days or risk being served a deportation order. But in recent years, Spain's state-run detention centers have all been overrun, as cases take longer and longer to reach review, and individuals are routinely denied their basic rights to legal counsel and emergency medical assistance. NGOs, like the Spanish Commission for the Assistance of Refugees (SCAR), have tried to fill the widening gap between the services guaranteed and the services provided by offering safe housing and legal guidance at discounted rates. But these organizations, too, are struggling to handle the number of new arrivals. The French Refugee Agency, like the Spanish, has admitted to being completely overwhelmed. Their review process now takes an average of 24 to 36 months and results in a rejection rate of over 90 percent.

The European Border and Coast Guard Agency, known as Frontex, claims that the European "crisis" began in 2014 when the number of asylum applications received by EU member states rose by 44 percent. In France and Spain, applications have increased by 73 percent and 64 percent, respectively, in the past five years.[4] There is no denying that the EU, especially its southern states, carries the weight of a great exodus of men, women, and children fleeing increasingly fractured political and economic systems across Africa and the Middle East. Southern member states make a powerful argument that this burden outweighs the size of their nations relative to the rest of the world. Given the realities of a failed asylum review system, it is not difficult to understand why Spanish officials, with the purported support of the EU, would attempt to mold Morocco into a final destination for all African migrations north. And it is not difficult to understand why Morocco would accept. North African nations are struggling under the weight of their own economic instability, making it difficult to turn down the significant funds received in exchange for their role in controlling migration flows into Europe. Last year alone, Morocco was paid over 30 million euros in the name of "development aid."

In the spring of 2015, then president of Melilla, Juan Jose Imbroda Ortiz, made a shocking announcement. Instead of properly repatriating migrants to their countries of origin as mandated by international human rights law, Spain would now return all Africans to Morocco in order to eliminate the "prize" of letting those who had migrated to the country "illegally" remain in Spain while their asylum applications were reviewed. This popular argument for "punishing" the journeys of "illegal" migrants is a far cry from Spain's legal conviction that every individual has "the right to apply for asylum."[5] Where, under international law, do we proclaim that those fleeing war-torn and impoverished regions of the world, that men, women, and children who have lost everything and sustained untold abuses in their long journeys toward safer shores, should arrive with neatly arranged dossiers with their claims for asylum? In too many cases, the migrant is the refugee, and the refugee is the migrant. Both arrive at the hands of the same smuggling rings, and rarely does either arrive with an application in hand. It is the obligation of the states receiving them to assemble the necessary information to disentangle the two. As Kia, a young mother from Mali, said in one of our last interviews together, "If I lose my children to war or I lose my children to disease or starvation, what's the difference? There is no way to survive in my country. I will not stay home and watch them die. Dying on the sea means that at least I died trying to reach something better for them." Her words highlight the arbitrary legal distinctions that states draw between those who feel they have no choice but to put their lives on the line.

President Ortiz's comments marked the moment when, for the first time, Spain publicly acknowledged its illegal practice of "push backs."[6] Spain acknowledged its literal pushing back of migrants at the Spanish borders surrounding Ceuta and Melilla and its symbolic pushing back of those like Alphonse who are forcibly returned from mainland Spain to Morocco rather than to their countries of origin. President Ortiz said he hoped that Ceuta and Melilla's routinizing of push backs would reduce the incentive for migrants to leave their homes, and the following day, Spain's cabinet quietly approved a €3 million "aid package" to be divided between the two enclaves, which have a combined population of under 150,000. According to the press release by Spanish Deputy Prime Minister Maria Teresa Fernandez de la Vega, Ortiz intended this package to "compensate the efforts of both cities to address illegal immigration before it reaches our shores." He failed to field questions from reporters about the six African migrants who had been fatally shot by security forces the previous weekend in their attempts to scale the fence surrounding Ceuta. In addition to structural changes to the border, security forces had recently been outfitted with new weapons, and Moroccan police forces were bolstered by the addition of Spanish border control teams.

Integrating studies of racial inequality with those of global inequality illuminates a world in which asylum, citizenship, and other state-sanctioned categories of belonging are no longer just markers of identity constructed to include and exclude. They are now the goods with which people barter. As more lose faith in the possibility of legal pathways to asylum, alternative routes have gained momentum. Passports are bought and sold. Smuggling businesses are thriving. And governments are auctioning citizenship off to the highest bidder, offering special visas to applicants willing to make million-dollar-plus investments, as is routinely done in the United States.[7] It should be no surprise that those at the bottom of our global economic pyramid end up paying the highest price for their chance at inclusion.

I know there is no easy solution. But having conducted research on migration at Europe's southernmost borders, embedded with smuggling rings and living in migrant camps across North Africa since 2007, I also know that externalizing border controls and asylum processing centers will not solve the problem. Seeking asylum in foreign countries is a human right guaranteed under international law to those fleeing the

African continent as much as it is to those fleeing the Middle East and elsewhere. With 54 countries in Africa and multiple factors contributing to the migration of citizens from each one, there is no single solution that could address the African migrant and refugee "crisis" as a whole. It is important to recognize that what would be the right solution for the large percentage of unaccompanied minors may not be the right solution for adults—the right solution for women may not be the right solution for men—and the right solution for those fleeing active conflict may not be the right solution for those fleeing the debilitating effects of extreme poverty, climate change, or political persecution. But unless international laws are amended, every citizen of the world is entitled to the same basic right to seek asylum. This right needs to be guaranteed with safe and legal pathways, with timely and objective asylum case review, and with proper repatriation practices for those whose claims are denied.

In the Moroccan prison where he sat waiting, Alphonse told me that he would not change a single decision he had made. With even the smallest chance of making it back to Europe someday, he would make the same decision to leave home and sacrifice everything he once knew for the promise of something better. "The hope keeps me alive," he said, a chain link fence separating his face from mine. Writing this conclusion one year ago, I would have made a stronger argument for us to recognize all displaced persons—documented and undocumented—as having the basic rights that are granted to refugees. But today, I am not sure if the language matters. What good does an inclusion of all displaced persons under the protected category of refugee matter if our world no longer protects the refugee?

My research has highlighted the failure of both North African and European governmental agencies to uphold international laws and provide those seeking a better life with basic human rights. But I do not overlook the burden that the states situated in our world's most critical border zones bear. The UK Royal Navy estimates that half a million migrants will attempt to cross the Mediterranean this year alone. Contrary to popular narrative, this strain is not only on the EU, which receives the majority of those crossing. In fact, the world's poorest countries shoulder the greatest burden of the global crisis. According to the UNHCR's latest annual Global Trends report (2018), "developing" regions host the vast majority of the world's refugees—a staggering 84 percent.[8] This is a weight that we all should bear.

"Like a magnet, Europe pulls them in, until suddenly, without warning, the magnet flips and they are pushed back out." Myriame, a refugee from Côte D'Ivoire, was living in Morocco and working with migrants like Alphonse when I first met her. She had held prestigious positions with both the UNHCR and the International Organization for Migration (IOM) in Europe before returning to Morocco to establish her own NGO. "I saw such suffering on my journey through North Africa," she said, remembering the migration she made alone at the age of 22, "that I felt compelled to return here and offer my hand. I've never seen suffering like this before." Myriame often spoke about Europe's desire to pull Africans—slaves, soldiers, and workers—from beyond their own borders when they were needed and to freely scavenge the African continent for natural resources. "Colonialism left our homes raped and fractured. Of course, we wanted to travel north to seek an education, to seek work, to seek what colonialism had taught us was good and right and civilized, to seek the future that had been stolen from us. But then there emerged a sacred thing they called a border." She paints a picture of a world in which colonial powers retreated securely behind the borders they had drawn, the humanitarians among them crying out, *We will now establish human rights! We will grant you asylum! We will protect and defend!* If only you can survive this deadly obstacle course to reach us.

Throughout my research, I applied "counter-mapping" as a tool for challenging the geopolitical map of Europe and investigating the bordering practices that are being enacted in spaces distinct from European territory. I documented the EU's expanding collaboration in border patrolling, surveillance, and interception and how this collaboration affects populations on the ground. I examined the very practices through which border externalization is enacted: training programs for third countries' coast guards and border patrols; technical equipment for monitoring migrants' journeys by land and sea; and the new alliances that are emerging daily between unlikely actors ranging from governmental officials and smuggling rings to NGO workers and police forces. But most central to my research was my exploration of the new spaces that border externalization is producing at the external frontiers of the global north and the embodied experiences of migrants who remain trapped behind externalized borders across the global south.

At the Threshold: Migration as a Sacrificial
Rite De Passage

Liminality comes from the Latin word *līmen,* which means "a threshold." During a ritual's liminal stage, participants "stand at the threshold" between their previous self and their new self, and liminality can be used to describe the quality of disorientation that occurs in this middle stage. In his now famous "Betwixt and Between: The Liminal Period in *Rites de Passage*" (1967), Victor Turner developed a way of understanding liminality that has since been applied to make sense of individual, political, and cultural upheaval. During the liminal stage, or the critical space that exists between the old (person, system, or nation) and the new (person, system, or nation), social hierarchies may be reversed, social bonds may be dissolved, and the continuity of tradition may be uncertain. The future is suddenly cast with doubt, as the person, system, or nation loses the very thing that once defined it. But it is through the dissolution of all established order—a moment that exists outside of our conceptions of time and place—that liminality creates the possibility for something new to be born. It is only through the migrant's burning of the past, a ritual throwing of the old self into the fire, that a new self can be born. New identities, institutions, and nations are established through completion of the ritual. Order is reestablished. The person is whole again. But how do we understand a continuation of the liminal?

Although it is less often applied in studies of migrant communities, the concept of liminality has been applied to refugee populations that are stuck "betwixt and between." Whether Afghans in Karachi or Syrians in Amman, the majority of the refugee populations that have been theorized as being in liminality are temporarily settled in official camps while awaiting the opportunity to move on to destinations in Europe or the United States. What is remarkable about those who remain trapped in Morocco for undetermined periods of time is their proximity to their imagined home. For migrants in Morocco, unlike Somalis in Nairobi or Burmese in Bangkok, their journeys have not been stalled thousands of miles from Europe or the United States, but rather at the very border of the nations they are so desperately seeking to enter. They can see the land of opportunity that they have sacrificed their pasts for, sustaining the dream and making it that much more difficult for them to turn away. One challenge to the theorization of constrained mobility through liminality is that it often neglects to take into account how the few migrants who "succeed" in reaching their desired destination countries continue to feel unsettled and remain largely unincorporated in social and economic life. The difficult truth is that racialization follows African migrants as they traverse international borders, as has been explored in exceptionally powerful recent scholarship (e.g., Besteman 2019; Lucht 2011; Andersson 2014). Even successful crossings and hard-won legal status will not resolve the liminality of migrants who are marked by their racial status as other.

Turner called on us to investigate the phenomenon of midtransition, claiming that it is here, in this "betwixt and between period," that we can find "the basic building blocks of culture" (1967: 55). Viewing the migrant as the transitional being or the *"liminal persona"* reveals the process of self-making through one individual's experience and illustrates the process of state-making through one nation-state's molding of social inclusion and exclusion. The state asks: Who are you? Who are we? Are you us? Are we becoming you? The lines of belonging are continually being drawn and redrawn to define the symbolic boundaries of the nation through those who are granted the title of citizen. Subjects who remain in states of liminality across North Africa have burned their pasts in exchange for a new self and a new state that has not yet been constructed. *Hrig*, the process of "illegal" immigration—the rite of "the burning"—is best understood as a ritual of sacrifice.

> *Click. Click. Click. The officers pass the hours pulling the trigger on the weapons at their hips. Every dry fire is a reminder of the seconds, the minutes, the months I've been locked in here. Their keys clang against the metal bars every time a new man enters. The door grates against the concrete floor every time it opens. The whole place is metal and concrete. Cold and hard. All I can do is listen. I don't know what's coming next. I can't see past the walls around me. I'm always on edge. After so many months, maybe I should expect that nothing is coming. That is the ultimate torture. Nothing.*
> —Alphonse

A Return to the Beginning

I began this book in one of the many hidden forest camps that I have been fortunate enough to call home over the past decade. I began it with two courageous individuals who have become like family to me— Moneba, the chief of the camp, and Bambino, the youngest member of their brotherhood. It is in this space and with this brotherhood that I would like to end it. In my final year of research, as I finished this book and moved on to complete the filming of my related documentary film project, *The Burning*, I was able to reconnect with many of those whose journeys bought these pages to life. Some of my final shoots took me to the European cities where they are now building new lives. Some took me back to their home countries where they are struggling to re-build old ones. And some took me to the burial grounds where their bodies lay, to the cells where they sit trapped, and to the camps where they remain, still hoping for a better tomorrow. Much like any journey, mine began with me unable to imagine all of the places that the fol-lowing years would take me. From the camps in Morocco's northern mountains to the prisons overflowing in Libya's capital city, I ended up spending the majority of my own journey in the spaces that lie in be-tween. Bringing to light the untold stories of the men, women, and chil-dren trapped along Africa's treacherous migratory routes has become my driving passion. I have put my own life on the line for this work because I believe that by raising awareness, inciting action at the indi-vidual level, and advocating for change at the policy level, we can bring positive change to our world's most critical borders and to the hundreds of thousands whose basic human rights are being denied there. As an-thropologist Margaret Mead famously said, "Never doubt that a small group of thoughtful, committed citizens can change the world. Indeed, it's the only thing that ever has."

Not all who successfully make it to the other side of the border set foot on Spanish shores like Alphonse. Some, like Bambino, only make it as far as Morocco's Spanish enclaves. There, they are housed in one of two overcrowded detention centers as they await their asylum case review. Melilla's detention center for unaccompanied minors is heav-ily patrolled. The building, a faded yellow color, is surrounded on all sides by a high fence. At the entrance, there is a guard in full uniform, gun at his side, lifting and lowering an automatic door that controls the passage of cars onto the property. I approached him and listened as he told me many variations of "No"—"No, you cannot enter the property," "No, you cannot speak with a detainee through the fence," "No, I will not call the superintendent"—before he finally passed me off to another guard who directed me to the social welfare office in downtown Melilla. Inside the office, I was told that visitation is a right reserved for "legal guardians" of detainees. Since Melilla's detention center is reserved for unaccompanied minors, the majority of them having lost their parents before leaving home, this means that visitation is a right reserved for almost no one. I spent the next six days speaking to various officials, who were all unwilling to let me enter the center under any circumstances. At the end of the week, it was arranged that I could see Bambino—but it would be on the other side of the fence, and our brief visit would be under the supervision of guards.

I hardly recognized his silhouette as he approached—his longer hair adding inches to his already lanky frame. But his body looked somehow shrunken, bones protruding from under his tattered clothes. Cautious at first, he walked toward me with his head down. Then he broke into a run, as a familiar smile crossed his face. He buried his face in my shoulder, his body shaking with tears. I had not seen him since my last visit to his camp on the other side of the Moroccan border, since before he had become one of the success stories—one of the few who survive the grueling feat that he and his brothers call "the crossing."

When I receive a phone call from the brotherhood in the early morning hours, I have come to expect only one thing—someone has died. Sometimes, the death comes as quickly as a border guard can break a wooden baton across the back of a head. But more often, it festers for weeks as lacerations grow infected. Back on the mountainside with little sustenance and no medical care, even a scraped knee from tumbling down a rocky path at night can turn fatal. In the time I spent living in Moneba's camp, I remember how he would instruct his brothers to focus on their hands and feet when conserving the few strips of duct tape they had left to use as their sole protection against the razor-wire fences. "Wrap the soles of your feet, but not so much that you can't use them!" He always paid special attention to Bambino, checking to see that his small feet were covered. "The pain will be great," Moneba would warn, "but don't let it distract you! Hold the ladder for the ones behind you." One brother reminded the others to cover their heads with one hand when descending. "A broken hand is better than a missing eye," had said, gesturing to his own left eye, still swollen shut. "When the beating is really bad, I tell them to play dead," Moneba explained to me one night. "If you're lucky, the guards might think they're done with you and drop you on the other side of the fence." "But it's hard to do!" Another said knowingly, "It's hard to stay silent when they drag you with broken ribs."

Moneba had many failed attempts under his belt, so he understood the risks involved. After more than one year in the camp, he thought that Bambino, who had just turned 14, was finally ready to move up to the second round of stormers. This would increase his chances of making it to Europe, but also his chances of sustaining a serious injury in his attempt. "He's bigger now, and he has a lot of motivation," he explained. It was true that Bambino's determination was palpable. Like many of the other boys, he was driven by the memory of the younger siblings he left behind and the desire to give them a better life. He felt the full weight of their survival on his shoulders.

In the camp, Bambino was rarely seen without his two closest friends, Bronx and France. They had each taken the names of the places where they envisioned their journeys ending, as is a common practice in the brotherhoods. "My older brother," one boy explained, "lives in New York City now. He lives in a place called the Bronx, and he says it's the most beautiful place in the world." Bronx is one year older than Bambino, but his voice is a high-pitched squeak. Standing just a hair over 5 feet tall, he is built as strong as he is short—solid muscle. His skin is a deep brown, almost black under the heavy Moroccan sun, and his speech is interrupted with a full-mouthed smile. His one shirt was black with pink flowers—the kind with pearl snaps down the front that another boy his age in Manhattan could very well be wearing. The other boy's one shirt had three faded stripes—red, black, and blue—and the word "France" printed in large block letters across the front. It was this old sweatshirt and not his love for France that had given him his name. But he had since decided that, being called France, he would like to end up there. "I always wanted to go to America," he explained over the fire one night, "but I think the people in France will like me. Maybe I should try to find a new life there first." France is tall and gangly, his skin light, his small eyes always on alert. He moved with a tentativeness unlike the others, but he, too, quickly took to following Bambino's lead.

Bambino decided that on their next attempted crossing, he was no longer going to play by the rules. He had been on water duty the morning he first told his friends about his plan. As the only one among them who had attempted a crossing before, he knew the place in the bush where Moneba stashed the ladders and he knew the safest path to the fence. He was convinced that if their group was small enough and they were stealthy enough, their best chance at evading the guards would be in breaking with the brotherhood. "I thought, 'I've been good, so God will reward me,'" he said. The three boys waited until the others had fallen asleep. Bambino knew the forest well, and he moved with confidence through the sparse trees that dot the rocky mountainside down to the border. Quietly, Bronx and France followed behind him.

Bambino recalled how he, and then Bronx, scrambled across the first fence, bloodied hand over foot. Bronx steadied the ladder for France, waiting to feel his brother's weight, prepared to use all of his strength to pull him up to the top of the fence beside him. But he never felt that weight. France had disappeared into the shadows, already retracing his footsteps back to their hidden home. Bambino knew that calling out for him would foil their plan, so he gestured to Bronx to keep moving forward. Like Moneba had taught him, if he was ever one of the lucky few, "Don't turn around. Keep your eyes in front of you. And if you reach the other side, RUN. You'll see the lights when you're getting close." The lights represent the two detention centers in Melilla.

When I arrived, I was told that there were only 10 detainees from sub-Saharan Africa. One of them went by the name "Bambino." I learned that all of the detainees were boys, ranging in age from 10 to 16, and that they came from Sierra Leone, Guinea, Côte d'Ivoire, and the DRC. They were far outnumbered by the more than 100 minors from across North Africa who were detained, and Bambino explained how within the center, he and his new brothers had grown accustomed to being abused by the other detainees. "Most of the guards are Moroccan, so they have no concern for our safety. They laugh at us, encouraging the beatings, and they even place bets on who will fall first." In addition to routinely beating the 10 boys of racial minority status, the North African detainees stole their clothing and daily food rations, leaving them to survive on scraps. In previous interviews, I heard similar stories, some of them more graphically addressing the verbal, physical, and sexual assault that detainees experience at the hands of fellow detainees and the guards who are tasked with protecting them.

Most of those arriving in Europe from across the African continent have already been instructed by their smugglers to burn any documentation that may trace them back to their countries of origin. With passports and other state-issued IDs long since destroyed, they arrive at Europe's southern borders without any papers in hand, their fates left to the subjective interactions that follow. Unlike Alphonse, who had the option of attempting to live as an undocumented migrant on mainland Spain, those who do not make it beyond Morocco's Spanish enclaves only have one path. The lucky few who are not beaten off the fences and "pushed back" into Morocco are instructed to nurse the wounds of their successful crossing, often tying lose articles of clothing around their limbs to stop the bleeding, and then run toward the lights. There, they are met by a Spanish police officer who will first assess their age. That determination, made in a matter of seconds, can make all the difference in shaping their path forward.

Bambino, with his lanky frame and smooth face, was quickly placed in the minor category. Yet his friend Bronx, only 15 years old, was taken to the adult detention center, where the chances of winning an asylum case are even lower. Those who end up in the detention center for unaccompanied minors, like Bambino, will be detained until they reach the age of 18, at which point their cases can begin. When asked how age is determined without papers, one worker shrugged and said, "We get crowded." For the hundreds of boys detained in centers for unaccompanied minors in Melilla and Ceuta, this can mean years waiting behind bars with no certainty of when the waiting will end. When it finally does, those whose cases are denied—as more than 80 percent will be—are sent back to Morocco, where they have no choice but to begin the cycle of attempted escapes once again.

In the small cell that Bambino shared with 11 others, he told me that they marked the passing time with scratches on the wall. "Otherwise, you forget how long you've been in here. There aren't any windows, so sometimes I don't know if it's day or night outside. They let some of the boys outside every day. But not all of us. If you've been bad, they keep you inside." One boy from Sierra Leone had been living behind bars for six years. In Bambino's cell, which is built to accommodate eight, there are metal bunk beds for a few and blankets on the floor for the rest. "The black boys are always on the floor," he explained.

When I was back in Moneba's camp the following week, the group was eager to hear about my brief reunion with their youngest brother. "Is Bambino learning English now?" France asked me. "Do they have a big soccer field?" "Is he fat off of all the food?" I struggled to answer—to tell them all about the prison that awaited them on the other side of the border. But I remembered Bambino's last words to me, as the guards signaled to us that our time was up. "Sometimes," he said, "I wish I was still in Morocco with my brothers. This isn't the Europe I expected to find." His words had become whispers, as the guards, one on either side, lifted him up from the rock we had been sitting on and pushed him back through the fence toward his cell. "Tell them I'm doing well!" was the last thing I heard him say.

From the edge of the camp, where Bambino once slept on the forest floor with hundreds of others, they could see the Mediterranean Sea below and the Spanish coast curving along its shores like a green blade of grass below the horizon. At one point, more than half of the camp was under the age of 16. "I see my little brother in them," Moneba said, explaining why he took in so many of the children that the other chiefs had turned away. He knew they would slow him down when outrunning the police, who routinely raided their camps. He knew they would make his chances of a successful crossing even lower. But he also knew they had nowhere else to go.

In late 2017, I received a phone call from Moneba letting me know that he, along with France and some of the other brothers, had successfully crossed by boat to mainland Spain. In his first months there, he was able to find work as a day laborer, and he sent all of the money he saved home to his mother, grandmother, sister, and younger brother in Guinea. With great pride he told me that in only a few months, he had sent enough for them to rent a home with "a real roof." When I visited that home in rural Guinea in the summer of 2018, his mother explained to me that Moneba means "one who sacrifices himself for others." Although it was not the name she had given him, she was not surprised to learn that the brotherhood he cared for in Morocco had chosen it for him and that people now know him as nothing else.

These days, Moneba shares a small apartment with five other undocumented migrants on the outskirts of Barcelona. He makes a few euros for a full day's work picking fruit. But this work is in high demand and some days, he finds nothing. While sitting together in his apartment a few months ago, he told me he had terrible news to share. His younger brother, Abdoulaye, was gone—Abdoulaye, the spitting image of Moneba, who had slept on the ground beside me in their home in Guinea the year before. He was 12 years old when he left home. Moneba showed me his picture, remembering how he had begged him not to follow in his footsteps, crying and shouting at him over the phone from Spain, "I sacrificed myself so you don't have to take the same risks with your life!"

Like so many migration journeys across the continent, Abdoulaye's had ended in Libya, where he was subjected to forced labor, daily beatings, and threats of being sold in the open marketplace. He made multiple attempts to escape the brutal prison where he was trapped with hundreds of other young migrants, but each time, his boat was turned around in the water, and he was forcibly returned to the place they called hell. After his final attempt, he was beaten to death by a guard who worked in the prison. I was not sure if Moneba would ever recover from the loss.

In the months that followed, as European leaders debated the future of migration policy at the annual EU Summit,[9] the voices of migrants like

Abdoulaye were absent. In their place were proposals to formalize the "offshoring" of detention centers and a complete disregard for the documented risks of trapping vulnerable populations in North Africa. If given a platform, I imagined how powerful stories like Abdoulaye's could be in proving the dangers of border externalization before it becomes the new approach to managing global migration flows in the Mediterranean and beyond. On the horizon is a future in which those seeking a better tomorrow are trapped in black sites just beyond the world's most trafficked borders—their names, their faces, and their stories trapped with them.

More than 68 million have been forced from their homes around the world this year, but Moneba reminds us that in the masses, there is still the story of one—one whose mother held tightly the shoes he wore when he was small and who wailed all through the night to any god who would listen. She begged for the months passed to be forgotten, for the miles walked to be revered, for her son Abdoulaye to be standing beside her again. She wails still, feeling the heavy weight of her mourning—the full weight of mourning a death the world is silent to. "Does no one know I lost my son?" she asks me. "Does no one cry with me? Does no one remember the way he used to tuck his shoelaces into his little shoes because he was too stubborn, too fast, too eager to run out into the world to ever learn how to tie them?" She remembers how he clung to her as a child, how he strayed from her as a boy, and how he hugged her that last time before he left—still too stubborn, too fast, too hopeful about what the world was holding for him to listen to her fears. In the millions, there is the story of one. One whose life is over before the age of 14. One whose small hands lifted him up and down, again and again, over fences and through trenches, whose small feet carried him 3,000 miles, across deserts and seas, toward the promise of a future that was just out of reach. Abdoulaye's life was over far too soon, but together, we can make a commitment to carry his story forward.

It is the storyteller who makes us what we are, who creates history. The storyteller creates the memory that the survivors must have—otherwise their surviving would have no meaning.

—Chinua Achebe

Notes

1. For the complete story, see Mattathias Schwartz, "The Anniversary of the Lampedusa Tragedy," *The New Yorker*, October 3, 2014.
2. Spain's Law on the Right to Asylum and Refugee Status was adopted in 1984.

3. Those who are granted asylum in Spain are also entitled to €51.60 a month and are able to file for additional funds to support any legal family members who have reunited with or accompanied them.

4. Germany continues to receive the largest number of asylum applications in Europe, followed by France, Sweden, Italy, and the UK.

5. In addition to violating Spain's Law on the Right to Asylum and Refugee Status, the deportation of migrants to Morocco, a country with minimal reception capacity to guarantee basic human rights, violates Article 3 of the Convention Against Torture and Other Cruel, Inhuman, or Degrading Treatment or Punishment, which maintains that "No State Party shall expel, return ("refouler") or extradite a person to another State where there are substantial grounds for believing that he would be in danger of being subjected to torture." Spain's refugee and asylum laws can be reviewed in greater detail at the Library of Congress: https://www.loc.gov/law/help/refugee-law/spain.php

6. "Push backs" were originally sanctioned under a little-used 1992 agreement allowing Spain to undertake "exceptional repatriation" of immigrants entering Spanish territory "illegally" from Morocco, even if those entering were not Moroccan nationals.

7. The "selling" of citizenship is best evidenced by special EB-5 visas that the United States offers to any applicants who make million-dollar-plus investments guaranteed to create 10 or more jobs (Schwartz 2014).

8. The world's top host countries, and the only countries to host more than 1 million refugees according to 2018 data, include: Turkey (3.7M) followed by Jordan (2.9M), Lebanon (1.4M), Pakistan (1.4M), Uganda (1.1M), and Germany (1M).

9. In June 2018, European leaders met for the annual EU Summit in Brussels, and migration was the central debate. They reached a deal, which threatens to solve the bloc's migrant "crisis" by pushing the issue south of European borders and abandoning international commitments to uphold the basic human rights of those who have been displaced. The main points they agreed to include the following:
   - Share the responsibilities of migrants rescued at sea among all member states.
   - Create new detention centers in Europe, where migrants will wait while their asylum claims are processed.
   - Tighten the EU's external borders and increase the rates of deportation for migrants and asylum seekers.
   - Set up processing centers outside the EU, where ships could disembark migrants rescued at sea and hold them while their asylum claims are reviewed.
   - Increase financing and infrastructure for Turkey and North African transit nations to control migration to Europe.
   - Channel more government aid and private investment toward the "socioeconomic transformation of the African continent."

EPILOGUE

....

The space that exists between Africa and Europe has become a graveyard. It now claims more than six lives every day. But behind every number, there is a name, a face, and a story that goes untold.

"Most of the bodies were floating face down. Some wore life jackets. But there were a lot of life jackets without any bodies inside. It was a moment I'll never forget." These are the words of the crew member who first alerted Spanish Maritime Rescue to a capsized boat in the Mediterranean on February 4, 2018. He was on board his ferry, making his daily trip between Almería, a city in Southern Spain, and Melilla, one of the two small Spanish enclaves in Morocco.

Four thousand miles away, my cell phone started ringing. I spent most of the following week on the phone with families across West Africa—parents, spouses, and children who were desperately searching for any information about their loved ones. *My son, is he alive? My wife, have they found her body yet? When will we know? How will we know? Is anyone looking for them?*

For tourists seeking a day trip to Morocco, there are a host of ferry options from Spain—most take 30 minutes and cost 25 euros per passenger. For African migrants seeking the chance for a future in Europe, there are a host of smuggling options running the same routes in reverse. Most take several days at sea and cost an average of 2,500 euros per passenger. Boarding one of the ferries, you might notice a small sign warning you of seasickness. Boarding one of the rafts or old fishing boats that leave from Morocco's rocky coast at night, migrants do not need a sign warning them that, as one 14-year-old boy told me, "You'll make it or you'll die trying."

After being alerted to the bodies found floating, Spanish Maritime Rescue sent a ship to begin searching for survivors. In the hours that followed, the Royal Navy of Morocco ended up recovering the majority of the bodies, which had already drifted back to the Moroccan coastline. They placed 20 bodies in one massive, blue plastic bag made for tragedies like this and took them to El Hassani Hospital in Nador. The one body recovered by the Spanish was taken to Melilla. At the morgue in Nador the following week, I was told that 16 of the 20 bodies still remained unidentified. "We have a poster hanging in the police station with pictures of each face, so the families can identify them," one officer said. But I knew that the victims' families were not in Morocco, and their friends live hidden in forest camps that are routinely under attack by the Moroccan police. I also knew that the lack of official reporting by Spain and Morocco leaves family members with more questions than answers, often learning about the passing of their loved ones from Facebook posts many months after a tragedy has occurred.

That same week, major news organizations from *The New York Times* to *El Mundo* covered the latest Mediterranean tragedy, but regardless of which source you followed, you read the same facts: 21 bodies. All Africans. All packed into a small wooden fishing boat that capsized off the coast of Morocco's Spanish enclave. There were no corrections made as the victim count grew, ultimately being more than double what was originally reported. As I followed the coverage by various sources, I noticed that there was never a single name released.

I needed more than a number. I did not want to simply break the news that it was 47 migrants, not 21, whose lives were lost to the sea last week. I wanted to report *who* had been lost. I enlisted the help of fellow migrants and longtime friends of mine who were still living in Morocco's hidden camps, and together we committed to the goal. We would find the name, the face, and the story of every one who had been lost. They knew better than anyone the group that had left their camp just after nightfall on February 3 to walk 16 miles to the meeting point their smugglers had given them.

The photograph of Abdul Karim Barry—a 17-year-old boy from Guinea—was one of the first I saw. I had been in Karim's camp only a month before the tragedy, and as more details poured in, I realized I knew many of the victims well. Karim had been in the camp awaiting his chance to escape for over two years. After his father died, he felt the responsibility of taking care of his younger siblings and helping his mother, who struggled to find work in their rural community. He wanted to give his siblings the chance to go to school like his father had given him. "Karim was smart and above all, he was generous," one of his closest friends told me over a crackling phone line. "He always risked the dangers of going into the street to beg for us when we couldn't find enough food to eat. It was Karim who prepared the one daily meal for our brotherhood every night." I posted a photograph of him and asked his friends in Morocco and Guinea to help me make him more than a number. Over the following days, I received dozens of responses.

"Karim studied hard before leaving home," wrote one friend, "and he used his education to speak up for the other boys who didn't have any. He was young, but he was a natural leader and he couldn't stand for anyone to be treated as less than human." Another wrote, "He dreamed of becoming a soccer player when he was little. He used to play on a team in Guinea, and he was really good. Sometimes, he played with me in the forest. We had a ball we made out of plastic bags and tape."

In the hours before the first bodies were spotted, Karim, along with 46 men, women, and children coming from Guinea, Côte d'Ivoire, Sierra Leone, Cameroon, Senegal, and Mali left their camps. Their smugglers, two Moroccan men, were waiting for them on a rocky beach in Arekmane. They carried a small wooden fishing boat that had been rigged with an outboard motor down to the water. A witness who traveled with them but did not board the boat that night told me the winds were too strong for a safe crossing—50 mph, according to official reports. So why would smugglers choose to travel, risking their own lives, under such rough conditions?

In previous years, they would not have made the same decision. But new systems established to protect migrants' financial investments have made tragedies like this one more likely. In 2016, I knew dozens of migrants who were devastated when they paid between 1,500 and 2,500 euros and failed to reach the other side. It left many trapped in Morocco for decades, struggling to save up enough money to try again. Last summer, I noticed a niche market had emerged, with some smugglers stepping into the business of transferring money from migrant to smuggler—only after their boats had reached Spanish soil. For a 10 to 15 percent increase in fee, migrants can now pay these third parties and secure their investments. Those who find themselves back in Morocco after a boat has capsized or after a rescue ship has forcibly rerouted them, as happens more often than not, have the money to try again. For the smugglers who captained the boat on February 4, a postponed departure would have meant the return of approximately 117,500 euros. Mounting surveillance efforts in the Mediterranean also mean more incentives for smugglers to call for last-minute departures when bad weather is on the horizon. They know that storms make it easier to evade the Guardia Civil.

With an overcrowded boat and waves reaching 10 feet high, the group's boat capsized less than one hour into their journey. All 47 passengers were thrown into the freezing water without enough life jackets to go around—many of those on board finding themselves in water for the first time and not knowing how to swim. The oldest reported passenger on board was 34. The youngest had just turned 14. There were eight women, one of whom was pregnant. Two days after the tragedy, the Royal Navy of Morocco reported that, miraculously, one young man from Mali had been found alive. After a series of interrogations, he was accused of taking part in an illegal smuggling operation and taken into police custody. The Nadori police told me they are still searching for the top-level smugglers thought to have masterminded the operation and many others like it.

In the following weeks, the poster was taken down at the police station, and the bodies were taken to a mass grave where they would be buried. But names, photographs, and stories continued to pour in from devastated family members. Along with them, I received final videos that were recorded by some of the young men and women, including Alpha Moron Diallo, 22, who told his mother, "I've suffered greatly in my journey to Morocco, but it's all been worthwhile, Mama, because soon I'll be calling you from Spain!" And Safourata "Sofia" Sow, 30, who told her three daughters how much she loved and missed them. "Be good girls while I'm away," she said. "Mama is proud of you." Again and again, I listened to the video recorded by Karim, who was one of the last boys I interviewed in person. Sitting by his makeshift tent, I remember him telling me, "I finally understand what my brothers meant when they told me, 'I'll make it to Europe or I'll die trying.' After you've endured the horrors of this journey to Morocco, there is only one way home."

I learned that Hassane and Houseine Traoré—28-year-old twin brothers from Côte d'Ivoire—had a similar story to tell. "They were the coolest guys," said a childhood friend I connected with by phone. "They were the best athletes our village had ever seen, they played music and sang, they did well in school. All the girls loved them. We knew they would become big men someday." "They were always together," explained another, "One never did anything without the other." Including their final crossing to Europe. Both boarded the boat, and neither body was found. Their mother called me day after day, hoping I would have some news to share. Months later, she was still waiting to bury her sons. Although Hassane and Houseine were adored in their camp in Morocco, it was difficult for me to find their actual names because everyone there knew the charismatic young men simply as "the twins."

The Traoré brothers were not the only twins on board. Alhassane Barry, 26, from Guinea was also among the victims. "Hassane was the quiet one. His twin was the outgoing one. Hassane always looked up to his brother, but, in a lot of ways, it was him who the rest of us admired," one of his closest friends, who survived the crossing from Morocco to Europe last year, told me as we sat side by side with a stack of old photographs between us. "They lost their father when they were young, and they were both devoted to their mother. She worked hard to send them to university, and they wanted to provide a better life for her. Hassane was one of the best students in his class, but when he graduated, he had nothing. In Guinea, it doesn't matter how smart you are. If you're not from a wealthy family, you can't find a good job. He didn't tell his brother he was leaving because he didn't want him to worry. I was the one who called him to tell him about the tragedy. I wanted him to hear it from a friend before he saw his brother's photo on Facebook. He couldn't breathe. I remember him choking back his tears, saying, 'How am I going to tell our mother?'"

Not everyone had family members at home waiting for news of their safe crossing. Oumou "Belle" Bah, 16, and her little brother, Mamadou Saliou Bah, 14, who was the youngest reported passenger on board, left their home after losing both of their parents. Back in their camp, one of the boys' friends told me he cried when he realized there was no one to notify of their death. Belle's friend, also 16, said, "I made a flower necklace and burned it in the fire last night. Belle and I used to make them together." Everyone remembered her as kind, beautiful, and fiercely protective of her brother.

Some had family members waiting for them on the other side. Tahirou Barry, 24, from Guinea was one of them. His friend told me, "He had a beautiful woman waiting for him in France. She was the love of his life. They had known each other since they were little, and they got married after university. Tahirou saved up all of his money to help her get a student visa so she could continue her studies in Europe after their wedding. He was working and trying to save more, so he could join her there, but it was difficult to find work and he couldn't wait any longer. After two years, he decided to cross through Morocco. Tahirou was counting down the days until he would see her again. She didn't know he had left."

Like the newlyweds, Marlyatou "Marly" Diallo, 26, was crossing to meet her husband, who had made it to Germany the year before and soon after, had fallen gravely ill. After her multiple requests for a visa had been denied, she, too, decided to cross through Morocco. "Marly wasn't just my sister—she was the smartest, kindest, most beautiful woman," said Fatima, her older sister, who was watching Marly's only child for her until her return. Her siblings passed the phone around, each sharing with me their memories of "the little one." She was adored. "She'll be deeply missed by us," her older brother, Barry, told me, "But most of all, by her husband and son, whom she loved with all her heart.

FIGURE E.1   A Sampling of the 39 photographs collected for the authors' "Names not Numbers" campaign, which included names, images, and stories of the 47 victims of the February 4th tragedy and can be viewed in full at www.twitter.com/isabella_writes. Places and dates vary.
Photographs courtesy of the victims' families.

How can we explain to this child how the world took his mother from him like this?" Marly's Facebook page is filled with albums documenting every moment of her son's life—from his first tooth to his most recent birthday—5 years old last month. The last image she posted was perhaps an answer to her brother's question. It read, "Son, I carried you for nine months in my body and I'll carry you always in my heart. If there's ever a day when I'm not beside you, know that my spirit is there." A sampling of the photographs provided by the family of Marly and the other victims is pictured in Figure E.1 above.

I hope people will look at the faces of Marly and Tahirou, Karim and Hassane, the twins and the siblings who had no parents to mourn them. I hope they see that on February 4, 2018, there were 47 individuals who packed what few belongings they had on their backs, handed their savings over to smugglers, and stepped onto a small, wooden fishing boat to begin their lives. They were proud and eager, like students at graduation.

I have about 47 students in my lecture hall on Wednesday afternoons. Most of them are the same age as those who are smuggled across the rough waters of the Mediterranean at night. I have thought about how much attention would be devoted to remembering each of their lives if a tragedy of this proportion ever struck. For months, I worked tirelessly, with the help of my friends in Morocco, collecting names, images, and stories, and yet in the end, we only had 39. To this day, there are still family members who do not have answers to their questions, who do not know if their loved ones are gone.

Twenty-six lives will never be a part of the statistics because no effort was made to recover their bodies from the water. Sixteen of the 21 recovered bodies were buried without names because no effort was made to identify them in the morgue. In the 24 hours following this one tragedy, another boat carrying 39 migrants arrived safely at the Chafarinas Islands off the coast of Morocco; 94 migrants were reported dead in a capsized boat off the coat of Libya; and the Guardia Civil intercepted 31 migrants en route to Spain, forcibly retuning their boat to Morocco. Migration across the Mediterranean is growing by the day. And so are the rates of drowning in the small stretch of sea that now serves as the world's deadliest border.

Before the waves overthrew the boat, before he fought for one last breath, I imagine Karim was thinking of how long it might take him to save up for a real soccer ball and if the ground in Spain would feel anything like the ground at home. What I know is that he and the others stepped onto that small boat carrying the dreams of supporting their parents and siblings, partners and children. In all of the years I have spent working with migrants across North Africa, I have never met a single one who did not dream of helping someone they loved. I do not think it is possible to endure the suffering they do without love motivating them to reach the other side.

I hope people will remember these stories the next time they read headlines about overcrowded boats and numbers, not names, of those who were lost at sea. The headlines never change, as if the same bodies are washing ashore again and again. But how could it be the same twins who brought music to their hidden camp, the same siblings who clung tightly to one another, the same big-hearted boy with dreams of being a soccer player? Those 47 are gone, soon to be replaced with others, proud and eager.

This book is dedicated to all those who remain unnamed.

May they finally find the refuge they were seeking.

GLOSSARY

....

A note on language: Research at the geographic and symbolic intersections known as borders often brings together a mixing of languages and cultures and requires moving fluidly between them. The primary languages used in research for this book were French, English, and *Derija*, or Moroccan Arabic, although there was rarely a conversation that did not interweave the three, and often, the conversations included words or phrases from other languages spoken by respondents, including most notably, Bambara, Lingala, and Fula.

Fula, also known as Fulani, Pular, or Peul, is a language with an estimated 24 million speakers spread out across 20 countries in West and Central Africa. For the purposes of this research, it was spoken with Moneba and his brotherhood. These individuals, representing some of my primary research subjects, are from Guinea and Sierra Leone, but all belong to the same ethnic group. The ethnic group, like the language, is known as Peul. Bambara is a Mande language with an estimated 3 million speakers throughout Mali, Burkina Faso, Côte D'Ivoire, Senegal, Gambia, Guinea, Sierra Leone, and Ghana. For the purposes of this research, it was spoken with other primary research subjects, including Kia and her children, who are from Mali. Lingala is a Bantu language with an estimated 70 million speakers throughout the Democratic Republic of the Congo (DRC) and the Republic of the Congo, as well as smaller populations in Angola and the Central African Republic. For the purposes of this research, it was spoken with other primary research subjects, including Phino, who is from the DRC.

At various points in my writing, I include words and phrases in their original language in order to avoid losing their meaning in translation and to better emplace readers in various scenes throughout Morocco. This glossary includes some of the words and phrases that can be found throughout the book.

Derija

Adhan: the call to prayer, heard throughout the Muslim world five times a day.

Amreekia: a foreigner from the United States.

Anduk: a common term for "Attention!" used frequently by street vendors and hawkers.

As-salaam alaikum: the standard greeting meaning "Peace be upon you."

Atay: black tea, traditionally served with mint and sugar.

Banlieue: (French origin) a suburb of the city.

Boza: (unknown origin) a common term used among migrant groups to describe "success" or the ultimate success of reaching Europe.

Camarade: (French origin) a common term used among migrant groups to describe one's friend or brother.

Cheri: (French origin) a common term for one's romantic interest.

Dirham: the national Moroccan currency.

Fatwa: an official ruling on a point of Islamic law.

Hajj: a pilgrimage to Mecca; one of the five pillars of Islam.

Hammam: a neighborhood bathhouse.

Hand of Fatima: also known as "*hamsa*," is the depiction of an open right hand, widely recognized as a sign of protection and used to decorate doors throughout the Middle East.

Hanout: a neighborhood stall selling food staples like bread.

Hashish: a drug made from the resin of cannabis.

Hawker: (English origin) a person who sells goods informally on the street.

Harsha: "worker's bread," made with a high-calorie mixture of cornmeal, eggs, sugar, salt, and animal fat.

Hijab: a head covering traditionally worn by Muslim women.

Imam: a Muslim religious leader who leads prayers in the mosque.

Insha'Allah: a common phrase meaning "God willing."

Jamal: camel, a common term used among migrant groups to describe a smuggler.

Khobz: bread, commonly served at all meals along with *atay* or black tea.

Madrassa: a neighborhood schoolhouse.

Medina: an old (precolonial) part of the city and often the center of informal commercial activity.

Moto: (French origin) a scooter commonly used for transportation in cities.

Mufti: a Muslim legal expert who gives rulings on religious matters.

Patera: (Spanish origin) a small wooden boat used for fishing and now commonly used by migrants and smugglers in the Mediterranean Sea.

Plage: (French origin) a beach.

Riad: a traditional Moroccan home with an interior courtyard.

Salat: prayer; one of the five pillars of Islam.

Sallah Allah 'alaihi wa sallam: a common phrase meaning "peace be upon him" (PBUH) and spoken after the name of the Prophet.

Salon: (French origin) the main gathering room in one's home.

Sawm: fasting; one of the five pillars of Islam.

Shahada: faith; one of the five pillars of Islam.

Souk: an outdoor marketplace.

Tagine: a clay dish traditionally used to cook over an open flame in a neighborhood oven.

Ville nouvelle: (French origin) a new (postcolonial) part of the city and often the center of formal commercial activity.

Zakāt: charity; one of the five pillars of Islam.

BIBLIOGRAPHY

....

Abu-Lughod, Lila. *Writing Women's Worlds: Bedouin Stories*. Berkeley: University of California Press, 1993.

Abum-Nasr, Jamil. *A History of the Maghrib in the Islamic Period*. London: Cambridge University Press, 1987.

Agier, Michel. "Between War and City: Towards an Urban Anthropology of Refugee Camps." *Ethnography* 3, no. 3 (2002): 317–341.

al Makhfi, Jalal. "Morocco's African Immigrants Fear Rising Racism Tide." *AFP*, September 6, 2013. https://voicesofafrica.co.za/moroccos-african-immigrants-fear-rising-racism-tide/

Andersson, Ruben. *Illegality, Inc.: Clandestine Migration and the Business of Bordering Europe*. Oakland: The California Series in Public Anthropology, 2014.

Anzaldúa, Goria. *Borderlands: The New Mestiza = La Frontera*. New York: Aunt Lute Books, 1987.

Appadurai, Arjun. "Putting Hierarchy in Its Place." *Cultural Anthropology* 3, no. 1 (1988): 36–49.

Bachelet, Sebastien. "Murder of Senegalese Migrant Overshadows 'Radically New' Politics of Migration in Morocco." *All Africa,* September 23, 2014. https://africanarguments.org/2014/09/23/murder-of-senegalese-migrant-overshadows-radically-new-politics-of-migration-in-morocco-sebastien-bachelet/

Bairoch, Paul. *Mythes Et Paradoxes De L'histoire Économique*. Paris: Decouverte, 1994.

Baldacchino, Godfrey. "The Coming of Age of Island Studies." *Journal of Economic and Social Geography* 95, no. 3 (2004): 272–283.

Baldwin-Edwards, Martin. "Between a Rock and a Hard Place: North Africa as a Region of Emigration, Immigration and Transit Migration." *Review of African Political Economy* 33:108 (2006): 311–324.

Balibar, Étienne. *We, the People of Europe?* Princeton, NJ: Princeton University Press, 2003.

Barth, Fredrik. *Cosmologies in the Making: A Generative Approach to Cultural Variation in Inner New Guinea*. Cambridge, UK: Cambridge University Press, 1987.

Barth, Fredrik. *Ethnic Groups and Boundaries*. Chicago: Waveland Press, 1969.

Basch, Linda, Nina Glick Schiller, and Cristina Szanton Blanc. *Nations Unbound: Transnational Projects, Postcolonial Predicaments and Deterritorialized Nation-States*. New York: Routledge, 1994.

Bateson, Gregory. "Culture Contact and Schismogenesis." *Man* 35 (1935): 178–183.

Bauman, Zygmunt. "In the Lowly Nowherevilles of Liquid Modernity: Comments on and Around Agier." *Ethnography* 3, no. 3 (2002): 343–349.

Bauman, Zygmunt. *Wasted Lives: Modernity and Its Outcasts*. Oxford: Blackwell, 2004.

Behar, Ruth. *Translated Woman: Crossing the Border with Esperanza's Story*. Boston: Beacon Press, 2003.

Behar, Ruth. *The Vulnerable Observer: Anthropology That Breaks Your Heart*. Boston: Beacon Press, 1996.

Benmehdi, Hassan. "Casablanca Conference Tackles Counterfeit Goods." *Morocco World News*, December 15, 2011.

Benslama, Fethi. "*Le geste de Bouazizi a changé le modèle du martyr*." *Jeune Afrique*, 4 March. 2011. https://www.jeuneafrique.com/192557/societe/fethi-benslama-le-geste-de-bouazizi-a-chang-le-mod-le-du-martyr/

Berger, John. 1992. *About Looking*. New York: Vintage.

Besteman, Catherine. "Militarized Global Apartheid." *Current Anthropology* 19 (2019): 26–38.

Bhabha, Homi. *The Location of Culture*. New York: Routledge, 1994.

Bonnet, J., and R. Bossard. "Aspects Géographiques De L'émigration Marocaine Vers l'Europe." *Revue De Géographie Du Maroc* 23–24 (1973): 5–50.

Bosniak, Linda. *The Citizen and the Alien: Dilemmas of Contemporary Membership*. Princeton, NJ: Princeton University Press, 2006.

Bourdieu, Pierre. *Language and Symbolic Power*. Cambridge, MA: Harvard University Press, 1999.

Bourqia, Rahma, and Susan Gilson Miller (eds.). *In the Shadow of the Sultan: Culture, Power, and Politics in Morocco*. Cambridge, MA: Harvard Center for Middle Eastern Studies, 1999.

Braudel, Fernand. *La Méditerranée et le Monde Méditerranéen a l'époque de Philippe II*. Paris; Armand Colin, 1949.

Brett, Mark. *Genesis: Procreation and the Politics of Identity*. New York: Routledge, 2000.

Brooks, Andrew. "The Hidden Trade in our Second-Hand Clothes Given to Charity." *The Guardian*. 13 Feb 2015. https://www.theguardian.com/sustainable-business/sustainable-fashion-blog/2015/feb/13/second-hand-clothes-charity-donations-africa

Brubaker, Rogers. *Citizenship and Nationhood in France and Germany.* Cambridge, MA: Harvard University Press, 1998.

Brubaker, Rogers. "Ethnicity, Race, and Nationalism." *Annual Review of Sociology* 35 (2009): 21–42.

Brubaker, Rogers. *Nationalism Reframed: Nationhood and the National Question in the New Europe.* Cambridge, UK: Cambridge University Press, 1996.

Brunhes, J. *Human Geography.* London: Methuen, 1920.

Cameron, C. "How People Moved among Ancient Societies: Broadening the View." *American Anthropologist* 15, no. 2 (2013): 218–231.

Canclini, Nestor Garcia. *Consumers and Citizens: Globalization and Multicultural Conflicts.* Minneapolis: University of Minnesota Press. 1995.

Castles, Stephen. *Ethnicity and Globalization: From Migrant Worker to Transnational Citizen.* London: Sage Publications, 2000.

Ceuppens, Bambi, and Peter Geschiere. "Autochthony: Local or Global? New Modes in the Struggle over Citizenship and Belonging in Africa and Europe." *Annual Review of Anthropology* 34 (2005): 385–409.

Chavez, Leo. "The Condition of Illegality." *International Migration* 45, no. 3 (2007): 192–196.

Chavez, Leo. *The Latino Threat: Constructing Immigrants, Citizens, and the Nation.* Palo Alto, CA: Stanford University Press, 2008.

Cherribi, Sam. *In the House of War: Dutch Islam Observed.* New York: Oxford University Press, 2010.

Cherribi, Sam, and Matthew Pesce. "Khatibi: A Sociologist in Literature." In Kirstin Bratt, Youness Elbousty, and Devin Stewart (eds.), *Vitality and Dynamism: Interstitial Dialogues of Language, Politics, and Religion in Morocco's Literary Tradition.* Leiden NL: Leiden University Press, (2014): 177–184.

Cherti, Myriam, and Michael Collyer. "Immigration and Pensée d'Etat: Moroccan Migration Policy Changes as Transformation of 'Geopolitical Culture.'" *Journal of North African Studies* 4 (2005): 590–604.

Chu, Julie. *Cosmologies of Credit: Transnational Mobility and the Politics of Destination in China.* Durham, NC: Duke University Press, 2010.

Clark-Ibañez, Marisol. 2004. "Framing the Social World with Photo-Elicitation Interviews." *American Behavioral Scientist* 47 (12) 1507–1527.

Collyer, Michael. "In-Between Places: Trans-Saharan Transit Migrants in Morocco and the Fragmented Journey to Europe." *Antipode* 39, no. 4 (2007): 668–690.

Collyer, Michael, Myriam Cherti, Thomas Lacroix & Anja van Heelsum. "Migration and Development: The Euro–Moroccan Experience." *Journal of Ethnic and Migration Studies* 35, no. 10 (2009) 1555–1570.

Combs-Schilling, M.E. *Sacred Performances: Islam, Sexuality, and Sacrifice.* New York: Columbia University Press, 1989.

Crapanzano, Vincent. *Tuhami: Portrait of a Moroccan.* Chicago: University of Chicago Press, 1985.

Crush, Jonathan, & Bruce Frayne. *Surviving on the Move: Migration, Poverty and Development in Southern Africa.* Oxford: African Books Collective, 2010.

D'Alisera, Joann. "I [heart] Islam: Popular Religious Commodities, Sites of Inscription, and Transnational Sierra Leonean Identity." *Journal of Material Culture* 6, no. 1 (2001): 91–110.

Da Silva, Denise Ferreira. *Toward a Global Idea of Race.* Minneapolis: University of Minnesota Press, 2007.

Davis, Robert. *Christian Slaves, Muslim Masters: White Slavery in the Mediterranean, The Barbary Coast, and Italy, 1500–1800.* London: Palgrave Macmillan, 2003.

De Alencastro, Luiz Felipe. "The African Slave Trade and the Construction of the Iberian Atlantic." In Kerry Bystrom and Joseph Slaughter (eds.), *The Global South Atlantic.* (pp. 33–45). New York: Fordham University Press. 2017.

De Almeida Mendes, Antonio. "The Foundations of the System: A Reassessment of the Slave Trade to the Spanish Americas in the Sixteenth and Seventeenth Centuries." In David Eltis and David Richardson (eds) *Extending the Frontiers: Essays on the New Transatlantic Slave Trade Database* (pp. 63–93). New Haven: Yale University Press, 2008.

De Genova, Nicholas. "Migrant 'Illegality' and Deportability in Everyday Life." *Annual Review of Anthropology* 31 (2002): 419–447.

De Genova, Nicholas. *Working the Boundaries: Race, Space and "Illegality" in Mexican Chicago.* Durham, NC: Duke University Press, 2005.

De Genova, Nicholas, and Nathalie Peutz. *The Deportation Regime: Sovereignty, Space, and the Freedom of Movement.* Durham, NC: Duke University Press, 2010.

De Genova, Nicholas, and Ana Ramos-Zayas. *Latino Crossings: Mexicans, Puerto Ricans, and the Politics of Race and Citizenship.* New York: Routledge, 2003.

De Haas, Hein. "Morocco's Migration Transition: Trends, Determinants and Future Scenarios." *Global Migration Perspectives* 28 (2005): 1–38.

De Haas, Hein. "Migration and Development: A Theoretical Perspective." *International Migration Institute: Working Paper Series, Paper 9* (2008): 1–61.

De Haas, Hein. "Trans-Saharan Migration to North Africa and the EU: Historical Roots and Current Trends." *The Migration Information Source* (2012): digital version. https://www.migrationpolicy.org/article/trans-saharan-migration-north-africa-and-eu-historical-roots-and-current-trends

De Haas, Hein, and Simona Vezzoli. "Time to Temper the Faith: Comparing the Migration and Development Experiences of Mexico and Morocco." *The Migration Information Source* (2012): digital version. https://www.migrationpolicy.org/article/time-temper-faith-comparing-migration-and-development-experiences-mexico-and-morocco

De Haldevang, Max. "Why Do We Still Use the Term 'Sub-Saharan Africa'?" *Quartz,* September 1, 2016. https://qz.com/africa/770350/why-do-we-still-say-subsaharan-africa/

De Saussure, Ferdinand. *Course in General Linguistics.* Chicago: Open Court, 1916.

De Tapia, Stéphane. "L'émigration turque: circulation migratoire et diasporas." *L'Espace géographique* 23, no. 1 (1994): 19–28.

Dwyer, Daisy Hilse. *Images and Self-Images: Male and Female in Morocco.* New York: Columbia University Press, 1978.

Dwyer, Kevin. *Moroccan Dialogues: Anthropology in Question*. Baltimore: Johns Hopkins University Press, 1982.

El Bouih, Fatna & Slyomovics, Susan. "'This Time I Choose When to Leave:' An Interview with Fatna El Bouih." *Middle East Report* 42 (2002): 42–43.

El Hamel, Chouki. *Black Morocco: A History of Slavery, Race, and Islam*. London: Cambridge University Press, 2014.

El Hamel, Chouki. "'Race,' Slavery and Islam in Maghribi Mediterranean Thought: The Question of the Haratin in Morocco." *Journal of North African Studies* 7, no. 3 (2002): 29–52.

Ennaji, Mohammed. *Soldats, domestiques et concubines. L'esclavage au Maroc au XIXe Siècle*. Casablanca: Editions Eddif, 1994.

Evans-Pritchard, E. E. *The Nuer: A Description of the Modes of Livelihood and Political Institutions of a Nilotic People*. Oxford: Clarendon Press, 1940.

Fábos, Anita. *'Brothers' or Others?: Propriety and Gender for Muslim Arab Sudanese in Egypt*. New York: Berghahn Books, 2010.

Fanon, Frantz. *Black Skin, White Masks*. New York: Grove Press, 1952.

Fanon, Frantz. *The Wretched of the Earth*. New York: Grove Press, 1963.

Fassin, Didier. "The Biopolitics of Otherness: Undocumented Foreigners and Racial Discrimination in French Public Debate." *Anthropology Today* 17, no. 1 (2001): 3–7.

Fassin, Didier. "Compassion and Repression: The Moral Economy of Immigration Policies in France." *Cultural Anthropology* 20, no. 3 (2005): 362–387.

Ferrer-Gallardo, Xavier. "The Spanish-Moroccan Border Complex: Processes of Geopolitical, Functional and Symbolic Rebordering." *Political Geography* 27 (2008): 301–321.

Fikes, Kesha. *Managing African Portugal: The Citizen-Migrant Distinction*. Durham, NC: Duke University Press, 2009.

Fisher, Michael, and Mehdi Abedi. *Debating Muslims: Cultural Dialogues in Postmodernity and Tradition*. Madison: University of Wisconsin Press, 2002.

Foner, Nancy. *Islands in the City: West Indian Migration to New York*. Berkeley: University of California Press, 2001.

Foucault, Michel. *The Birth of Biopolitics: Lectures at the Collège de France, 1978–1979*. London: Picador, 2004.

Foucault, Michel. *Discipline and Punish: The Birth of the Prison*. New York: Random House, 1977.

Foucault, Michel. *Power/Knowledge: Selected Interviews and Other Writings, 1972–1977*. New York: Pantheon Books, 1980.

Freeman, Carla. "Is Local: Global as Feminine: Masculine? Rethinking the Gender of Globalization." *Signs* 26, no. 4 (2001): 1007–1037.

Geschiere, Peter. *The Perils of Belonging: Autochthony, Citizenship, and Exclusion in Africa and Europe*. Chicago: University of Chicago Press, 2009.

Gilson Miller, Susan. *A History of Modern Morocco*. Cambridge, UK: Cambridge University Press, 2013.

Gledhill, John. "Rights and the Poor." In Richard Wilson and Jon Mitchell (eds.), *Human Rights in Global Perspective: Anthropological Studies of Rights, Claims and Entitlements* (pp. 209–228). London and New York: Routledge, 2003.

Glick Schiller, Nina, Linda Basch, and Cristina Szanton Blanc. *Towards a Transnational Perspective on Migration: Race, Class, Ethnicity, and Nationalism Reconsidered.* New York: New York Academy of Sciences, 1992.

Glick Schiller, Nina, and Georges Fouron. *Georges Woke Up Laughing: Long Distance Nationalism and the Search for Home.* Durham, NC: Duke University Press Books, 2001.

Glissant, Édouard. *Philosophie de la relation: Poésie en étendue.* Paris: Gallimard, 2008.

Goldenberg, David. *The Curse of Ham: Race and Slavery in Early Judaism, Christianity, and Islam.* Princeton, NJ: Princeton University Press, 2003.

Gupta, Akhil, and James Ferguson. "Beyond 'Culture': Space, Identity, and the Politics of Difference." *Cultural Anthropology* 7, no. 1 (1992): 6–23.

Hall, Bruce. *A History of Race in Muslim West Africa, 1600–1960.* Cambridge, UK: Cambridge University Press, 2011.

Hall, Stuart. *Representation: Cultural Representations and Signifying Practices.* New York: Sage Publications, 1997.

Hall, Stuart. "Who Needs 'Identity'?" *Identity: A Reader.* In Peter du Gay, Jessica Evans, and Paul Redman (eds.), *Identity: A Reader* (pp. 15–30). New York: Sage Publications, 2000.

Hammoudi, Abdellah. *Master and Disciple: The Cultural Foundations of Moroccan Authoritarianism.* Chicago: University of Chicago Press, 1997.

Hannaford, Dinah. *Marriage Without Borders: Transnational Spouses in Neoliberal Senegal.* Philadelphia: University of Pennsylvania Press, 2017.

Harper, Douglas. "Talking about Pictures: A Case for Photo Elicitation." *Visual Studies* 17 (2002): 13–26.

Hart, David. *Tribe and Society in Rural Morocco.* New York: Routledge, 2000.

Hazan, Pierre. *Judging War, Judging History: Behind Truth and Reconciliation.* Palo Alto, CA: Stanford University Press, 2010.

Hazan, Pierre. "The Nature of Sanctions: The Case of Morocco's Equity and Reconciliation Commission." *International Review of the Red Cross* 90, no. 870 (June 2008): 399–407.

Hellie, Richard. *Slavery in Russia, 1450–1725.* Chicago: University of Chicago Press, 1984.

Hirschberg, H. Z. *A History of the Jews of North Africa.* Leiden: Brill, 1974.

Hochstadt Steven. *Mobility and Modernity: Migration in Germany, 1820–1989.* Ann Arbor: University of Michigan Press, 1999.

hooks, bell. *Black Looks: Race and Representation.* Cambridge, UK: South End Press, 1999.

Horst, Cindy, and Katarzyna Grabska. "Flight and Exile—Uncertainty in the Context of Conflict-Induced Displacement." *Social Analysis: Journal of Cultural and Social Practice* 59, no. 1 (2015): 1–18.

Inhorn, Marcia. *The New Arab Man: Emergent Masculinities, Technologies, and Islam in the Middle East*. Princeton, NJ: Princeton University Press, 2012.

Kearney, Michael. "From the Invisible Hand to Visible Feet: Anthropological Studies of Migration and Development." *Annual Review of Anthropology* 15 (1986): 331–361.

Kearney, Michael. "The Local and the Global: The Anthropology of Globalization and Transnationalism." *Annual Review of Anthropology*. 24 (1995): 547–565.

Khatibi, Abdelkebir. *Maghreb Pluriel*. Paris: Denoel, 1983.

Krasniqi, Gëzim. "Contested States as Liminal Spaces of Citizenship: Comparing Kosovo and the Turkish Republic of Northern Cyprus." *Ethnopolitics* 18, no. 3 (2019): 298–314.

Kusenbach, Margarethe. "Street Phenomenology: The Go-Along as Ethnographic Research Tool." *Ethnography* 4, no. 3 (2004): 455–485.

Lalami, Laila. "Arab Uprisings: What the February 20 Protests Tell Us about Morocco." *The Nation*, February 17, 2011a.

Lalami, Laila. "The Moroccan 'Exception.'" *The Nation*. 24 Aug. 2011b.

Laroui, Abdallah. *The History of the Maghrib: An Interpretive Essay*. Princeton, NJ: Princeton University Press, 1983.

Levitt, Peggy. *The Transnational Villagers*. Berkeley: University of California Press, 2001.

Levitt, Peggy. "Transnational Migrants: When 'Home' Means More Than One Country." *Migration Information Source*, 2004.

Levitt, Peggy, and Nadya Jaworsky. "Transnational Migration Studies: Past Developments and Future Trends." *Annual Review of Sociology* 33 (2007): 129–156.

Levitt, Peggy, and Rafael de la Dehesa. "Transnational Migration and the Redefinition of the State: Variations and Explanations." *Ethnic and Racial Studies* 26, no. 4 (2003): 587–611.

Lewis, Bernard. *Race and Color in Islam*. New York: Octagon Books, 1979.

Lewis, Bernard. *Race and Slavery in the Middle East: an Historical Enquiry*. New York: Oxford University Press, 1990.

Lucassen, Jan, and Leo Lucassen. "The Mobility Transition Revisited, 1500–1900: What the Case of Europe Can Offer to Global History." *Journal of Global History* 4 (2009): 347–377.

Lucassen, Leo. "Where Do We Go from Here? New Perspectives on Global Migration History." *International Review of Social History* 49, no. 3 (2004): 505–510.

Lucht, Hans. *Darkness Before Daybreak: African Migrants Living on the Margins in Southern Italy Today*. Los Angeles: University of California Press, 2011.

Mahmood, Saba. *Politics of Piety: The Islamic Revival and the Feminist Subject*. Princeton, NJ: Princeton University Press, 2004.

Malkki, Liisa. "Citizens of Humanity: Internationalism and the Imagined Community of Nations." *Diaspora* 3, no. 1 (1994): 41–68.

Malkki, Liisa. "Refugees and Exile: From 'Refugee Studies' to the National Order of Things." *Annual Review of Anthropology* 24 (1995): 495–523.

Mamdani, Mahmood. *Citizen and Subject: Contemporary Africa and the Legacy of Late Colonialism.* Princeton, NJ: Princeton University Press, 1996.

Manning, Patrick. *Migration in World History.* New York: Routledge, 2005.

Martin, Philip. "Trade and Migration: NAFTA and Agriculture." Washington, DC: Institute for International Economics, 1993, pp. 457–476.

Martin, Philip, and Edward Taylor. "The Anatomy of a Migration Hump." In J. E. Taylor (ed.), *Development Strategy, Employment, and Migration: Insights from Models.* (pp. 43–62). Paris: OECD, Development Centre, 1996.

Massey, Douglas. *Worlds in Motion : Understanding International Migration at the End of the Millennium.* London: Oxford University Press, 2005.

Mauss, Marcel. *The Gift: Forms and Functions of Exchange in Archaic Societies.* New York: Norton, 1967.

McDougall, James, and Judith Scheele. *Saharan Frontiers: Space and Mobility in Northwest Africa.* Bloomington: Indiana University Press, 2012.

McMurray, David. *In and Out of Morocco: Smuggling and Migration in a Frontier Boomtown.* Minneapolis: University of Minnesota Press, 2001.

Munholland, Kim. *The Emergence of the Colonial Military in France, 1880–1905.* Ph.D. Thesis, Princeton University, 1964.

Natter, Katharina. "The Formation of Morocco's Policy towards Irregular Migration (2000–2007): Political Rationale and Policy Processes." *International Migration* 52, no. 5 (2013): 15–28.

Nelson, Katie. "Viewing Migration as a Key Human Adaptive Strategy." *General Anthropology* 25, no. 2 (2018): 1–11.

Newcomb, Rachel. "Gendering the City, Gendering the Nation: Contesting Urban Space in Fes, Morocco." *City and Society* 18, no. 2 (2006): 288–311.

Ngai, Mae. *Impossible Subjects: Illegal Aliens and the Making of Modern America.* Princeton, NJ: Princeton University Press, 2005.

Oliver, Douglas. *The Pacific Islands.* Honolulu: University of Hawaii Press, 1951.

Olwig, Karen. *Caribbean Journeys: An Ethnography of Migration and Home in Three Family Networks.* Durham, NC: Duke University Press, 2007.

Ong, Aihwa. *Buddha Is Hiding: Refugees, Citizenship, the New America.* Berkeley: University of California Press, 2003.

Ong, Aihwa. "Citizenship as Subject Making: New Immigrants Negotiate Racial and Ethnic Boundaries." *Current Anthropology* 37, no. 5 (1996): 737–762.

Ong, Aihwa. *Flexible Citizenship: The Cultural Logics of Transnationality.* Durham, NC: Duke University Press, 1999.

Ong, Aihwa, and Michael Peletz (eds.). *Bewitching Women, Pious Men: Gender and Body Politics in Southeast Asia.* Berkeley: University of California Press, 1995.

Ouzgane, Lahoucine. *Islamic Masculinities.* London: Zed Books, 2006.

Pandolfo, Stefania. "'The Burning': Finitude and the Politico-Theological Imagination of Illegal Migration." *Anthropological Theory* 7 (2007): 329–363.

Parker, Geoffrey. *The Military Revolution: Military Innovation and the Rise of the West, 1500–1800.* Cambridge, UK: Cambridge University Press, 1988.

Peletz, Michael. "Neither Reasonable Nor Responsible: Contrasting Representations of Masculinity in a Malay Society." *Cultural Anthropology* 9, no. 2 (1994): 133–176.

Phillip, William. *Slavery from Roman Times to the Early Transatlantic Trade.* Minneapolis: University of Minnesota Press, 1985.

Pierre, Jemima. "The Predicament of Blackness: Postcolonial Ghana and the Politics of Race." Chicago: University of Chicago Press, 2012.

Ramsay, Georgina. "Incommensurable Futures and Displaced Lives: Sovereignty as Control over Time." *Public Culture* 29 no. 3 (2017): 515–538.

Rippingale, James. "Are Moroccan Gangsters Being Paid to Beat Up Sub-Saharan Migrants?" *Vice*, November 22, 2014. https://www.vice.com/en_us/article/dp-ww9x/are-moroccan-gangsters-being-paid-to-beat-up-african-migrants-803

Robben, Antonius, and Jeffrey Sluka. *Ethnographic Fieldwork: An Anthropological Reader.* Malden, MA: Blackwell Publishers, 2007.

Sadiqi, Fatima. "Migration Related Policies and Institutions in Morocco." *Euro-Mediterranean Consortium for Applied Research on International Migration* (2004): 1–15. http://hdl.handle.net/1814/11698

Schwartz, Mattathias. "The Anniversary of the Lampedusa Tragedy." *The New Yorker*, October 3, 2014. https://www.newyorker.com/news/news-desk/anniversary-lampedusa-tragedy

Segalla, Spencer. *The Moroccan Soul: French Education, Colonial Ethnology, and Muslim Resistance, 1912–1956.* Lincoln: University of Nebraska Press, 2009.

Shaw, Rosalind, and Lars Waldorf. *Localizing Transitional: Justice Interventions and Priorities after Mass Violence.* Palo Alto, CA: Stanford University Press, 2010.

Skeldon, Ronald. *Migration and Development: A Global Perspective.* New York: Routledge, 1997.

Slyomovics, Susan. *The Performance of Human Rights in Morocco.* Philadelphia: University of Pennsylvania Press, 2005.

Stanfield, John. *Rethinking Race and Ethnicity in Research Methods.* New York: Routledge, 2011.

Stoller, Paul. *The Power of the Between: An Anthropological Odyssey.* Chicago: University of Chicago Press, 2008.

Szakolczai, Arpad. *Reflexive Historical Sociology.* London: Routledge, 2000.

Szakolczai, Arpad. "Liminality and Experience: Structuring Transitory Situations and Transformative Events." *International Political Anthropology* 2, no. 1(2009): 141–172.

Thomassen, Bjorn. "Liminality." In A. Harrington, B. Marshall and H. P. Müller (eds.) *Routledge Encyclopedia of Social Theory* (pp. 322–323). London: Routledge, 2006.

Thomassen, Bjorn. "The Uses and Meanings of Liminality." *International Political Anthropology* 2 (2009): 5–27.

Ticktin, Miriam. "Where Ethics and Politics Meet: The Violence of Humanitarianism in France." *American Ethnologist* 33 (2006): 33–49.

Tilly, Charles. *From Mobilization to Revolution.* Boston: Addison-Wesley, 1978.

Todorova, Maria. "Historiography of the countries of Eastern Europe: Bulgaria." *American Historical Review* 97, no. 4 (1992): 1105–1117.

Toynbee, A. J. *A Study of History, Vol.1.* London: Oxford University Press, 1934.

Turner, Victor. *The Forest of Symbols: Aspects of Ndembu Ritual.* Ithaca: Cornell University Press, 1967.

Turner, Victor. *The Ritual Process: Structure and Anti-structure.* Chicago: Aldine Publishing, 1969.

Turner, Victor, and Edith Turner. *Image and Pilgrimage in Christian Culture.* New York: Columbia University Press, 1978.

Van Gennep, Arnold. *The Rites of Passage.* Chicago: University of Chicago Press, 1909.

Vink, Markus. "'The World's Oldest Trade': Dutch Slavery and Slave Trade in the Indian Ocean in the Seventeenth Century." *Journal of World History* 14, no. 2 (2003): 131–177.

Wikan, Unni. "Toward an Experience-Near Anthropology." *Cultural Anthropology* 6, no. 3 (1991): 285–305.

Wilkinson, Isambard. "Abandoned to die on the desert road of despair." *The Telegraph.* Nov 11, 2005. https://www.telegraph.co.uk/news/worldnews/africaandindianocean/morocco/1500412/Abandoned-to-die-on-the-desert-road-of-despair.html

Willen, Sarah. *Transnational Migration to Israel in Global Comparative Context.* Lexington, MA: Lexington Press, 2007a.

Willen, Sarah. "Toward a Critical Phenomenology of 'Illegality': State Power, Criminalization, and Abjectivity among Undocumented Migrant Workers in Tel Aviv, Israel." *International Migration* 45, no. 3 (2007b): 8–38.

Williams, Brackette. "A Class Act: Anthropology and the Race to Nation across Ethnic Terrain." *Annual Review of Anthropology* 18 (1989): 401–444.

Wilson, Richard. *The Politics of Truth and Reconciliation in South Africa: Legitimizing the Post-Apartheid State.* Cambridge, UK: Cambridge University Press, 2001.

Wolf, Eric. *The Human Condition in Latin America.* Oxford: Oxford University Press, 1972.

Yow, Valerie. *Recording Oral History: A Guide for the Humanities and Social Sciences.* Los Angeles: Altamira Press, 2005.

Zelinsky, Wilbur. "The Hypothesis of the Mobility Transition." *Geographical Review* 61, no. 2 (1971): 219–249.

Zemer, Bob. *Kif: Hashish from Morocco.* Kindle Books, 2010.

Zuluaga, Jonathan Echeverri. "Errance and Elsewheres among Africans Waiting to Restart Their Journeys in Dakar, Senegal." *Cultural Anthropology* 30, no. 4 (2015): 589–610.

INDEX

....

Algeria, xxxiv, 50, 58, 60, 62–63, 130
    Western Mediterranean route, 207
    See also border (between Algeria-
        Morocco)
anthropological methods
See interviewing; participant observation;
    photo elicitation; oral history (and
    "oral future") collection; visual life
    history collection
Arab Spring, 90, 95, 121
asylum, xxix–xxxiii, 41, 65, 80, 83, 88, 125,
    130, 143, 156–157, 187, 196–201,
    207–211, 215
    legal process to, xxxi
Australia
    border security model, xxxiii–xxxiv
    See also border externalization (Australia
        to South Pacific Islands); immigration
        policy (Australian)

Barca Nostra ("Our Ship") by Christophe
    Büchel, 206
blackness (as a marked category), 41, 47, 76,
    107, 128–129, 181, 196
    black Moroccans, 181–186
border
    anthropological study of, 191–193
    between Algeria-Morocco, 81, 102

between Spain-Morocco, 43, 48, 106,
    125, 193
between United States-Mexico, 43, 48,
    187–189, 193
border externalization, xxxii, 4, 40–41,
    212, 221
    Australia to South Pacific Islands
        (Manus and Nauru), xxxiii
    European Union to North Africa, 41,
        205–208
    United States to Mexico, xxxiii, 129
brotherhoods (informal communities of
    migrants), xxiii, 115–117, 121, 217
    structure of, xxiii, 118, 121
    See also forest camps

Ceuta, xxix, 60, 62, 82, 116, 192, 210
    See also border (between Spain-Morocco)
Christianity, 52, 108–109, 112, 129,
    churches (community centers), 125, 178
class, 35, 174–176
    lower-class Moroccan laborers, 15,
        106–107, 175, 183–184
    upper-class African migrants, 21, 52,
        165–173, 186
    See also labor (division of)
colonialism, 60–62, 90, 97, 212
    neocolonialism, 76, 98

Constellations by Bouchra Khalili, 162

De Genova, Nicholas (an ethnographic study
   of Latino migrants in the United
   States), 188–190
Democratic Republic of the Congo (DRC),
   139
   Congolese migrant experience, 149–155,
   195–204
deportation, 81, 86, 102, 163, 198–199,
   207–108
debt (accrued for the cost of migration), 170,
   126–127
detention centers (official migrant housing),
   3, 191, 221
   Australian, xxxiii
   Melilla's detention center for
   unaccompanied minors, 215–219
   Moroccan, 197, 215
   Spanish, xxix–xxx, 199, 208
Doctors Without Borders (also referred to as
   Médecins Sans Frontières or MSF),
   xxxiv, 86–87
   annual report, 87–88
   search and rescue (SAR) in the
   Mediterranean Sea, 207–208

education, 90, 97, 166, 174
   basic rights to, 40, 110–111, 133, 179–180,
   198, 208
European Union (EU)
   partnership with Morocco, 88, 209
   See also border externalization (European
   Union to North Africa); immigration
   policy (European)

forest camps (unofficial migrant housing), 3,
   74, 108, 197, 214
   structure of, xxiii, 118, 121
   police raids of, xxii, 114,
   rock art, 122
   See also brotherhoods
femininity (female migrants), 100, 110–113
   in Islam, 178–179
   in migrant communities, 107–109, 127,
   112
   in the labor market, 15, 105–107
   See also labor (division of)

Fikes, Kesha (an ethnographic study of
   African migrants in the EU), 188–190

gender
   anthropological study of, 15–16, 20–23,
   117–118
   See also labor (division of); femininity;
   masculinity
Greece, xxxi
   Eastern Mediterranean route, 207
Guardia Civil (also referred to as the Civil
   Guard)
   patrol at the Spain-Morocco border,
   xxviii, xxxii, 81
   history and mission of, xxviii
   search and rescue (SAR) in the
   Mediterranean Sea, 226, 229
   use of force on migrants, xxviii, xxx, 83
Guinea
   Guinean migrant experience, xxi–xxxvi,
   214–221

Hassan II, king of Morocco (1961-1999),
   91–94
   "Years of Lead," 91–93
healthcare
   basic rights to, 110, 198, 208
Hein, De Haas, 49
hrig ("the burning"), xxxv–xxxvi,
   120, 214

immigration policy, 38–40
   American, xxxiii, 210
   Australian, xxxiii–xxxiv
   European, xxxiii, 88, 208–211, 221
   Moroccan, 88
international human rights, xxx, 38–41, 174,
   197, 199–201, 209–211
   establishment of, xxxii
International Organization for Migration
   (IOM)
   history and mission of, 51
   Missing Migrants Project, 207
interviewing, 119, 145, 200
   "go-along" interviewing, 102
Islam
   mosques (community centers), 178–179
   pillars of, 103

Islam (*continued*)
   See also femininity (in Islam); masculinity (in Islam); race (as referenced in Islamic texts); slavery (as referenced in Islamic texts)
Italy, xxxi, 35, 47, 53, 139, 206–207
   Central Mediterranean route, 207
labor
   division of, 102–103, 179, 184–185
   migrant-dominated labor markets (also referred to as informal economies), 102, 105–06
   migrant-laborer, 49–51, 105–106, 112, 189
   See also femininity (in the labor market); masculinity (in the labor market)

Lampedusa
   tragedy, 205–206
Libya, xxxiv, 58, 63, 206, 208, 220, 229
   Central Mediterranean route, 207
liminality, 3, 114, 128, 133, 213–214
   anthropological origins of, 4–8
   Turner's research on, 108–109, 117, 213–214
   Van Gennep's research on, 5–6

Mali
   Malian migrant experience, 100–113
Martin, Phillip & Taylor, Edward (migration hump theory), 48–49
masculinity (male migrants), 22–23, 138
   in Islam, 117–122
   in migrant communities, 111–112
   in the labor market, 137, 139, 172–173
   See also labor (division of)
media
   Australian anti-migrant and anti-refugee campaign, xxxiii–xxxiv
   censorship of media in North Africa, xxxiv, 117
   European coverage of migrant and refugee deaths, xxxix, 210
   global coverage of the migrant and refugee "crisis," xxxi–xxxii, 41–43, 208
   influence of media on migrant communities, 33, 53–54
   Moroccan anti-immigration campaign, 79
   Moroccan anti-racism campaign, 72

Moroccan coverage of migrant and refugee deaths, 72–74, 165, 186
   portrayals of Islam, 118
   See also social media
Mediterranean Sea, xxxi
   tragedies in, 223–230
   See also Lampedusa (tragedy); search and rescue (in the Mediterranean Sea)
Melilla, xxix, 60, 62, 82, 116, 192, 210
See also border (between Spain-Morocco)
Mexico
   Mexican migrant communities, 187–189
   See also border (United States-Mexico); border externalization (United States to Mexico)
migrant (immigrant, emigrant), 2, 49–51, 97, 123–127
   definition of, 132
Mohammed VI, king of Morocco (1999-present), 93–96, 167
   Equity and Reconciliation Commission (IER), 94
Morocco
   Moroccan migrant experience, 31–37, 53, 72, 118–120, 129
   partnership with Senegal, 167
   Western Mediterranean route, 207
   See also border (between Algeria-Morocco); border (between Spain-Morocco); border externalization (European Union to North Africa); European Union (partnership with Morocco); United States (partnership with Morocco)

nongovernmental organizations (NGO), 12
   La Fondation Orient-Occident (Moroccan NGO), 79–81
   Spanish Commission for the Assistance of Refugees (Spanish NGO), 208–209

oral history (and "oral future") collection, 145–148

participant observation, 102
photo elicitation, 144–148
police, Moroccan police force, xxii, 76, 81, 210

"pat-downs" (street harassment), 75
raids, xxii, xxxv, 75, 114
illicit repatriation by, xxx, 81, 86, 88
    See also forest camps (police raids of)

race
    anthropological study of, 176–180
    as referenced in Islamic texts, 54–57
    North African history of, 57–60
    See also blackness; labor (division of);
        whiteness
refugee
    definition of, 132
    studies, 132–133
    See also United States (refugee
        resettlement)
remittances, 33, 124, 126–127, 148, 153–155
repatriation, 211
    illicit practice of, xxx, xxxii, 27, 81–86, 88
    See also police (illicit repatriation by)

search and rescue (SAR)
    criminalization of, 207
    in the Mediterranean Sea, 198
Senegal
    exchange of university students from,
        165–171
    trade of goods from, 105
    See also Morocco (partnership with
        Senegal)
Sierra Leone
    Sierra Leonean migrant experience,
        155–160
slavery, 72, 158
    as referenced in Islamic texts, 58–59
    European history of, 45, 47, 57
    North African history of, 57–60
smuggling
    of drugs, 77–79
    of humans, 77, 81–82, 85, 115, 139,
        225–226
    of illicit goods, 77, 105
    routes, 139
social media, 155–160
Spain, xxxi, 47–48, 60–62, 80, 93, 161,
        207–208

Law on the Right to Asylum and Refugee
        Status, 208–209
    Western Mediterranean route, 207
    See also border (between Spain-Morocco)
Sub-Saharan Africa
    origins of term, 63–65

transnationalism, 160, 192
    anthropological origins of, 122–128
    American model, 123
    French model, 123
trans-Saharan trade, 47, 52
Tunisia, 50, 58, 60–61, 63, 95, 121
    Central Mediterranean route, 207
Turkey, 47, 211
    Eastern Mediterranean route, 207
Turner, Victor, 5–8, 108–109, 117,
        213–214
    See also liminality (Turner's research on)

United Nations Refugee Agency (also
        referred to as the United Nations High
        Commissioner for Refugees or the
        UNHCR), xxxii, 83, 130, 156–157,
        207, 211
    history and mission of, 51
    UNHCR definition of a refugee, 132
    UNHCR definition of a migrant, 132
United States
    migrant and refugee communities in,
        124–128, 188–189
    partnership with Morocco, 95
    refugee resettlement, xxxii–xxxiii
    See also border (between United
        States-Mexico); border externalization
        (United States to Mexico); immigration
        policy (American)

visual life history collection, 144–148,
        149 (example 1), 155 (example 2)

whiteness (and an unmarked category), 41,
        107, 168

youth (migrants under the age of 18), 79, 133,
        179–180